Dictionaries of Civilization

Africa

Ivan Bargna

Translated by Rosanna M. Giammanco Frongia, Ph.D.

University of California Press

Berkeley   Los Angeles   London

Dictionaries of Civilization
Series edited by Ada Gabucci

University of California Press, one of the most distinguished university presses in the United States, enriches lives around the world by advancing scholarship in the humanities, social sciences, and natural sciences. Its activities are supported by the UC Press Foundation and by philanthropic contributions from individuals and institutions. For more information, visit www.ucpress.edu.

University of California Press
Berkeley and Los Angeles, California

University of California Press, Ltd.
London, England

Cataloging-in-Publication Data for this title is on file with the Library of Congress.

ISBN-13: 978-0-520-25974-4 (pbk.: alk. paper)

Manufactured in Spain

16   15   14   13   12   11   10   09
10   9   8   7   6   5   4   3   2   1

Art direction: Dario Tagliabue

Design: Anna Piccarreta

Editorial coordination: Caterina Giavotto

E-ducation.it S.p.A., Florence
Editorial direction: Cinzia Caiazzo

Chief editor: Filippo Melli

Technical coordination: Sibilla Pierallini

Picture research: Eva-Shaaron Magrelli

Layout: Edimedia Sas, Florence

Photo touch-up: Francesca Lunardi, Andrea Pacileo, Federico Pandolfini

English-language translation: Rosanna M. Giammanco Frongia, Ph.D.

English-language typesetting: Michael Shaw

Cover
Mask, Chokwe (Democratic Republic of the Congo), wood, vegetable fibers, metal and pigments. Tervuren, Musée Royal de l'Afrique Centrale.
Page 2
Ndebele woman wearing a traditional costume (South Africa).

Contents

6   Introduction

11   Peoples

113   Power and Society

179   Divinities and Religion

231   Ancestor Worship

251   Everyday Life

337   Human Habitats

References

376   Map of Pre-colonial Sub-Saharan Africa

378   Chronology

379   Museums

381   Index

382   Bibliography

386   Photo Credits

Introduction

In 2003, at the 50th Venice Biennale, in the American wing built in a classically inspired style, the Afro-American artist Fred Wilson exhibited an installation called Safe Home: *a clay jar resting on a black-and-white checkered floor inside which were objects such as a table lamp, a TV, a tea cup, and some books on Africa, including one of my works on African art.*

With this ensemble of disparate objects, in the padded cocoon of an egg-shaped container, the work of the anthropologist was displayed as a practice that intended to confine the Other in the finite, reassuring space of discourse and of a book's objective materiality.

To enclose a world inside a book and put it in one's pocket is the implicit promise of the dictionary: it is a history that began a long time ago in the West as the Civilization of the Book, in the role played by the written word in building knowledge and power, canonizing cultural tradition, and developing historiography and modern science. Scientific knowledge in particular, though it no longer bases its legitimizing principle on the authority of the written word, continues to investigate the world starting from the premise that the world is, indeed, "readable."

Insofar as today we still write books, and specifically this one on Africa, we are still, at least partially, inside this history where knowledge and power intersect and enhance one another. Anthropological knowledge about Africa, and the ethnographic museum that puts it on display, were made possible by the Western dominance of the world, by the material and symbolic expropriating and appropriating practices of colonial governments, and by the legitimacy that accrued to the social sciences as a knowledge useful for governing the conquered territories.

To list, classify, order, or regulate means to assign a place to the Other, putting it in its place and making it into an object of our knowledge; it means attributing a binding identity as to what *Africa* is and who *the Africans* are.

Subdivided into tribes and ethnic groups that can be located on a map, like butterflies pinned to a showcase and classified in a taxonomic outline, "Africans" stop being persons *and their individuality becomes subsumed under their "typicality," part of a "culture" whose major and allegedly immutable traits they exemplify. Individuals, groups, dynamic and complex societies are thus reduced to "things" inside definite boundaries, removed from time and change. Instead of a starting point, "tribes" and "ethnicities" seem the result of tribalization and ethnicization policies that were meant to break up, divide, and simplify the social space, making it easier to be ruled.*

Historically, these reification processes

fed the vision of a "primitive" Africa that still has a toehold on the Western imagination: the media, the tourist industry, and the art market mostly continue to label Africa as "primitive," a mark that simultaneously repels and attracts, like the threat of savagery and the promise of redemption.

Fortunately, this monologue conducted by the West on an object, "Africa," that had been reduced to silence, lost much of its credibility after the demise of colonialism. Post-colonial studies by scholars from the South of the world now offer multiple points of view that give a voice to subaltern groups and "provincialize" Europe and the West, uprooting our presumption of being the center of the world.

Thus we become aware of how socially constructed differences of race and gender, social class and cultural group, and our various involvement in colonialism and its effects, contribute to trace a horizon inside which another Africa may be glimpsed.

Still, as much as the awareness of this historical conditioning ruptures our illusion of a rational, free, transparent objectivity, it does not follow that we must be sentenced to relativism and the non-communicability of viewpoints, or that we can only affirm our individual identity. On the contrary, the awareness of our one-sided, incomplete viewpoint implies the possibility and the

need of listening to the Other, of acknowledging that we are made by otherness, that we are what we are precisely through the relations we establish with others.

In our era of globalization, cultural identities are being increasingly defined from within inter-cultural relations, unequal exchanges, and appropriation and recontextualization dynamics. To try and say what the West and Africa are, or to treat them as if they were separate, self-subsistent entities, no longer makes any sense, if it ever did.

For this reason, this book emphasizes neither otherness nor exoticism, but tries to show how differences always occur inside relations and histories that also build similarities.

In particular, we tried to develop our discourse inside the two broad rhetorics that still inform writings on Africa, not so much in scholarly circles, as in the popular image that still prevails: the two contrasting visions of Africa – as a unitary civilization, or as a continent broken up into a myriad ethnic differences. In the former, different cultures are jumbled together and the similarity lies only in the perception of a far-away observer (the West), or of someone with a plan (such as Pan-Africanist or Afrocentrist intellectuals). In the latter vision, we risk treating ethnicities like natural organisms, forgetting that they are political constructions (often the work of colonialism or post-colonialism) and cutting the ties that bind African societies to each other and to broader worldwide dynamics.

The issue, at any rate, is not to find a theoretical synthesis between these two paradigms or narratives, but to deconstruct them at the level of popular communication, stimulating a greater awareness of the limitation of our discourse and the stereotypes that subtend it.

This partiality, the notion of construction and "fiction" that is proper to every representation, is also visible in the structure of this book and the conventional limits of the subject matter, for we do not cover the entire continent but only parts of sub-Saharan Africa. We left out the north and the Horn of Africa somewhat arbitrarily because, peculiar and distinct from the rest of the continent as their history might be, we still could have integrated them (as others have) into an overall view – for example, by stressing the relationship between Egyptian civilization and the African hinterland; but this would have required more space.

Still, the awareness of the limits imposed on this book translates positively into an open-ended structure that, while showing its inevitable shortcomings, does underline the dynamic, manifold, complex nature of African societies.

Today books are at the frontier of the Gutenberg galaxy, of the printed-book era, as images and multimediality undermine the primacy of reading, creating new traps along with new possibilities. This dictionary, wedding as it does words to images, self-consciously places itself at this frontier.

We have given priority to the image. While the text does not disappear and is more than just captions, the image has its own autonomy and does not just illustrate the text. This makes the book more attractive and responsive to the needs of publishing, but has implications as well that go beyond that of being a teaching aid or a marketing ploy.

The fact is that images play an increasingly central role in defining what we mean by Africa at a time when the media infiltrates every corner with layers of images that inevitably affect our life, wishes, and aspirations, in the West as well as in Africa.

By giving more weight to images, we do not simply follow contemporary sensibility but come closer to the multimedial nature of "traditional" African societies because, as is the case with electronic media, communication does not just rely on writing, but also on music, images, objects, dance, etc.

More than words (at least, more than academic essays), images can evoke something of the concrete sense experience of life – not its totality, for images are two-dimensional, fixed, and frozen in time, but more than simply the written word.

But here we run the risk implicit in the use of images, of creating the illusion that they are a faithful mirror of reality, thus replacing reality with its representation.

Starting from an image and building the text around it entails another risk, of reducing discourse to a comment about the material aspects of culture; for although the immaterial aspect is often expressed in visible, physical forms, it is not reduced to them.

More specifically, we cannot hide the fact that in selecting the images, their capacity to attract the reader and meet his or her taste also plays a role: for this reason, landscapes and "works of art" are preferred while objects and places that are not as significant aesthetically but are still culturally important are left out. Among the inevitable distortions of this approach is the fact that cultures with a strong visual arts tradition loom larger than others and come to have a weight they would not have if other criteria (for example, demography) were adopted.

To overcome, at least partially, these obstacles, we tried to mitigate their power of seduction, for example by discarding "too beautiful" or "too ugly" pictures that could suggest a Garden of Eden image of Africa, or an equally stereotypical savage one – pictures that instead of conforming to "reality," satisfy our search for the sublime. In particular, we tried to reject the aestheticization of poverty that is often applied to Africa (images of refugee camps, famine, massacres), choosing instead pictures that suggest suffering without exhibiting it crudely or directly in a celebratory manner.

Still, this is more than a photography book: it is a "dictionary" even if not laid out alphabetically in linear succession from A to Z. The topics do follow a commonsensical order, by sections. The reader can skip between them or follow the suggested references, or even read it in the order in which it appears.

This book has its own architecture (a sort of "cosmological" frame) and narrative, because, unlike a dictionary, in addition to its parts it also expresses a whole. It is not our intention to restore a vision of knowledge as a self-enclosed totality, but rather to question the meaning of the information presented, in order to be guided into that reality. These minimal, provisional guidelines are starting points that put the reader on a path along with other readings and experiences, so he can form his own idea of Africa.

Have we perhaps gone somewhat beyond the Safe Home into which Fred Wilson relegated books on Africa?

Peoples

Western Guinea's Coast
Mande
Volta Populations
Fulani (Peul)
Akan Peoples
Nigerian Region
Kongo
Chokwe
Luba-Lunda
Kuba
Zande
Mangbetu
Lega
Mbuti
Maasai
Kikuyu
Nyamwezi
Makonde
Swahili
Madagascar
San
Shona
Ndebele
Nguni

◀ Chi Wara helmet, Bamana
(Mali). New York, Brooklyn
Museum of Art.

"When you see a palm tree, the palm tree ... saw you first"
(Wolof proverb, Senegal)

Western Guinea's Coast

Peoples
Wolof, Baga, Bidjogo,
Shebro, We

Geographic locations
Senegal, Guinea,
Guinea-Bissau, Sierra
Leone, Liberia, Ivory
Coast, western Africa

Related entries
Mande, Black Islam,
farmers, traditional
artists

The area stretching from the Casamance region and the Gambia River Valley in southern Senegal down to the Ivory Coast never had large states, unlike the Sahel region of western Africa. Still, it was the site of broad historical processes that affected tribes like the Baga in Guinea, the Bidjogo in Guinea-Bissau, and the Shebro in Sierra Leone, who were pushed into the area by Mande-speaking people: thus this forest area with a marshy coastline became a haven for them. The Baga live on the coast, where the men fish and grow kola nuts and the women grow rice. The Bidjogo today number about fifteen thousand and live on the islands of the Bijagos Archipelago facing the Guinea-Bissau coastline, where they mainly grow rice.

► Man standing next to his canoe. Bijagos Islands (Guinea-Bissau).

This figure was consecrated by pouring blood from an ox, a noble animal, on it. Young men wear masks with ox horns as a visible sign of success in raiding cattle, which raises their prestige in their age class and supplies them with the wherewithal to marry.

These statuettes also served as containers. They are topped by a half-length or full-length anthropomorphic figure, or by a seated figure, a position that signified high status.

These Iran statues are the receptacles of spiritual beings, especially the guardian spirits of clans and villages.

▲ Statuette, Bidjogo (Guineau-Bissau). Paris, Musée du Quay Branly.

The snake is one form under which the fertile spirit of the waters appears; the rainbow (often called "snake-in-the-sky" in Africa) is also associated with the snake, which plays a cosmological role by reconciling the water kingdom with that of the jungle.

The diamond pattern and the alternating colors mark the snake's undulating shape and suggest a hypnotic movement, further heightened by the round eyes.

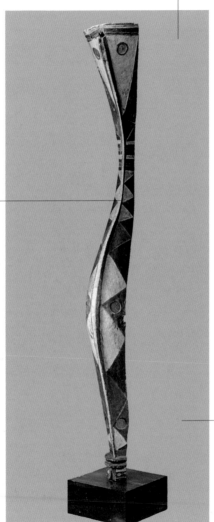

The snake is positioned vertically on the head of a masked male dancer during the initiation rituals that escort boys into adulthood, or during funerals.

▲ Basonyi helmet, Baga (Guinea-Bissau). Paris, Musée du Quay Branly.

The mask in the shape of a bird's beak evokes a spirit that moves between earth, water, and air.

This mask, worn at harvest celebrations, is an ideal representation of motherhood. The large, elongated breasts that suggest nursing are a sign of mature womanhood; the woman who touches them as the mask dances can expect healthy children and rich harvests.

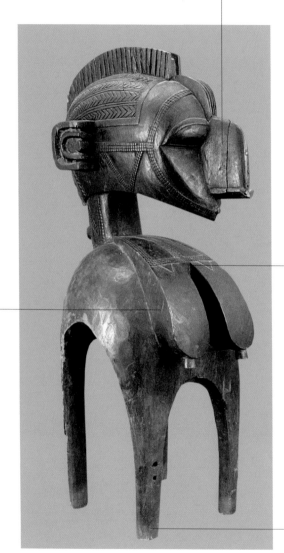

Two holes between the breasts allow the dancer to see.

The dancer wears the mask on his shoulders, his body hidden from the waist down by a wide raffia-fiber skirt. The mask's weight and size require unusual athletic skills of the dancer, who must move with the appropriate elegance.

▲ *Nimba* mask, Baga (Guinea-Bissau). Seattle, Seattle Art Museum.

This mask embodies the terrible jungle spirits; it is used in war, against witchcraft, and to mete out justice, which thus finds its legitimacy in a superhuman source.

The hair is made of cowrie shells from the Indian Ocean: used in the past as currency, they were a symbol of power.

The use of human hair contributes to the disturbing look, as it adds a familiar, domestic element to a foreign and faraway reality.

The use of animal elements such as hair reaffirms the distance between men and the jungle spirits.

The convex forehead, large bulging eyes, red, dilated nostrils, and open mouth all work to project a threatening look.

The sleigh bells increase the size of the mask and with their sound call forth the ancestors to mediate between men and spirits.

The mask enables the spirits to approach men and exercise some control over them, including providing visible, anthropomorphic assistance.

▲ Mask, We (Ivory Coast).
Private Collection.

"Even if you leave it in the river for a long time, a boat will never become a crocodile" (Bamana proverb, Mali)

Mande

The term *Mande* designates a broad linguistic family centered in the Bamako region and stretching towards Burkina Faso, Senegal, Gambia, Guinea, Sierra Leone, Liberia, Ivory Coast, and Ghana. Belonging to the Mande family are savannah ethnic groups such as Bamana, Malinke, Diula, Bozo, Kagoro, Marka, and Soninke, and jungle people such as Kuranki, Kono, Vai, Susu, and Dan. They live on millet, sorghum, rice, and maize farming. Cattle is kept primarily for prestige, for paying the "bridal price," and for sacrifices. The Bozo fish along the Niger River, while the Soninke and the Diula are wholesale traders. There is an important distinction between farmers, craftsmen, and slaves, though this "caste" structure does allow for some social mobility, such that even slaves can reach powerful positions. There is an important distinction between the Honrow, who are tied to the land and to agriculture and consist of noblemen, warriors, and farmers, and the Nyamakalaw, an endogamous group that controls the vital forces of nature (*nyama*). Although wary of each other, they are closely codependent, for while the former provide the food, the latter produce the iron, wood, and leather implements and cult objects used in everyday life and in rituals.

Peoples
Bamana, Malinke, Diula, Bozo, Kagoro, Marka, Soninke, Kuranki, Kono, Vai, Susu, Dan

Geographic locations
Mali, Burkina Faso, Senegal, Gambia, Guinea, Liberia, Sierra Leone, Ivory Coast, Ghana, western Africa

Chronology
13th–16th centuries: Mali empire
18th century: Segou and Kaarta kingdoms

Related entries
Kingdoms and empires of the Sudan, chiefless societies, age-sets and initiation, blacksmiths, male and female, Black Islam, farmers, theater

◀ Village on the Niger River (Mali).

The Saga mask represents a ram, the animal that
God sacrificed to wash away Musokoroni's guilt,
the female deity that had turned the earth barren.
The myth of a primordial fault followed by an
act of reparation is also found in the beliefs of
other local populations, such as the Dogon.

These masks are
polychrome;
some also have
metal plate
decorations.

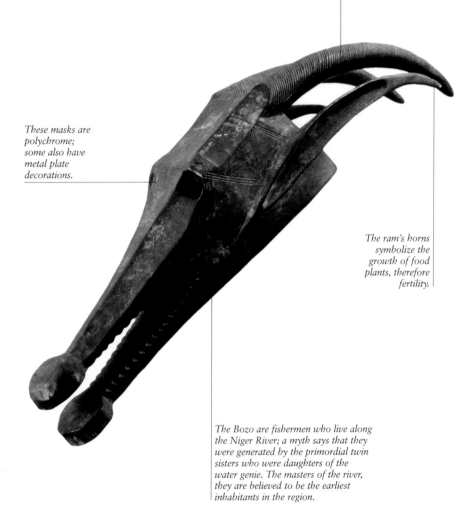

The ram's horns
symbolize the
growth of food
plants, therefore
fertility.

The Bozo are fishermen who live along
the Niger River; a myth says that they
were generated by the primordial twin
sisters who were daughters of the
water genie. The masters of the river,
they are believed to be the earliest
inhabitants in the region.

▲ Mask, Bozo (Mali). Seattle,
Seattle Art Museum.

The Bamana, about two million people, live in western and southern Mali, where they apparently settled in the 17th century. In the late 18th century the Segou and Kaarta kingdoms achieved regional power, but fell under the attacks of the Toucouleur Muslims in 1860. Having converted to Islam only then, they maintain many traditional beliefs. In 1890 Segou fell to the French.

The puppet theater, sometimes performed on boats, plays scenes from everyday life.

The Bamana live in villages under chiefs whose role is legitimized by their families and the level achieved in their initiation society. Descent is patrilineal, and the choice of a home follows patrilocal principles, with the bride moving into her husband's house.

▲ Puppet of the Sogow society,
Bamana (Mali). Private Collection.

19

These wooden statues, carved by blacksmiths, have multiple uses. When carved as maternity figures (gwandusu) with a gently rounded shape, they represent the female deity Musokoroni and are used by the Gwan and Jo initiation societies, where women with sterility or pregnancy problems, or whose children are ill, find support.

The body is highly stylized, reduced to elementary geometric shapes. Particular emphasis is placed on the breasts, the prominent hips, buttocks, and navel, all allusions to woman's fertility. Another characteristic is the crest-like headdress.

This type of statuette reminds the elderly and young girls that young men are looking for wives. Sometimes these statues are also used to commemorate dead twins.

▲ Female statue, Bamana (Mali), 19th–20th century. New York, Metropolitan Museum of Art.

The anthropomorphic shapes of the oil lamps forged by Mande blacksmiths contain symbols that are also found elsewhere, as pieces of an initiatory language. For the Bamana, and the Dogon as well, these signs correspond to the divine design: they precede the existence of things and are revealed in myth.

"Son of the tree" refers to the wish for progeny of a recently circumcised boy.

"The keeper of truth" is a symbol found at important meetings.

"The old woman's corpse" sign is used when burying the corpse of a very old woman.

This sign refers to "the sacrificial offering."

This sign marks the members of the Hausa ethnic group.

This is "the heavenly fire" sign that is placed on the head of the household's altar before readying the fields for sowing; it propitiates the rain.

"The wind" represents the movement of the soul in all things.

"Your two hands" refers to the farmer's hands and the hope for a rich harvest.

▲ Symbolism of textile motifs and Mande lamp shapes, Bamana (Mali) (from McNaughton, 1988).

"Let everyone learn to carry their bundle on their naked head, for sometimes no rags can be found" (Mossi proverb, Burkina Faso)

Volta Populations

Peoples
Mossi, Gurma, Bobo, Dogon, Senufo, Kulango, Lobi

Geographic locations
Burkina Faso, northern Ghana, northern Ivory Coast, northern Togo and Benin, western Africa

Chronology
14th century: Mamprusi kingdom
17th–18th centuries: rise and apex of Mossi kingdoms

Related entries
Fulani, kingdoms and empires of the Sudan, chiefless societies, Black Islam, farmers

The people speaking the Voltaic languages live between Burkina Faso and the northern regions of Ghana, the Ivory Coast, Togo, and Benin. They include the Mossi, Gurma, Bobo, Dogon, Senufo, Kulango, and Lobi tribes. Their economy and culture is akin to that of the Mande-language peoples, though unlike them they did not build great empires through conquest, and even Islam had a lower rate of penetration here. But state-type societies did exist in antiquity in this vast region, such as the state founded by the Mossi, horsemen who reached the White Volta River Valley in the 15th and 16th centuries. Their leader and founder, Naaba Ouedrago (the "stallion chief") was the son of a princess from the Mamprusi kingdom, a state in northern Ghana founded in the late 14th century. As was the case for other parts of Africa, while the ruling dynasty was foreign (the Mossi converted to Islam in the 18th century), the aboriginals maintained sacral power over the land. A centralized, caste-based state controlled the village societies and the clans. Starting in the 17th century, the Mossi split into kingdoms, the leading ones being the Fada N'Gurma, the Ouadagougu, and the Yatenga, who reached their apogee in the 18th century, only to wane first under the jihad of the Fulani of Samori, and later under French occupation.

▶ Family altar (*doba*), Bobo (Burkina Faso).

*These statues (*bouthiba*) are carved under the guidance of priests and soothsayers, often after a dream: they are said to collect the will of the gods (*thila*), for the gods themselves have dictated what form they are to take.*

These ancestor figures act as middlemen between human beings and gods in rituals that try to trace the cause of a disgrace or an illness, usually attributable to a flawed ritual that must be remedied.

The statuettes protect their owner; sometimes, when he is in mourning, they also take charge of his sorrow. For this reason, they are carved with raised arms to stop evil. They can also oppose witchcraft, find a wife, or increase fertility.

The Lobi people today number about 180,000 and are organized in clans without a chief. They grow cereals and raise cattle, the latter being given as dowry or offered in sacrifice. They are known as savage warriors who successfully resisted both Islam's and Christianity's penetration.

▲ Female statue, wood, Lobi (Burkina Faso). Paris, Musée des Arts d'Afrique et d'Océanie.

If masks made of leaves represent the savannah, wooden masks correspond to villages. Used by families and clans, wooden masks personify animals such as the antelope, the buffalo, the monkey, the crocodile, and the butterfly.

The Bwa people number about 300,000 and live between Mali and Burkina Faso. They lack a centralized authority and live in villages ruled by elder councils. In the 18th and 19th centuries, they were the victims of raids by the Bamana and Fulani people. They were later invaded by the French.

The Bwa religion is based on the clan's ancestor worship. Their god is Do, son of the creator god Difini, who deserted men after being hit with a pestle by a woman who was crushing millet. Do is a god of the generating forces of nature; he becomes visible in masks made of branches.

▲ Male dancer wearing a butterfly mask, Bwa (Burkina Faso).

The half-circle on top is the "mask moon," alluding to the ceremonial hour.

The protruding hooks allude to the circumcised penis and the rhinoceros hornbill, a bird used in divination.

The "X"-shaped motifs signify the scarifications that men and women wear on their forehead.

This mask represents a water or air spirit and dances in agrarian rituals and at funerals, initiations, and market days.

The eyes' concentric circles also remind the viewer of the owl, a bird that symbolizes magical powers.

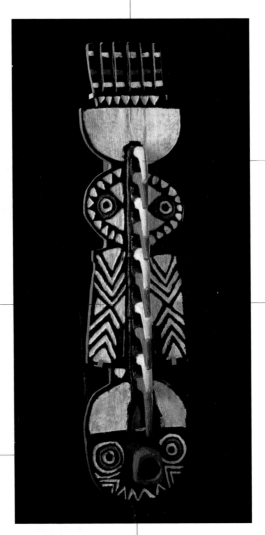

The hole for the mouth and the concentric circles for the eyes recall water ponds.

▲ *Nwantantay* mask, Bwa (Burkina Faso). London, Horniman Museum.

This type of mask, with a vertical fretwork panel and a figure on top of the face, is also used by the Dogon of Mali (the masks are called satimbe and sirige). They commemorate events that took place when Mossi horsemen took over the region, pushing some Dogon people to the northwest toward the Bandiagara cliffs. Those who did not leave were assimilated but kept their masks.

This figure represents a woman ancestor. Masks were a prerogative of the tribes that already inhabited a certain place when a new ruling dynasty took over. The new rulers would use statues instead for worship.

▲ *Karan wemba* mask, Mossi (Burkina Faso). Seattle, Seattle Art Museum.

Kpelye masks represent ideal feminine beauty. Appearing in pairs at initiation rites of the Poro society, they evoke the event of man's creation.

On top of the mask are emblematic figures that mark membership in a social class: here, the rhinoceros hornbill is a symbol of blacksmiths.

The lateral projections are headdress decorations.

The lower extensions would seem to represent the legs.

▲ *Kpelye* mask, Senufo (Ivory Coast). Private Collection.

The Senufo people number about one and a half million and live in an area that includes parts of the Ivory Coast, Mali, and Burkina Faso. The Poro society is their central social, political, religious, and educational institution: it is organized by age classes, to which all the Senufo males belong. Women belong to the Sandogo society.

Fulani (Peul)

Geographic locations
Guinea, Senegal, Mali,
Burkina Faso, Niger,
Nigeria, Cameroon,
western Africa

Chronology
19th century: Fulani
jihad

Related entries
Nigerian region,
Black Islam, herders,
body arts

The Fulani (known as Peul by the French and also Fula or Fulbe) are herders and number about six million people, many of them still nomads. They are scattered in western Africa, from Senegal to Cameroon. Because of their physical features and mysterious language, the Europeans were intrigued by their origins, speculating that they must have come from India, Malaysia, Polynesia, Palestine, ancient Egypt, or Ethiopia. Some even theorized an Indo-European, gypsy origin. The Fulani still migrate seasonally with their livestock and follow their traditions, living peacefully side by side with the many tribes they meet in their wandering, with whom they barter milk products in exchange for food staples and craft implements. Their woolen blankets (*khasa*), woven by the Mabube caste, are in high demand. The Fulani who became urbanized and converted to Islam built centralized states ruled by Koranic law, such as Fouta Jallon (Guinea), Macina (Mali), Sokoto (northern Nigeria, where the Fulani are also called Bororo), and Adamawa (Cameroon). In Nigeria in particular, they came to rule over the Hausa city-states born from the rerouting to the east of the trans-Saharan caravan routes, after the Shongay empire was invaded by the Moroccans in 1591.

▼ Fulani woman tending cattle (Niger).

Normally, the life of the Fulani is not conducive to producing or owning many material goods because they are a burden to the Fulanis' wandering. They express themselves artistically through poetry and care for their appearance.

The headgear is made of gold, glass beads, and amber.

The large earrings are in hammered gold.

The Fulani take constant care of their hairdo, jewelry, and clothing. These aristocrats disdain manual work, preferring to employ craftsmen from other ethnic groups.

▲ Fulani woman wearing traditional garb (Mali).

Rings, bracelets, and anklets of gold, copper, or silver identify a woman's age and social status. For each new baby girl, the mother removes some of her rings and gives them to her daughters; she removes all of them when the oldest daughter reaches ten to twelve years of age.

The care that the Fulani (Bororo) devote to their physical appearance is especially visible during the gerewol, festivals held in the rainy season, when herders from different clans meet and young men dance in beauty contests to win over their girl.

This male head covering is embellished with a row of cowrie shells and an ostrich feather.

The eyes, another key element of beauty, are kept wide open.

The face is painted and made shiny by spreading butter over it.

Lips are painted black, with lines, triangles, and dots painted on each side to heighten the teeth's whiteness, a key feature of male beauty.

The tunic is embroidered by the women with geometric spider and snake motifs.

▲ Young Fulani man with painted face (Niger).

"Even a small bird cannot be swallowed whole" (Ashanti proverb, Ghana)

Akan Peoples

The Akan-language tribes live between Ghana and the Ivory Coast. The principal groups are the Ashanti, Fante, Baoulé, Abron, and Anyi. Notwithstanding their historical relationship and the similarity of their art forms (in goldsmithery in particular) and of symbols of power such as thrones and fabrics, there are strong differences in social and political organization. While in the 17th–18th centuries the Ashanti founded a highly structured monarchy, the Baoulé founded egalitarian, individualistic societies based on the extended family. In the 19th century, two forms of government existed in the Ashanti kingdom: a "federal" structure dealt with relations between the Kumasi king and neighboring chiefs, while a centralized bureaucracy dealt with the subject populations, collecting tributes and organizing manpower in the farms and the gold mines, even using slaves. Originally from Ghana, the Baoulé migrated to the Ivory Coast in the 18th century when the Ashanti came to power, and merged with the aboriginals, from whom they learned to use masks, which the Ashanti did not use. The Akan tribes built their historical identity by incorporating aspects of Muslim culture (though without converting to Islam), to which they were exposed by the caravan traders who crossed the Sahara and the Europeans who used the ports-of-call on the Gulf of Guinea.

Peoples
Ashanti, Fante, Baoulé, Abron, Anyi

Geographic locations
Ghana, Ivory Coast, western Africa

Chronology
17th–18th centuries: rise of the Ashanti kingdom
18th century: Baoulé migration from Ghana to Ivory Coast
18th–19th centuries: expansion of the Ashanti kingdom

Related entries
Mande, hunters and warriors, Black Islam, farmers, trade, Kumasi

◀ King (*ashantene*) Nama Opuko Ware II, Ashanti (Ghana).

The seat embodies part of the individual's spiritual essence, therefore must be treated with care and never left unguarded; only its legitimate owner may sit on it. At his death, the seat is buried with him or blackened and used as an ancestor altar by his progeny.

The figured and geometric motifs refer to proverbs, in this case, an allusion to the "knot of wisdom," to problems whose unknotting requires thinking.

Sometimes an empty niche at the bottom hides a protective "medicine."

Ashanti seats are carved from a single piece of wood: they symbolize a nobleman's power and evoke the golden throne of their king, who embodies the unity of the Ashanti nation.

▲ Wooden throne, Ashanti (Ghana). Private Collection.

Gold weights were made in geometric or figured shapes often associated with adages or moral precepts about the appropriate way of living one's life. They were made of brass using the lost-wax technique first introduced in the northern savannahs by Mande traders in the 14th or 15th century.

The images used for gold weights were usually of wild animals; missing are the domesticated animals or those that live closer to the village such as hyenas. The elephant is a symbol of royal power.

Because of its brightness and incorruptibility, and the advantages of trading it with Europeans, gold was the symbol of the Ashanti king's power and its bedrock. It was also used for jewelry, using the lost-wax technique or worked into thin sheets that were overlaid on wood sculptures.

▲ Gold weight, Ashanti (Ghana).
Paris, Private Collection.

Two-faced masks allude to the marriage of the Sun and the Moon, or to twins, their being alike and different simultaneously, as marked by their resemblance and the different details used on each mask, such as hairdo and scarifications.

These masks are meant to amuse and are used in dances for happy events, the birth of twins being considered an auspicious event.

Probably the Ashanti have no masks because they lack the male initiation rites where they are often used; masks are very important in the Baoulé culture.

The use of different colors, black and red, may indicate that the twins are of different genders, though there is no hard and fast association between a color and a gender. "Red" skin is considered more beautiful and is seen as a symbol of purity and excellence.

▲ Mask, Baoulé (Ivory Coast). Geneva, Musée Barbier-Müller.

The head (the seat of freedom, intelligence, and clairvoyance) and sexual features, such as a woman's breasts and buttocks and a man's chest or calves, are emphasized. These traits do not mark a purely physical beauty, but instead allude to woman's fertility and man's hard labor.

When a Baoulé child is born, he deserts his otherworldly bride, causing her resentment and jealousy. Statues represent this complex relationship. The disagreements with the supernatural brides and grooms are manifested in nightmares or in sexual problems such as impotence or sterility, and cause tensions with one's earthly spouse.

Statues are used to placate a moody, otherworldly spouse, by sacrificing to him or her. The statues adhere to Baoulé beauty canons and their serene, quiet mien is meant to secure the spouse's favor. The sculptor's hand is guided by the soothsayer, who receives the wishes of the otherworldly lover about the features to be given to his or her portrait.

▲ Sitting male figure, Baoulé (Ivory Coast). Seattle, Seattle Art Museum.

"If the big mask refuses to see the little mask, the latter will refuse to see the former" (Yoruba proverb, Nigeria)

Nigerian Region

Peoples
Hausa, Fulani, Igbo, Yoruba

Geographic locations
Nigeria, western Africa

Chronology
6th century BC–5th century AD: Nok culture
5th century: Ile-Ife begins to be populated
9th–11th centuries: Igbo-Ukwu culture
12th–16th centuries: great Ile-Ife sculpture period
17th–19th centuries: rise of Oyo's Yoruba kingdom
19th century: Sokoto caliphate

Related entries
Kingdoms of Niger, African religions, water spirits, twin worship, Shango the thunder god, Eshu the rogue god, Black Islam, African Christianity, Egungun masks, Ogboni cult, literature, African cities

▶ Sitting male statue. Paris, Musée du Quai Branly.

Approximately two hundred and fifty ethnic groups live in today's Nigeria, though about eighty percent of the population is composed of Hausa and Fulani in the north, Yoruba in the west, and Igbo in the eastern part of the country. While the Hausa and the Fulani are Muslim, the Yoruba and Igbo are animists as well as Christians. This difference between the Islamic north and the Christian south is one line of division in today's Nigeria. The Yoruba were never united politically: in the past, they were a conglomerate of kingdoms and cities fighting each other. They were united only in their mythology and in their common lineage traceable to the city of Ile-Ife. The most powerful Yoruba kingdom was that of Oyo, whose military strength rested on the cavalry; it controlled the Middle Niger River down to the coast until

the 19th century, when it withdrew before the advancing Fulani jihad. The Oyo kingdom was a politically centralized federation of crowned cities and trading towns. The Igbo, on the other hand, were one of the major tribes subjected to the Atlantic slave trade; they were organized in independent villages governed by elder councils and societies that conferred titles of prestige. Like the Hausa and the Yoruba, the Igbo are known for their trading skills. The earliest Igbo artifacts were found in Igbo-Ukwu, an archaeological site that has yielded refined bronze objects from the tenth century.

Findings of the Nok culture, which flourished on the border of the southern Nigerian Savannah and was named after the village where the first artifacts were found in 1928, date from the 6th century BC to the 5th century AD. These people knew how to cast iron, having probably discovered the technique independently.

The eyes are the focus of this statue, magnified by the pierced pupils, the wide arch of the eyebrows, and the lower eyelids. The navel, ears, nostrils, and sometimes the mouth were also pierced.

The heads of Nok statues are easily recognizable for their spherical, conical, or cylindrical shape and elaborate headdresses.

The size of these statues (this one is 23 inches high) varies from a few inches to almost natural size.

According to some scholars, an analysis of style and iconography would seem to link the ancient Nok culture to today's Yoruba.

▲ Sitting female statuette, Nok (Nigeria). Private Collection.

While among the Igbo only the men are wood carvers, uli *painting is women's work: they paint their bodies and the walls of homes and shrines.*

Women's painting follows its own aesthetic: while carved objects are mostly angular, women's drawings are curvilinear.

▲ Woman painting a wall, Igbo (Nigeria).

The python, an animal that comes from the depths of the earth, represents the ancestors and links both worlds. The rainbow also joins the sky to the earth, and for this reason is called "python-in-the-sky." A coiled snake alludes to the cyclical time of rebirths.

These divinities stand for the elements of nature, and are portrayed in human form with all the attributes of influential people, such as headgear, scarifications, and decorations.

The statues of the north-central Igbo are moderately realistic, with good proportions and all the bodily parts represented. Made for being viewed frontally, they are symmetrical, with the legs slightly apart and the arms away from the body. The volumes are full and rounded, with strong shoulders and vigorous neck.

A recurring element is the palms turned upwards to signify frankness – openness to give and to receive – which is the reciprocal relationship between man and god.

The attention to detail is especially visible in the head, while hands and feet are carved summarily on purpose.

The Igbo portray their gods following the family model: sculpted individually, they are nevertheless displayed in groups in the shrines.

▲ *Alusi* deity, Igbo (Nigeria).
Private Collection.

The bird clutching the snake alludes to the dark power of the "mothers" who can turn into birds at night.

The knives on each side stand for the courage and aggressiveness of hunters and warriors and of Ogun, the god of metal wars. The leather sheaths are a Hausa influence and highlight the importance of the Muslim militia that served under the Yoruba kings.

This mask is used as a headdress, hooked to the costume (which hides the face) through holes at the bottom.

The Efe gold masks are used in the gelede *cult, when the "mothers" as "mistresses of the world" are paid homage and beseeched to use their powers to create, not destroy; their assent is required for ritually reordering the cosmos and to condemn anti-social behavior.*

▲ Efe Baba Ako gold mask, Yoruba (Nigeria). Seattle, Seattle Art Museum.

Decorations on building façades in the cities of Kano and Zaria, or in Zinder (Niger), are based on Arabic script and motifs, and are also found in embroidery work. They were built for the Fulani aristocracy by skilled Hausa craftsmen.

The inscriptions carved on doors and windows are meant to protect the home with their magical powers.

Abstract geometric patterns sometimes become figurative, such that the door becomes a mouth, the pinnacles ears, and so forth.

The decorating techniques used include shaping the fresh plaster by hand, carving designs in plaster, or painting them on the wall.

▲ Building façade, city of Kano, Hausa (Nigeria).

"The lizard runs so fast that it overtakes its own den" (Kongo proverb, Democratic Republic of the Congo)

Kongo

Populations
Vili, Woyo, Bembe, Yombe

Geographic locations
DRC, central Africa

Chronology
13th century: Kongo migration
14th century: birth of the Kongo kingdom
1482: first Portuguese settlement
1491: Nzinga a Nkuwu, the Kongo king, converts to Christianity
16th century: reign of Alphonse I
18th century: fall of the Kongo kingdom

Related entries
Colonialism, African Christianity, trade

The Kongo populations, currently numbering about three million, migrated from the northeast to their current settlements at the mouth of the Congo River in the 13th century. They are subdivided into several tribes which include the Vili, Woyo, Bembe, and Yombe. In the 14th century they unified the region (Kabinda and northwestern Angola) under one kingdom, probably the most powerful in central Africa when the Portuguese reached it in 1482. Although King Nzinga a Nkuwu converted to Christianity in 1491, taking the name of John I, the population continued in their traditional beliefs, though incorporating Christian imagery. In the 16th century, under the leadership of Alphonse I, the kingdom expanded and reached international renown, even sending diplomatic missions to Europe and Brazil. In the meantime, power was becoming increasingly centralized, and the powers of the aristocracy were reduced, in the election of the king, to a mere symbolic ratification. The kingdom reached its apogee in the 17th century but was torn apart soon after by succession infighting, the slave trade, and attacks from Angola, which it tried to resist by enlisting the help of the Portuguese. In the 18th century, though still united culturally, Kongo became fragmented politically and was reduced to a Portuguese colony in 1885.

▶ View of the Congo River (DRC).

This fabric is made of woven raffia, a fiber obtained from the leaves of the raffia palm; the women then traced the embroidery pattern on it.

The symmetrical design is usually monochrome in the natural raffia color and diamond-shaped.

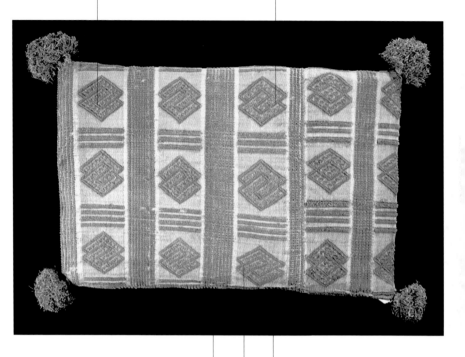

Bakongo weaving design and tradition also influenced the shoowa fabrics produced by the Bakuba, a population that flourished farther inland during the 18th and 19th centuries.

The Kongo aristocracy used these fabrics as signs of prestige.

These Kongo embroidery patterns are probably European-influenced (adapted from coats-of-arms and priestly garments), grafted on an older tradition that already existed in 1508. A 1611 European report estimated that the city of Loango produced annually about twelve to fifteen thousand high-quality cloths and forty to fifty thousand medium-quality ones.

▲ Raffia fabric, Kongo (DRC), 16th century. Rome, Museo Nazionale Preistorico Etnografico Luigi Pigorini.

The vertical axis links the world of the living with that of the dead; the two worlds are separated by the horizontal water line in which the sun sets, only to be reborn in the other world, from which ancestors come back as newborns.

The highest point alludes to the sun at noon, to the kingdom of God, to the male element, to the king sitting on the highest summit of his kingdom, thus defining himself as the most vital of human beings. It also alludes to the highest point in a human life.

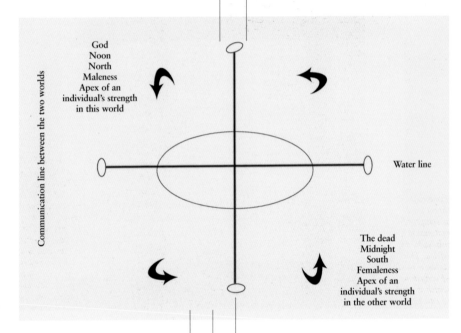

God
Noon
North
Maleness
Apex of an individual's strength in this world

Water line

The dead
Midnight
South
Femaleness
Apex of an individual's strength in the other world

Communication line between the two worlds

Crucifixes were used like the local "fetishes" (nkisi), to ward off evil and to heal.

The base of the cross signifies midnight, femaleness, the fullness of one's strength in the afterworld, the summit of the ancestors' mountain.

▲ Cosmogram (bidimbu), Kongo (DRC) (from Thompson, 1984).

The Kongo easily accepted the Christian crucifix without implying their conversion, because the cross motif was already part of their tradition, as it signifies the cyclical movement of the sun from east to west in its four principal positions.

These statuettes probably date to the 16th century; they are placed on the graves of those who led distinguished lives, thus bequeathing them to memory.

Stone was rarely used as sculpture material in sub-Saharan Africa. This statue is made of soapstone, which is easy to carve.

Figures with a hand supporting a head slightly bent seem to depict a "thinker," a chief meditating on how to best achieve the welfare of his people. Or it could express the sadness of someone in mourning.

▲ Ntadi figure, Kongo (DRC). Tervuren, Musée Royal de l'Afrique Centrale.

These statuettes were made in a variety of poses: the arms raised to the mouth signify grief and wailing; when held tightly against the body, loneliness; when crossed on the chest, they express icy silence. Still, once they are removed from their original context, guessing their meaning is not easy.

White is also used in initiation rituals, when the boys die a symbolic death only to be reborn as adults. Both the dead and children come from the other world and are "white" (note how in effect, black children have a lighter skin color at birth).

This mask with obvious female traits was carried by the Kongo priests (nganga) who used it to enter the netherworld and benefit from their ancestors' powers.

The color white is associated with the dead and is used for memorial statues that adorn graves and for dancing masks at funerals.

▲ Mask, Kongo (DRC). Tervuren, Musée Royal de l'Afrique Centrale.

When the Portuguese reached the shores of the Kongo kingdom, they were greeted not as foreigners, but as the dead come back to life, as their ancestors, for like the dead they were coming from the sea, spoke an incomprehensible tongue, had superior powers and were white.

"The coils of a basket always begin with a knot" (Chokwe proverb, Angola)

Chokwe

According to oral tradition, the Chokwe kingdom was born from the fallout of the marriage between Lweji and the Luba prince Chibinda Ilunga, who acquired mastery over the Chokwe. The unrest that followed caused part of the local nobility to flee the Lunda kingdom in what is now the southeastern Democratic Republic of the Congo around the end of the 15th century and settle in present-day Angola. Here they subjected the aboriginals, organized them into chiefdoms, each one ruled by a chief-king, and fused with them, adopting their customs. Still, the distinction between the descendants of the conquerors and of the subjected natives survived in each village. In the 17th and 18th centuries, the Chokwe kingdom was still under Lunda influence, but a century later it seized more power by, among other things, joining the ivory and rubber trades that had opened on the Angolan coast. Its power was short lived, for the sudden growth led to fragmentation and the final loss of independence at the hands of the Portuguese.

Geographic locations
Angola, central Africa

Chronology
15th century: flight of the Lunda aristocracy who found the Chokwe kingdom
19th century: the Chokwe engage in Atlantic trade

Related entries
Luba-Lunda, hunters and warriors, trade, traditional music

◀ Female statue, Chokwe (Angola). Private Collection.

The Luba Prince Chibinda Ilunga is a recurring theme in Chokwe iconography, where he appears as the founding hero who taught his people hunting and the use of magic. He also introduced the idea of the sacredness of the monarchy, and more refined customs at court.

Although he was a foreigner, Chibinda Ilunga is here portrayed wearing the Chokwe headdress known as mwanangana.

*The strap on the chest (*mukata) *is used to hang the pouch containing magic substances.*

*The large hands denote the hero's great strength. In the right hand he holds the traditional insignia of power (*cisokolu).

In the left hand the prince holds a flint rifle, a weapon introduced in Angola in the 18th century.

One custom introduced by the prince is the king's solemn walk: slowly raising his foot, he imitates the turtle's walk, the sacred animal of the Luba and the Lunda people; the foot's generous size indicates the hunter's strength as he continuously moves about.

▲ Statue of Chibinda Ilunga, Chokwe (Angola). Berlin, Ethnologisches Museum.

The Cihongo dance masks represent the spirit of plenty, here depicted as a long-bearded elder. In the past, this mask was apparently used to collect tributes from village to village.

Drum players (mukhundu).

Mungonge initiation scene with three elders stealthily advancing so as to frighten the initiates.

Sword-carrying drum players (mukupela).

The chair's legs symbolize the support that ancestors give to the king.

The carved figures depict rituals and everyday activities: masks, drum players, elders at initiation rites, monkey hunters, women with children, and men smoking the pipe.

These thrones echo the lines of Portuguese chairs (the first contacts with Europeans date to the 17th century), with the addition of carved figures in the typical Chokwe style on the back and between the legs. This mixture of local and foreign style made it a major symbol of royal power.

▲ Throne, Chokwe (Angola).
Berlin, Museum für Volkerkunde.

Chokwe

Hunters and warriors used whistles of this type for long-distance communication using agreed-upon sounds or to frighten the enemy.

Whistles come in many shapes: from the total lack of figurative forms to masks and full-length figures.

Applying pressure on the side holes modulates the sound.

The center hole is the mouthpiece.

▲ Whistle, Chokwe (Angola).
Paris, Musée du Quai Branly.

"The leopard's skin is lovely, but his heart evil" (Luba proverb, Democratic Republic of the Congo)

Luba-Lunda

The Luba kingdom was born in the southern savannahs of the present-day eastern Democratic Republic of the Congo; it reached its zenith in the 17th century but fell as a result of wars against the Chokwe and the effects of the Arab slave trade in the region. The king's sacral power was reined in by several institutions, including the Bambudye society (the "men of memory"), whose task it was to orally transmit the history of the kingdom and whose interpretation could influence the ruler's decisions. The culture of the Luba kingdom influenced other ethnic groups, such as the Kusu, the Songye, the Chokwe, and the Lunda. The chieftains of neighboring regions often claimed to have economic and political ties with the Luba kings by dis-

Geographic locations
DRC, central Africa

Chronology
16th century: beginning
of Luba expansion
17th century: apex of
Luba kingdom's power
1870: King Ilunga
Kabale dies; the Luba
kingdom starts its
decline

Related entries
Chokwe, male and
female, slavery

playing objects that might have proved an exchange of gifts with, and thus diplomatic recognition from, them. Such pervasive cultural influence led to the incorrect belief that it was a true empire in the political sense. According to oral tradition, the union of the Lunda and the Luba began with the marriage of Chibinda Ilunga, son of the first Luba king, to Lweji, daughter of a Lunda lord. The political unrest that followed this marriage led to a diaspora that extended the Lunda's dominance over the region.

◀ Arrow holder, Luba (DRC). Tervuren, Musée Royal de l'Afrique Centrale.

The "waterfall hairdo" was popular in Luba country from the late 19th to the early 20th centuries. It was shaped around a reed frame and decorated with hairpins whose shape recalled the sacred anvil associated with the Luba monarchs' power.

Hairdos such as these required up to fifty hours of work; this explains the need of a headrest to avoid spoiling it.

These hairdos were not simply pleasing to the eye, but distinguishing marks of social and professional rank.

An analysis of this headrest's style dates it to the 19th century. The artist has been called "the master of the waterfall hairdo" for he has reproduced a mikanda (stepped, or waterfall) hairstyle.

▲ Headrest, Luba (DRC).
Paris, Musée du Quai Branly.

The support that ancestors give to their descendants is rendered symbolically by the caryatid supporting the chief's body with her hands and head.

The expression is composed, thoughtful: the eyes and mouth are half-open and the face's projection is balanced by that of the hairdo.

The belly (whose symbolic centrality is highlighted by the scarifications) and the bare breasts allude to fertility.

▲ Seat, Luba (DRC). Private Collection.

The female figure appears often on Luba royal insignia and could depict the king's daughters and sisters married to lesser chiefs for the purposes of cementing political alliances. In rendering women, the volumes and curves are accentuated, along with symmetry and balance and neat, polished surfaces.

These tablets were memory aids for the wise men of the Mdbye society who were consulted by kings and noblemen for enlightenment on myths and on the complex rituals of court life.

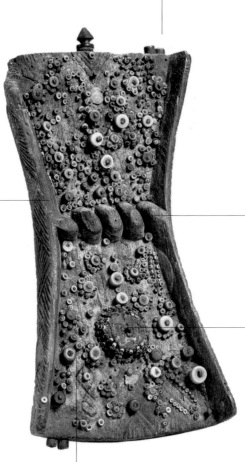

The dividing line in the center is the "threshold" that must be crossed during initiation rituals.

The rectangular shape represents the royal court, the human body, and the turtle, which is the royal emblem.

The large round projection in the lower part of the tablet represents the capital of the kingdom.

Beads and shells applied to the surface stand, by size and color, for the places and the protagonists of the oral history, thus readying the stage and the characters for the narratives that recount and reconcile the disputes and conflicts of the Luba kingdom.

▲ *Lukasa* tablet, Luba (DRC).
Private Collection.

Musumba, capital of the Lunda kingdom, was built according
to a zoomorphic layout that for unknown reasons followed
the shape of a turtle. The animal body, like that of humans,
allowed for a hierarchical placement of the different clans,
stressing each one's role and the organic unity of the whole.

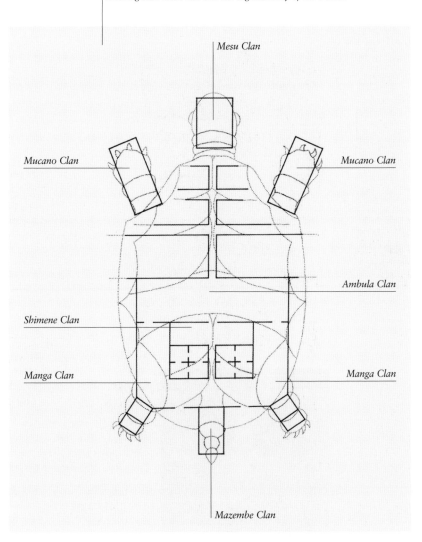

Mesu Clan

Mucano Clan

Mucano Clan

Ambula Clan

Shimene Clan

Manga Clan

Manga Clan

Mazembe Clan

▲ Map of the capital of the Lunda
kingdom (from Guidoni, 1975).

"Even a large animal cannot be bigger than the elephant"
(Kuba proverb, Democratic Republic of the Congo)

Kuba

Geographic locations
DRC, central Africa

Chronology
17th century: rise of
the Bushongo dynasty
1650: Shyaam aMbul
aNgoong seizes power
1750: the Kuba reach
maximum power
1870–1890: expansion
of the ivory trade
End 19th century: the
Nsapo invade the Kuba
kingdom

Related entries
Luba-Lunda, weaving
and clothing

According to oral tradition, the Kuba settled in the Congolese Kasai region by migrating there on canoes from the Atlantic Congo region. This highly structured society was ruled in the early 17th century by the Bushongo dynasty, the dominant clan that had come to rule over the native Kete. The Kuba in effect are not a homogeneous ethnic group but an ensemble of about twenty different clans. *Kuba* is what the neighboring Luba and the Europeans called them, while they referred to themselves as "the king's people." The fate of the kingdom took a decisive turn around 1650, when Shyaam aMbul aNgoong came from the west with a band of adventurers and usurped the throne. He introduced American crops such as maize, peanuts, and tobacco. But the central power was weak and the chiefdoms that made up the kingdom had great autonomy, which led to frequent uprisings. The king was responsible to a court council of all the chiefdoms. It was believed that the king (*nyim*) was of divine origin and that his power, drawn from the ancestors and from witchcraft, could influence the weather, the crops, and even fertility. The kingdom reached its greatest territorial expansion around 1750, and was still growing wealthy in the 19th century, especially from 1870 to 1890, when it became the main supplier of the ivory sold to Angola.

▶ King Kok Mabiintsh III, Kuba (DRC).

This type of statuette had a memorial purpose, but because it embodied the king's spirit it also guaranteed that his power would be handed down to his successor. These statuettes might also have been used to propitiate the gods for pregnancies for the king's many wives.

The square pedestal echoes the typical visor-headdress of the Bushongo kings, the dynasty that rules over the Kuba people.

Royal statuettes had a set iconographic repertoire: one arm rests on the knee while the other holds a sword pointed backward; at the center of the pedestal, a specific royal symbol identified each king.

▲ *Ndop* statuette of a Kuba king (DRC), 17th century. London, Museum of Mankind.

The emblem of Shyaam aMbul aNgoong, a merchant and medicine man who founded the Bushongo dynasty in the 17th century, is the board of a popular African game, mancala: the board is divided in two rows of boxes with forty-eight seeds, nuts, or pebbles distributed four per box. The player who seizes all the pawns wins.

This mask is associated with Woot, the mythical founder of the Bushongo royal lineage: it is used in many rituals, including the king's funeral.

An animal skin is sown on top of a woven raffia frame and decorated with rows of beads and cowries (the Indian Ocean shells used as currency in Africa) that trace male features and wide jaw.

There are no holes for the eyes, hence the mask must dance in majestic slow motions.

This is the most important of the Bushongo royal masks. It personifies a threatening ngesh spirit, and is used to maintain law and order. Because it has the terrible powers of blinding those who wear it, it is not worn by the king but by someone close to him. When the mask performs, the king stays at a distance, making believe that he is on a trip.

▲ *Mwashamboy* mask, Kuba (DRC). Private Collection.

According to oral tradition, this mask with a broad, convex forehead variously represents a jungle spirit (ngesh) or a pygmy, or a hydrocephalic prince; or even the brother of Woot, the mythical ancestor.

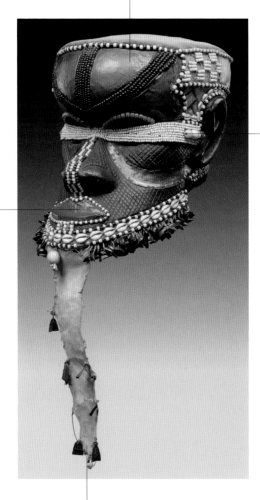

The horizontal line of beads highlights the blindness of the mask, even though the dancer can see from the nostril holes.

Copper plates, rows of glass beads, and cowries, all elements that signify the king's wealth and his power, are applied to the wooden surface of the forehead, cheeks, and lips.

▲ Bwoom mask, Kuba (DRC). Tervuren, Musée Royal de l'Afrique Centrale.

The strip of animal skin attached to the chin stands for a beard.

"A snake cannot get around its name" (Zande proverb, Democratic Republic of the Congo)

Zande

Geographic locations
DRC, central Africa

Chronology
18th century: the
Zande settle in Uele

Related entries
Mangbetu, hunters and
warriors, farmers

The Zande settled in the Uele River region (in the present-day DRC) in the late 18th century, subjugating the natives, whom they reorganized into kingdoms and chiefdoms. Even though the Zande assimilated dozens of different tribes and peoples, they themselves underwent cultural fusion, for they adopted farming and gradually gave up hunting in the 19th century. This mutual assimilation, however, was insufficient to remove the social distinction between conquered and conqueror, the originally foreign ruling aristocracy and the common people. Another important social distinction existed between freemen and slaves (prisoners of war, refugees who had no kin in the village hosting them, or people originally sentenced to death who had been pardoned). There was probably a reciprocal influence between the Zande and the Mangbetu, though the former live in the savannah and the latter in the forest, where in addition to raising cassava and banana trees, they are hunter-gatherers. The monarchy was not a sacred institution, and many kingdoms were set up by princes in exile who had lost the fight for the succession to the throne.

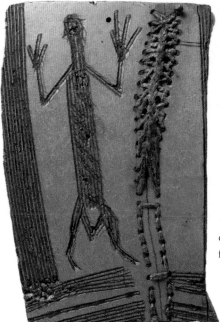

▶ Pumpkin piece, Zande (DRC). Paris, Musée du Quai Branly.

The conical head at the top of the harp's neck identifies it as Zande art.

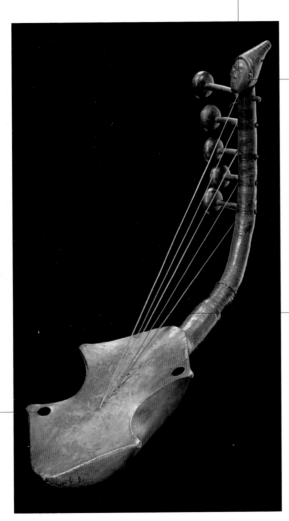

The ears are perforated and the eyes are made with beads.

The five chords made of plant fibers are attached to the wooden neck under the animal skin.

The soundbox is made of wood sheathed with animal skin, and has two sound holes.

▲ Harp with a head shape, Zande (DRC). Tervuren, Musée Royal de l'Afrique Centrale.

Zande

Even though these blades are shaped like throwing knives, they are not weapons but a sort of local "currency" in which copper replaced the original iron.

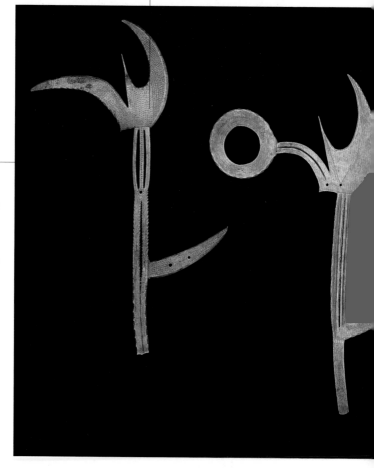

Weapons are a sign of the importance assigned to wars of conquest among the Zande people; the court pages supplied officers and elite corps to the army.

▲ Ngbandi and Nzakara blades, kingdom of Zande (DRC), 19th century. London, British Museum.

The blades were not traded on the regular market, but through a network of diplomatic relations between the Zande kingdoms, as luxury objects that contributed to reinforce the bonds between the different realms of the Zande empire.

The Ngbandi and Nzakara people who made these blades live on the outskirts of the Zande area of influence.

"Now I could delight my eyes in the fantastic figure of the king, who, I had been told, ate human flesh every day"
(G. Schweinfurth)

Mangbetu

Geographic locations
Democratic Republic of
the Congo, central
Africa

Chronology
19th century: birth
of the Mangbetu
kingdoms
Mid-19th century:
Arab and Sudanese
slave traders arrive; the
Mangbetu kingdoms
are split into sultanates

Related entries
Zande, slavery

Today numbering about eight hundred thousand people, the Mangbetu were probably aboriginal to the area occupied by today's Sudan; from there, they migrated to the northwestern forests of today's DRC, where they intermarried with the Bantu and the Pigmy (Mbuti) populations. The word *Mangbetu* actually only designates the aristocracy of the reigning lineage, not the entire population. The Mangbetu were mostly hunter-gatherers and manioc and banana farmers. Although forest fruit could be foraged all year round, still the Mangbetu built silos for storing dried or smoked bananas, meat, and fish. During the 19th century, chief Nabiembali transformed the government into a kingdom; in the 1850s, weakened by the repeated attacks of the neighboring Zande, the kingdom split in two. At about the same time, the Muslim Nubians began to include the Zande and Mangbetu chiefs in the ivory and slave trades, fragmenting the kingdom into sultanates. At the end of the 19th century, the Belgians, French, and English reached the area, driving the slave merchants away and subjugating the Mangbetu.

▶ Human-shaped
box, Mangbetu
(DRC). New York,
Harold Rome
Collection.

Mangbetu vases are an example of court art produced for a political purpose and devoid of religious meaning. First appearing when the Belgians took over the land, they were shown to the invaders to prove the pomp of the Mangbetu courts, whose members hoped to become political intermediaries.

The elongated head shape recalls the aesthetically induced cranial deformations of Mangbetu women, further emphasized by the elongated headdress.

The base also becomes figured, turning into a woman's body.

▲ Water pitcher, Mangbetu (DRC). Berlin, Museum für Volkerkunde.

This "contact art" form developed from two separate currents in the Mangbetu artistic tradition: non-figured terracottas and figurative wooden sculpture. The arrival of the Europeans led to a foreign demand for figured objects, which influenced the local arts.

The Mangbetu practice of elongating the head for aesthetic reasons lasted until the mid-1950s, when the Belgian government outlawed it. To achieve this effect, the heads of the newborns were wrapped with raffia and hair from the day they were born. At first fashionable among the nobility, it became a mark of beauty for all social strata, even among neighboring tribes.

The "basket headdress," which emphasizes the elongated head, is supported by a reed frame and completed with hair extensions taken from corpses.

The aesthetic effect is completed with ivory (or bone, wood, brass, iron, or copper) hairpins. For men, the pins are used to hold the hat firmly on the head.

In times of mourning, the headdress is "broken"; sometimes the head is shaved.

▲ Traditional headdress, Mangbetu (DRC).

King Mbunza dances before his wives in the audience hall.

The artist probably exaggerated the size of the audience hall to astonish the European reader. This mixture of reality and fantasy was aided by the Mangbetu themselves, who wanted the Europeans to believe that they were the most politically and artistically evolved tribe in the region.

The king's one hundred and twenty wives sit on sculpted seats: their typical headdresses and geometric body art are clearly visible.

The German botanist Georg Schweinfurth, who spent about three weeks in Mangbetu land, made several drawings that were to be a lasting influence on the Western imagination, helping to create a stereotype that guided later travelers: the nobility of the Mangbetu kings and the splendor of their court is exalted, but there is also revulsion at their "cannibalism."

▲ *King Mounza Dances before His Wives* (from Schweinfurth, 1875).

Lega

"He who for the first time sees lusembe *finds it useless" – Only the initiated can grasp the meaning of a Bwami emblem (Lega saying, Democratic Republic of the Congo)*

Geographic location
DRC

Chronology
16th century: the Lega settle in present-day East DRC
19th century: clashes with Arab traders

Related entries
Swahili, chiefless societies, age-sets and initiation, slavery

The Lega people live in the forests of the eastern DRC between the Great Lakes and the Lualaba River, where they migrated in the 16th century from what is now Uganda. In the past they were warriors who subsisted on hunting and gathering, fishing, and banana and manioc farming. Their only known crafts were blacksmithing and pottery (done by women potters), with very little trading (they had no markets). They were ruled by segmented, patrilineal clans with no centralized authority and a lineage-based power structure. Political authority was exercised by a village chief, who drew his power from his relationship with the village ancestors. The Bwami society filled an important role in each clan and unified its members: the society developed and transmitted the clan's ethics, conferring titles of prestige through a five-step initiation system and both secret and public ceremonies in which the entire village was involved. Women also could be inducted

and played different roles according to the husband's rank. The region was ravaged in the late 19th century by the slave and ivory trades: the Lega clashed with the Arabs, who had come from the northeast to set up commercial outposts along the border with their lands.

▶ Ivory mask, Lega (DRC). London, Entwistle Gallery.

These ivory figurines are owned only by the members of the two highest ranks of the Bwami society.

A recurring element in Lega figurative art is the heart-shaped face with a long nose.

These anthropomorphic ivory figurines are called iginga, *"objects that uphold Bwami teaching and precepts." Each portrays a specific character with distinct good or bad qualities, associated with dances or proverbs: depending on the context in which they appear, they assume different meanings and identities.*

▲ Bwami society statuettes, Lega (DRC). New York, Friede Collection.

Animal wood figurines. The objects in the basket are associated with sayings that change depending on the context or the collection of objects.

In the Lega clan-based society, solidarity is reinforced by the Bwami cult society that transmits their values and chooses their leaders. Those who reach the highest level by demonstrating strength and wisdom receive from their clan the goods needed for the initiation ceremony. Access to authority is temporarily bestowed on an elder whom the group holds in high regard.

Anthropomorphic wood figurines used in Bwami teaching. They represent characters to which good or bad moral qualities are attributed.

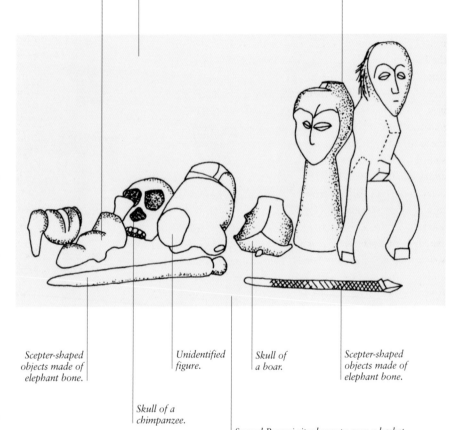

Scepter-shaped objects made of elephant bone.

Unidentified figure.

Skull of a boar.

Scepter-shaped objects made of elephant bone.

Skull of a chimpanzee.

▲ Drawing with contents of initiation baskets, Lega (from Layton, 1983).

Several Bwami ritual groups own a basket containing objects made at the initiation ceremony for the highest ranks; it is kept by the last candidate admitted. Upon receiving the basket, he must distribute to all the society members the goods that he accumulated with the help of his relatives to gain admittance to the new initiatory level.

"Unless it is here and now, it has no meaning" (Mbuti proverb, Democratic Republic of the Congo)

Mbuti

The Mbuti are one of the rainforest tribes (like the Baka, Bongo, Cwa, Twa, etc.) known as "Pygmies," from a Greek word meaning "short." About forty thousand surviving Mbuti live in the Ituri region of the eastern DRC, organized in semi-nomadic bands that hunt and forage, sometimes bartering wild game with Bantu farmers in exchange for bananas, manioc, salt, and iron tools. Men hunt while women forage, collecting honey in particular, an important food staple; about seventy percent of the food is supplied by women. As a rule, the vegetables are consumed by each family, while the hunted meat is shared by the entire band; in any case, the band practices solidarity so that everyone's needs can be met. Apart from the gender-based division of labor, there is no trade specialty and a fluid, egalitarian social structure prevails: the "bands" may split or regroup, especially for collective activities such as hunting treks. The only solid group is the nuclear family. While some individuals exert authority, it is never permanent or institutionalized, but results from their concrete contribution to the life of the band.

Geographic locations
DRC, central Africa

Related entries
Mangbetu, chiefless societies, hunters and gatherers

▼ Man making a drum, Mbuti (DRC).

These textiles are produced jointly by men and women: the men pound the inner layer of the ficus tree's bark into a length of fabric, and the women paint it.

A mixture of wood charcoal and the juice of the kange fruit yields black dye. Red dye is produced by grinding a plant's stem; lemon juice is used to trace the delicate drawings.

The multi-pattern designs of these fabrics, with their seeming lack of coordination, are almost a visual transposition of the intertwined structure and freedom that inform Mbuti polyphonic songs.

The textile patterns echo body art design and the signs traced on the ground during the hunting rituals. The patterns are divided into two main groups: "forest objects" (animals, trees, lianas, stars) and "camp objects" (mortars, combs, arrows, hunting nets, and ropes); zigzag lines can refer to snakes, ropes, or nets.

▲ *Murumba* fabric made of pounded and painted bark, Mbuti (DRC). Paris, Musée du Quai Branly.

The camps, inhabited by bands of a few dozen people each, are moved five or six times a year, based on food availability, within a circumscribed territory. The camp dwellers return to the same site once the forest resources have regenerated themselves. Moving is also one way of resolving conflict.

The camps are connected by ritual meetings and a continuous coming and going of visits, with visitors being accommodated for months at a time.

The wife moved and built a new hut upon the arrival of her husband's sister's son.

The back entrance was shut on the twelfth day.

The back of the camp was shut on the twelfth day.

The shared hearth was removed on the twelfth day.

This hut was built on the second day, abandoned on the third, and reoccupied on the fifth.

Transferred on the eleventh day.

Moved to another camp.

The camp layout corresponds to the changing composition of Mbuti bands; it does not reflect a hierarchical or family structure, but the status of inter-family relations. The egalitarianism of the Mbuti society is expressed by the ring-like layout of the huts that leaves a free area at the center. The entrance of each hut faces the huts of the friendly families and may change position based on their relationship.

▲ Village, Mbuti (DRC) (from Guidoni, 1975).

73

"One head alone cannot contain all the wisdom" (Maasai proverb, Kenya)

Maasai

Geographic locations
Kenya, Tanzania, eastern Africa

Chronology
1895: Kenya becomes a British protectorate
1915: the Maasai are expelled and their lands seized

Related entries
Kikuyu, chiefless societies, age-sets and initiation, hunters and warriors, herders, beads, dance

The Maasai are not a homogeneous people, but a conglomerate of distinct tribes of about one hundred and fifty thousand people scattered in Kenya and Tanzania; they share the Maa language and some socio-cultural traits such as a semi-nomadic pastoralist life. Their wealth is constituted by livestock, a sign of social prestige that is sometimes acquired through raids. The former English colonial government and the current Tanzanian government pressured the Maasai to treat livestock simply as a source of currency (to pay taxes), thus altering social relations, for men have always considered it their own property, not their women's. Theirs is a chiefless society organized in patrilineal clans and a system of age-based classes that groups men in fifteen-year age-sets, the building blocks of the Maasai military organization. These regiments are organized in two groups, based on the method of circumcision. From the ages of fourteen to thirty, the young warriors (*moran*) live isolated in the bush, where they learn the art of war and the duties of adult life. The Maasai have in turn allied, traded, and fought with the Bantu populations in the area, such as the Kikuyu, often forcing them to take shelter in the forest to escape Maasai raids.

► Young Maasai in isolation after circumcision (Kenya).

The Maasai military organization is based on different age-sets, with an entire age group being recruited at a specific time. The fact that the age-set is a closed group for long periods of time helps develop an esprit de corps and maximizes the warriors' effectiveness.

Each age-set is headed by a leader (labon), whom the colonial administrators mistook for chiefs, though their role is that of councilors without coercive powers.

When induction time comes for a class-set, circumcision rituals are performed for the young men between the ages of fifteen and twenty being inducted into the warrior group (moran).

Striking a balance between elder power and warrior power was not always easy, especially under English domination, as the administration increased the former and limited the latter, preferring to employ the warriors as a labor force.

▲ Maasai warrior (Kenya).

After serving ten years in villages specifically built for them, the young warriors become elder warriors, destroy the village where they lived and marry. The e-unoto ceremony marks this rite of passage, in which the mothers cut their sons' long hair and the ban on eating meat and milk in the presence of others ceases.

Each generation is divided in two warrior groups: the second group ("the left hand") is circumcised about six or seven years after the first ("the right hand"). Seven years after their circumcision, the "right hand" warriors become elder warriors, moving the incoming group into the phase they just vacated, of adulthood.

▲ *E-unoto* ceremony, Maasai (Kenya).

The concluding phase of the ceremony is the White Dance Day, which follows the Red Dance Day: at dawn, the warriors recede in the bush, paint their bodies with white chalk, and march in two files towards the village where the mothers welcome them; then they bow before the sacred hut (O-Singira) where a wild olive branch has been planted (the term e-unoto comes from the verb a-un, "to plant straight"), an allusion to the incoming age-set.

The most popular bead colors of the Maasai are black, white, blue, red, and pink, though in the 20th century the array of colors has widened. Of these, red, white, and black (or dark blue) have symbolic value. Red, associated with youth and the blood's vital force, is the color with which the bodies of the brides and the young initiated are painted.

Black is reserved for the elders and for God.

White has protective powers, and is used to paint the body of those undergoing a trial.

▲ Woman with bead necklace, Maasai (Kenya).

Recently added colors such as orange or green may stand for the base colors, with orange replacing red, and green replacing black and blue.

"When wrath fills the heart, it comes out of one's mouth"
(Kikuyu proverb, Kenya)

Kikuyu

Geographic location
Kenya

Chronology
1952–1956: the Mau
Mau rebel against
colonialism

Related entries
Chiefless societies,
age-sets and initiation,
colonialism, farmers

The Kikuyu are a people of Bantu-speaking farmers who live in central Kenya. Theirs is a patrilineal society with a system of age classes that includes the warriors (*anake*) and the council elders (*kiama*). Power is exercised by alternating generations, a method aimed at preventing any one group from becoming entrenched in power: each community is divided into two classes, the *mwangi* and the *maina*, with the children of a *mwangi* generation becoming *maina*, the grandchildren *mwangi* again, and so forth.

The British confiscated the Kikuyu lands in the early 20th century, turning the Kikuyu into "illegal squatters" and confining them to reservations. As a result, the Kikuyu were already among the more active groups in the anti-colonial liberation war in the 1920s, when they established the Kikuyu Central Association that included Jomo Kenyatta, who would become president of Kenya. The Mau Mau, the secret terrorist society made up of the impoverished unemployed, people who had been banished from their lands, and reservation farmers, were mostly Kikuyu.

▶ Ceremonial
shield, Kikuyu
(Kenya). London,
British Museum.

The shields are painted in geometric patterns on both sides. The patterns vary depending on the group of initiates; often the design on the back recalls an eye with eyelid.

The shields that the warriors use in their initiation dances are made of wood or bark, unlike those used in war, which are made of animal hide.

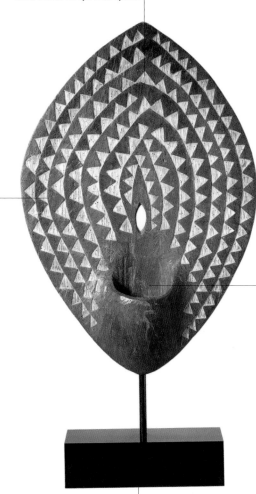

The back of the shield has a cavity for the arm, and thus is moved by flexing the arm, not the hand.

▲ Ceremonial shield (back), Kikuyu (Kenya). Private Collection.

When the English invaded what is now present-day Kenya, instead of meeting resistance from the Maasai, as they had expected, they had to fight the Kikuyu warriors. Given the superiority of firearms, the struggle was brief, but it left a deep mark in the collective memory of the Kikuyu.

"The wind will not break the tree that knows how to bend"
(Sukuma-Nyamwezi proverb, Tanzania)

Nyamwezi

Geographic locations
Tanzania, eastern
Africa

Chronology
18th century: the
Nyamwezi join the
Swahili trade circuit
1860–1884: birth of
the Nyamwezi
"empire"
End 19th century:
dissolution of the
Nyamwezi "empire"

Related entries
Swahili, slavery

The Nyamwezi today number about one million and a half people. They are Bantu-speaking farmers settled in central-western Tanzania, and were at one time divided into small kingdoms. Starting in the 18th century they were active in the ivory and slave trades that linked the hinterland to the coastal areas. From 1860 to 1884, Mirambo, a Nyamwezi military chief, fought the Arabs and the neighboring kingdom of Buganda for control of the long-distance trade routes and built an "empire" by unifying under his rule a number of small kingdoms. He bartered ivory and slaves for textiles (which he distributed to followers and allies) and firearms. He even formed alliances with the sultan of Zanzibar. His reign came apart upon his death. "Nyamwezi" is a Swahili word that literally means "people of the moon," signifying that they came from the west, where the moon rises. The name later was applied to ethnically diverse people whom the Swahili merchants recruited in central Tanganyika to work as porters and mercenary troops.

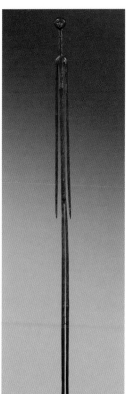

▶ Ceremonial insignia,
Nyamwezi (Tanzania)
(from Rubin, 1985).

Nyamwezi

The protruding ears, the prominent lips, and the eyes finished with beads are recurring traits of Nyamwezi sculpture.

This seat is carved from a single block of wood, differing from European chairs that are made of several parts joined together.

These high-backed, anthropomorphic carved seats with clearly rendered sexual features were probably meant to portray the clan's primordial ancestor mother. They were reserved for the chiefs, who sat on them to hear and adjudge legal matters.

▲ Seat, Nyamwezi (Tanzania). Private Collection.

The three curved legs with three jutting projections are typical of Nyamwezi seats.

"Multitudes to the wind / the earth is pale / the shout can be ploughed" (Luis Carlos Petraquin)

Makonde

Geographic locations
Mozambique,
Tanzania, Kenya,
eastern Africa

Chronology
1910: first contact
with Europeans
1960s: war of
liberation

Related entries
Swahili, colonialism,
trade, contemporary
visual arts, dance

The Makonde, over a million people, are a Bantu-speaking tribe settled between northeastern Mozambique and southeastern Tanzania (where they migrated in the 1950s), with small enclaves in Kenya as well. They are a matrilineal society organized in autonomous villages, with no central authority. They practice slash-and-burn farming. Although as coast dwellers they were active in the Swahili trade network, they came into contact with the Europeans quite late, in 1910. They have also resisted Islamic

penetration; their religion revolves around traditional ancestor worship. The Mapico mask society to which men are initiated fills an important role for this people. In the 1960s, the Makonde joined the Frelimo movement in the struggle for the liberation of Mozambique. In the West they are renowned for their ebony wood carvings (*shetani* and *ujamaa*), a craft that now supplies tourist demand.

▶ Belly mask, Makonde (Tanzania). Private Collection.

The Makonde masks of Mozambique are worn like helmets and differ from Tanzania's face masks. Real hair is inserted on the top of the head.

The Mapico dances also attract spectators from neighboring villages. Thus in addition to strengthening cohesion inside the group, they are an occasion for cementing relations with other groups that are not blood related.

Some of these masks have European, Arabic, or Asiatic features, perhaps in an effort to capture the foreigners' power, or as a strong form of social critique.

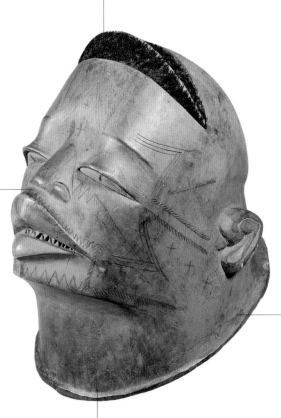

Mapico masks are believed to be the dead reincarnate, both men and women. For this reason, although frightful, they are not evil, occupying a category midway between benign ancestors (machinamu) and evil spirits (machatwani). Associated with the power of the men who have been initiated into their secrets, Mapico masks also appear at female puberty rituals.

▲ Mask, Makonde (Mozambique).
Private Collection.

George Lilanga, a contemporary painter, was influenced by the self-taught Edward Saidi Tingatinga (1932–1972), whose style, imitated by other artists as well, gave rise to a true genre, known as tingatinga. Subjects of this genre are animals (for which there is a high tourist demand), urban life scenes, and historical themes. Another frequent subject is the deformed representation of shetani spirits, influenced by Makonde beliefs and European painting, thus satisfying at the same time the exotic and aesthetic tastes of Westerners.

The use of highly contrasting and brilliant pure enamel colors on a monochromatic background is typical of the genre. Lilanga's "alien" figures, portrayed in scenes of everyday African life, lack the frightening quality of the shetani spirits.

George Lilanga was born in 1934 in Klkwetu, a village in Tanzania. He moved to Dar es Salaam, where he studied art. His work ranges from painting to sculpture. He died in June 2005.

▲ George Lilanga, Women Vendors, 2000.

"A patient man eats ripe fruit" (Swahili proverb, eastern Africa)

Swahili

The Swahili culture grew over the centuries from exchanges between the native coastal population and Arabs, Persians, and, later, Indian merchants. This urban culture thrived on trading seaports such as Manda, which reached its splendor in the 12th century, Mombasa, Pemba, Mafia, Kilwa, and Zanzibar. These ports acted as middle ground between the Indian Ocean merchants and the Congo hinterland that sent slaves and ivory tusks. The Swahili economy began to decline in the 16th century, when the Portuguese set up trading depots on the coast, to be replaced in turn at the end of the 17th century by the sultan of Oman, who lorded over the region for about two hundred years. In the 1830s, Swahili merchants even traveled to Angola, where they set up an exchange network that stretched from the Indian Ocean to the Atlantic. The "Swahili culture" rests on a common language but is not homogeneous, as many who identify with the culture do not call themselves "Swahili." The language is a mixture of Bantu and Arabic, with the latter adapted phonetically and syntactically to Bantu. The language of trade, Swahili has become a sort of lingua franca in much of eastern Africa and is the national language of Tanzania. The missionaries had no small part in spreading it, having chosen to preach in Swahili. A modified Arabic script is used in Swahili literature that hails back to at least the 17th century.

Geographic locations
Eastern coast (cities of Mombasa, Pemba, Mafia, Kilwa, and Zanzibar), eastern Africa

Chronology
12th century: apogee of Manda City
15th century: trade with China
16th century: the Portuguese arrive
17th century: rule by the sultan of Oman
19th century: Swahili traders reach Angola
19th century: apogee of door-carving art

Related entries
Black Islam, trade

◄ Swahili craftsmen carving a door, Zanzibar (Tanzania).

These boats of Arabic origin populate the coasts of the Arabian Peninsula, India, and eastern Africa. They sail by following the monsoons, traveling southward in winter and northward in late spring and early summer.

The dependency on long-distance trade and the failure to diversify their economy are related reasons for the decline of Swahili cities after the maritime trade collapsed with the arrival of Portuguese ships.

▲ Swahili boat (*dhow*), Zanzibar (Tanzania).

The Swahili cities derived their power and wealth from the commerce between East and West that passed through the Red Sea. They exchanged goods with the Arab, the Persian, and the Indian worlds, and starting in the 15th century with China as well. This business gave rise to a merchant class that vied for power with the traditional clan authorities; in the early 8th century, it converted to Islam.

This dispensary was built by a Delhi architect for Tharia Topan, an Indian merchant who intended to turn it into a hospital for the people of Zanzibar as a homage to Queen Victoria on the occasion of her jubilee. Begun in 1885, the building was completed only in 1894, after the merchant's death. The eclectic style mixes Arabic, Indian, African, and European motifs and is symbolic of Zanzibar's multicultural character.

The pointed tympani roofs are reminiscent of European architecture.

The wood railing of the balconies is reminiscent of Arabic shutters.

The portico's carved posts on the ground floor and the trefoil arches are in the Indian style.

▲ The old dispensary, Zanzibar (Tanzania).

The stone houses that filled the Swahili cities testified to the power of the leading families and contrasted dramatically with the surrounding straw huts. The father would build such a house for the daughter when she married. If the parents' and daughter's houses were adjacent, a sky-bridge would connect them.

The decorating motifs are partially local (the date palm, the incense cedar, the wave motif) and partially Indian (rosettes, lotus flowers).

It was customary, when a house was built, to start from the door: once it was in place, the house was built around it.

The door-carving tradition on the eastern coast blossomed in the 19th century. The double door opens inward; the central post, the doorjamb, and the lintel are carved.

▲ The old dispensary, Zanzibar (Tanzania).

"An empty belly is not good company" (Madagascar proverb)

Madagascar

Over the centuries, the culture of Madagascar became layered with Bantu, Arabic, and Indonesian elements. The Indonesians first reached the island in the sixth century. There are several theories about the origins of the kingdoms and chiefdoms that developed in the 17th century in the southwest of the island from the preexisting communities: some claim they were founded by Indonesians, and mention in support of their theory the outrigger canoe, the rice paddies, and even the Malagasy tongues; others stress the Arabic contributions or the Bantu influence (for example, in the role of magic to maintain the king's power). The plateau is home to the Merina, the Betsileo, and the Bezanozano, who possibly descend from a single tribe, but who look to the Merina as an aristocratic group whose ancestors hailed from southeast Asia. These populations reached the highlands in the 15th century, driven by the constant influx of small bands from Asia. Traditional lore mentions wars between the newcomers (the Merina) and the Vazimba (the "ancestors," who were Bantu), who were pushed farther inland. However, the Merina kings needed to make peace with the local divinities and thus with the "aboriginal" priests, which led to marriage alliances. The Arabic and Muslim influence touched the northwestern part of the island as the Swahili culture spread along the coast starting in the 11th century.

Peoples
Merina, Betsileo, Bezanozano, Mahafaly, Sakalava, Zafimaniry

Geographic locations
Madagascar, southern Africa

Chronology
6th century: earliest Indonesian presence
11th century: the Swahili expand their influence
12th century: rise of early kingdoms and chiefdoms
15th century: Merina, Betsileo, and Bezanozano settle on hinterland plateaus
18th century: rise of the Merina kingdom
19th century: the Merina kingdom becomes dominant

Related entries
Swahili, Black Islam

◀ Woman at the market (Madagascar).

The use of vertical funerary insignia, extending as it did from eastern Africa to Indonesia, passing through Madagascar, is evidence of the extensive contacts between these different cultural areas.

Like the Sakalava, the Mahafaly, who live in the south of the island, are renowned for their funerary art. The ancestor tombs are placed inside square areas enclosed by wood or stone fences and filled with stones, into which the funeral insignia are stuck.

The carved scenes illustrate the life and achievements of the deceased, personalizing the figure and creating a memory for the descendants.

The horns of the animals sacrificed at the funeral are arranged on the stones around the insignia. The Mahafaly shape the animals' horns as they grow, into unusual shapes.

▲ Funeral insignia (alo alo),
Mahafaly (Madagascar).

Villages are built on hills. The different altitudes of the houses imply a hierarchical and temporal difference, for in principle, the progenitors live higher up on the hill, the descendants below. To look at a landscape means to visually reconstruct the history and relations of one's own people in the space where they have made their home.

Man inserts himself in the natural environment, a manifestation of God, and by building his home leaves a lasting mark on the landscape. The success of a marriage is manifested in the house, especially the house of the village ancestors, which is sanctified: the central wood post and the three hearth stones become the meeting place of all the descendants.

The Zafimaniry, consisting of about twenty thousand people, live in eastern Madagascar in a mountainous, wooded area. The progressive cutting down of trees is modifying the landscape as the woodland is replaced by grassland and by rice fields cultivated on irrigated terraces. This is bringing about a change of life style, which the Zafimaniry interpret as a change in "ethnicity": because it is the Betsileo tribe that traditionally has cultivated rice, they themselves are becoming "Betsileo" as their environment changes.

▲ Zafimaniry village
(Madagascar).

These cloths are commonly used as shawls and to wrap the dead for the "second funeral" when, after a first burial in a temporary grave, the bodies are exhumed, washed, and wrapped in the length of cloth, then buried again, this time with the remains of the ancestors.

In the 19th century, fabrics with more complex weave patterns became fashionable among the Merina aristocracy. This was achieved by adding heddles to the looms and coloring the textiles with red aniline dyes imported from Europe.

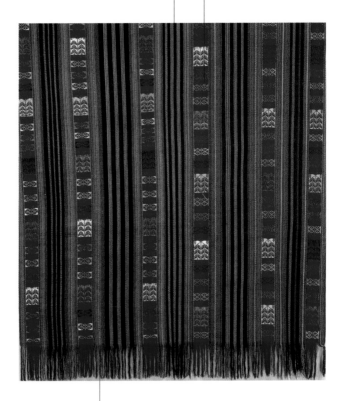

The Merina kingdom arose in the 18th century in the central tablelands of Madagascar. They were a farming people, divided in castes: a light-skinned nobility, the freemen, and the slaves. The expansion of rice farming in the swampy hinterland provided more and better nourishment for the slaves, who became goods to be exchanged for European firearms. Ravaged by civil war in the 18th century, the kingdom was unified again around 1780; in the 19th century it became the political leading force of Madagascar.

▲ Silk fabric (lamba akotofahana), Merina (Madagascar). London, British Museum.

"Soon they shall be reduced to a mere curiosity of nature: already in England and in Paris, there are stuffed samples"
(Charles Robert Knox)

San

The names *San* and *Bushman* refer to hunter-gatherer clans organized in small villages of usually less than fifty people that the Europeans found when they reached southern Africa. The San created most of the rock paintings and carvings scattered in about fifteen thousand sites in the mountains of South Africa, Namibia, Zimbabwe, Botswana, and Lesotho. Many of these works of art cannot be dated, while others are recent. The earliest rock painting was discovered in southern Namibia in the early 20th century at the Apollo Site 11, and dates to 25,000 BC: it is the first example of African painting. The paintings and carvings have different characteristics and are found in various places: while carvings are mostly of isolated figures, mostly animals rendered somewhat geometrically, the paintings have a more varied iconography of animals, human figures, deformed beings, hand prints, and abstract forms and also reproduce hunting or camp scenes, sometimes in narrative fashion. San rock artworks are thought to have had magic-religious purposes: they are representations of past events and propitiatory evocations of trance-inducing rituals through which the San priests and the witch doctors mastered the rain, wild game, and sickness.

Geographic locations
South Africa, Namibia, Zimbabwe, Botswana, Lesotho, southern Africa

Chronology
25,000 BC: Namibia, oldest rock painting

Related entries
Hunters and warriors

◄ Rock painting, San, Kamberg Natural Reservation (Namibia).

Figures of animals and human beings appear together in interrelated contexts. The alcina antelope is a frequent subject: more than any other animal, it was believed to embody the vital force. Interestingly, traces of blood have been found on these paintings.

About six hundred rock-painting sites have been found in the Drakensberg Mountains, with about thirty-five thousand works of art.

▲ Rock painting, San, Kamberg Natural Reservation (Namibia).

Colors were made with clay (white), charcoal and manganese for black, and ocher for red and yellow.

The beliefs of today's !Kung, a San group that lives in the Kalahari desert, confirm the magical-religious importance of the antelope: they perform trance-inducing dances around the sacrificed animal's carcass and believe that the shaman becomes an antelope in order to enter the otherworld.

Ethnological research on shaman rites among
hunting-gathering peoples has been used tentatively
to formulate theories about the function of rock
paintings and carvings; in particular, the meaning
of the giraffe, a recurring motif.

According to
these theories,
the stylization
of the figures
should not be
interpreted as
a lack of
realism, but
rather as a
faithful
representation
of the altered
state of
perception
induced by the
trance.

The importance
that the shamans
attribute to the
backbone as a
conduit of the
vital force would
explain the
symbolic
importance of
the giraffe.

The patches on the giraffe could
signify the fragmented state of
perception during a trance.

▲ Rock carving of a giraffe,
3000 BC–1000 AD, San
(Namibia). Windhoek,
Namibia State Museum.

Ostrich eggshells can survive intact for thousands of years; the hunting-gathering San, who until recently were still using them to store water or food, began to use them at least fifteen thousand years ago.

The patterns traced with stone tools first, then with iron chisels, are made by both men and women: ocher is used for red and charcoal for black.

Usually the designs consist of curves, triangles, and zigzag lines. In the 20th century, animal drawings began to appear, though the geometric decoration continued to prevail. No meaning has been found for this art, which could simply have a decorative purpose.

The relative rarity of eggs with traced drawings suggests that they were reserved for special purposes: fragments of traced eggs have been found in funerary furnishings; but they could also have been made for the tourist trade that developed quite early in South Africa.

▲ Ostrich eggs, San (Namibia).
Private Collection.

"Cross a big lake only once because if you go back, crocodiles will be on the alert" (Shona proverb, Zimbabwe)

Shona

Geographic locations
Zimbabwe,
Mozambique,
southern Africa

Chronology
5th century BC: first
settlements in the
Great Zimbabwe area
14th–15th centuries:
apogee of Great
Zimbabwe's power
16th century: fall of
the Great Zimbabwe
kingdom
16th century: kingdoms
of Khami and
Monomotapa
19th century: Ndebele
invasion

Related entries
Swahili, male and
female, beads

The Shona are a Bantu-speaking people who live between Zimbabwe and Mozambique. When the Portuguese reached this area in the 16th century, they met the Karanga (a Shona clan), from whom they learned about the vanished Great Zimbabwe kingdom whose monumental ruins were still standing: in particular, a stone complex in a highland valley between the Zambesi and Limpopo rivers. Great Zimbabwe reached its splendor between 1300 and 1450; its economy was based on agriculture, livestock breeding, gold extraction, and trade with the Swahili (as evidenced by Chinese porcelain and thousands of southeast Asian beads found among the ruins). The earliest settlements date to the fifth century BC and the oldest walls to the middle of the 13th century AD. The compound, which included the royal palace, was probably abandoned after 1550, when the Great Zimbabwe kingdom was displaced by the Khami and the Monomotapa. The main site, surrounded by walls, was home to the royal family, while the twenty to thirty stone houses surrounding it were for the nobility. The image of Great Zimbabwe as a great empire, however, is incorrect: the abundant land, the small population, and the subsistence economy were not conducive to building a great concentration of power. Great Zimbabwe was just one of the many kingdoms of about the same size and power that populated the region at one time.

▶ Upper part of Great Zimbabwe's fortified walls (Zimbabwe).

These ruins were built with blocks of granite from rocks subjected to natural cleavage by climatic change, or detached by warming the rock, then quickly cooling it with water.

In contrast with their imposing presence, the walls' interior spaces are narrow, which has only increased the mystery surrounding this monumental site, suggesting that it might have been an initiation locale.

The small entrance towers shaped like Shona silos were probably capped with monoliths in the shape of birds.

▲ Entrance in Great Zimbabwe's fortified walls (Zimbabwe).

The rocks were cut into regular blocks of varying thickness and neatly aligned to build dry walls to a height of thirty feet and a width of fifteen. Their imposing nature suggests that they were bulwarks, though the available data seem to rule it out, since there are no clearly recognizable military structures and many walls simply trace short arches around which one can easily walk. Perhaps they had a symbolic function and were signs of royal authority.

Only a few Great Zimbabwe sculptures exist. Because they were found accidentally, we lack precise information about their original sites and their use. They were presumably altar pieces, or stood on top of gates or walls.

This is the upper part of a steatite monolith of a bird, probably an eagle or a vulture, as may be presumed from the broken hooked beak.

The standing posture and the legs' unusual position suggest that the artist's intent was not to portray a specific bird, but a fantastic being embodied in animal form.

▲ Soapstone sculpture, 13th–15th century (Great Zimbabwe). Private Collection.

Currently, Shona people consider the birds messengers of the gods or incarnations of ancestors, but we do not know if these or similar beliefs were also part of Great Zimbabwean cults. According to some theories, these statues represented the king, for both the king and the bird link the sky to the earth.

African headrests are quite comfortable because by reducing the contact surface to a minimum, they make perspiration easier and keep the head cool.

Anyone using this headrest would not flatten or ruin his or her elaborate headdress.

The overall shape and the triangular and circular motifs of the base suggest, apparent abstraction notwithstanding, a female figure with legs, breasts, and shoulders showing. A person who used this headrest would complete the figure by adding the head.

Among the Shona, it is mostly men who use headrests. While they sleep, they visit their ancestors, on whose favors the wellbeing and prosperity of the family depends. Sometimes diviners also use them, to make contact with the netherworld.

▲ Headrest, Shona (Zimbabwe).
Raleigh, North Carolina Museum of Art.

"The elephant is not burdened by the weight of his tusks"
(Ndebele proverb, Zimbabwe)

Ndebele

Geographic locations
Zimbabwe, South
Africa, southern Africa

Chronology
1821: the Zulu empire
splits and the Ndebele
kingdom is born
1893: fall of the
Ndebele kingdom

Related entries
Shona, Nguni, hunters
and warriors, beads

The Ndebele are a Bantu-speaking group (part of the Nguni popu-lation), at one time a nation that split from the Zulu empire under Shaka after Mzilikazi, one of their military chiefs, rebelled in 1821. As a result, the Ndebele migrated to the north and set up a military state based on the Zulu model in the southern part of today's Zim-babwe, where they subjected the Shona people. Their social struc-ture rested on three distinct groups: Zansi, Enhla, and Hole.

The first group was the ruling aristocracy that claimed descent from the fellow warriors of the founding hero; the second was more numerous and was composed of the Sotho, Venda, and Tswana tribes, who had been subjected and assimilated before the Ndebele settled in Zimbabwe; the third and largest group included the Shona and other tribes that had voluntarily submitted in exchange for protec-tion from neighboring raids, or prisoners of war who would be forced into the Nde-bele regiments or to work as slaves. The Ndebele nation fell in 1893, when it was attacked by the English.

▶ Ndebele woman
painting a wall
(South Africa).

Nyoka *means "snake," an animal associated with the
ancestors, hence with fertility. The different styles of the beaded
garments reflect the steps of a woman's coming to maturity and
her changing social duties: at one time worn daily, these dresses
are now worn only on important occasions.*

The women
transfer the designs
of their murals to
beadwork; an
interesting detail is
the use of black
contours to trace
the shapes. In
recent decades the
characteristic white
background has
been replaced by
colored ones.

The manufacturing
of beads in
southern Africa
has local origins;
to these were
added glass beads
from Europe that
acquired the same
meaning and use
as the native ones.

As in mural painting, some geometric forms take on
a figurative identity (such as architectural elements
or sections of houses), even composing veritable
landscapes. The house is an element of stability for
a people that since the end of the 19th century has
been forced by war to move time and again.

▲ *Nyoka* garment, Ndebele
(South Africa). London,
British Museum.

Ndebele houses are decorated in brightly colored geometric frescoes whose shapes are heightened with black outlining. Sometimes they also include stylized figurative elements, such as airplanes, that evoke modernity and the West.

This art was born about one hundred years ago, after the English defeated the Ndebele and dispersed them in Sotho land. Mural painting and its unusual style became an identifying element, a sign of cultural membership in a group in a foreign land.

▲ Ndebele woman in traditional garb (South Africa).

These frescoes were painted by women and express their vision in a society that allows them little decision-making power. The symbolic heart of the compositions are the allusions to fertility, the earth, and the cosmic order.

Only apparently abstract, these compositions are symbolic representations of villages and landscapes and are associated with specific sites, especially in their current revival in urban settings, where they become political and identifying symbols.

"Hot water doesn't stay hot forever" (Zulu proverb, South Africa)

Nguni

Peoples
Nguni, Zulu, Sotho, Swazi, Xhosa, Ndebele

Geographic locations
South Africa, Zimbabwe, Lesotho, southern Africa

Chronology
19th century: rise of centralized military governments
1816–1828: Shaka forms the Zulu kingdom
1879: fall of the Zulu kingdom

Related entries
Ndebele, hunters and warriors, male and female, divination, dance

The name *Nguni* refers to an aggregate of Bantu-speaking peoples who live on the eastern coast of southern Africa, presently numbering about eighteen million. Organized in patrilineal, mostly pastoralist, chiefdoms at the turn of the 19th century, as land was becoming scarce, commerce was intensifying, and the area was racked by political upheavals, the chiefdoms became small, centralized military states, such as those of the Zulu, Sotho, Swazi, Xhosa, and Ndebele, that expanded to the center and south of Tanzania, subjugating and assimilating a number of ethnically different groups. The Zulu state was founded by Shaka: from 1816 to 1828 he turned a small clan into a powerful kingdom that held on to its independence until 1879, when it fell under English rule. Its strength was ensured by a system of age-sets as a basis for forced conscription and the formation of regiments that progressively included the young men of the conquered and assimilated tribes. A key element in this state-building process was the creation of a symbolic, political unity around the figure of the monarch, who was looked upon as a mediator between the living and the ancestors, thus as a creator of his people's prosperity.

► Men dancing in Soweto, Zulu (South Africa).

Spoons such as these, when privately owned, were buried with the owner in his grave, but if they were gifts from the bride's family exchanged during the prenuptial negotiations, upon the man's death they were returned to his wife.

The concave part of the spoon corresponds figuratively to the head.

The elongated shape of the handle suggests a female body with emphasis on the breasts, buttocks, pubis, and belly.

Spoons also have a symbolic function: as signs of a person's social status, they can be quite elaborate. In southern Africa artistic forms are generally geometric, but sometimes the link between an object and its owner is made more explicit by figurative forms.

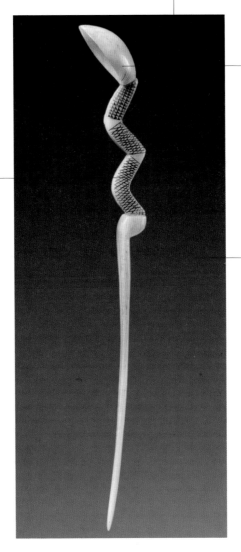

▲ Spoon, Zulu (South Africa), 19th century. Private Collection.

The Sotho number about ten million people, seven million of whom live in South Africa, and the rest in neighboring countries. Originally from the Transvaal, they settled in these lands in the 15th century. They are divided into northern Sotho (Puni), southern Sotho, and Tswana. Their languages, Sesotho, are similar, though each of the three groups is composed of heterogeneous tribes.

When the white man came and began to occupy the land, many were forced to migrate and to give up herding to work in the mines.

▲ A soothsayer, Sotho (South Africa).

The Sotho kingdom (known as Lesotho) was born out of the resistance to the Zulu invasion: a clan led by Moshoeshoe took the helm of the resistance movement and founded the reigning dynasty. Unlike other Nguni groups who prefer to live in scattered settlements, the Sotho live in villages and towns of several thousand residents, which has increased their defense capabilities.

Each year in the spring, thousands of young Swazi women visit the queen mother's village: they dance bare-breasted and offer her in tribute bunches of freshly cut reeds, to show their strength and their adaptability to labor.

The girls wear colored tassels or cloths to indicate whether they are betrothed or still unattached.

On the eighth and last day of the ceremony, the girls appear before the king, who offers them meat.

▲ Dance of the reeds (*umhlanga*), Swazi (South Africa).

The Incwala (the king's ceremony), an annual ritual, reinforces the bonds of solidarity and unity in the Swazi kingdom: first the capital is symbolically plundered and the king is accused of being an enemy of the people; then, during the eating of the first fruits, order and authority are restored.

The Incwala helps to defuse the social tensions caused by the hierarchical structure and by the harvest that suddenly brings to an end a time of hardship, and is at once a ritual of rebellion and of purification.

▲ Incwala ceremony, Swazi (South Africa).

The ceremony is twofold, with the Small Incwala taking place fifteen days before the Great Incwala. In the first ritual, during the new moon, the queens, the priest closest to the king, the princes, and the royal regiments sing and dance ritually (simemo), disparaging the king. This is followed by other chants that reconfirm the people's support of the king. The second ritual resembles the first, but is on a grander scale.

The king is confined to the cattle pen and watched by his most trusted warriors. There he gains strength from the seawater and the water of the principal local rivers. He reaches maximum strength and transforms himself into Silo, a monster who has no relations with human society and represents chaos, a dangerous state. Then the ritual reintroduces the king into society, ensuring that his powers will be used for the good of the nation.

Power and Society

Kingdoms and Empires of the Sudan
Kingdoms of the Niger
Kingdoms of the Great Lakes
Grassland Chiefdoms
Chiefless Societies
Age-sets and Initiation
Secret Societies
Blacksmiths
Women Potters
Griots
Hunters and Warriors
Male and Female
Slavery
Colonialism
Post-colonialism
Images of Power

◀ Ivory mask, Benin (Nigeria), 16th century. London, British Museum.

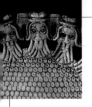

"Mansa Musa, emperor of Mali, flooded Cairo with his munificence. He left no emir or court notable without gifts of piles of gold" (Al-Umari)

Kingdoms and Empires of the Sudan

Kingdoms
Ghana, Mali, Shongay

Geographic location
Western Africa

Chronology
3rd–11th centuries:
kingdom of Ghana
9th–15th centuries:
statue art of Middle
Niger
9th–16th centuries: rise
and fall of the Shongay
kingdom (1591)
13th century: Sunjata
Keita founds the
kingdom of Mali
14th century: apogee
of the empire of Mali
1324: King Mansa
Musa makes a
pilgrimage to Mecca
16th century: fall of
the empire of Mali

Related entries
Mande, Akan peoples,
Black Islam, trade,
beads

▶ Clay male statue,
Djenné-Mopti (Mali).
Detroit, Detroit Institute
of Arts.

The savannahs of western Africa have historically been a portal between the Sahara and the Gulf of Guinea's forests. Especially after the Maghreb was converted to Islam, the northern regions supplied salt, textiles, tools, beads, and manuscripts, while the south provided primarily gold, but also kola, natural rubber, ivory, and hides. Islam marched southward, while slaves and pilgrims leaving for Mecca went northward. Sub-Saharan Africa, with its gold deposits in the Upper Niger and Upper Senegal Valleys and, more to the south, in the Volta River region and Akan country, was the main source of gold for Europe until the discovery and conquest of America. The same favorable geographical conditions that promoted economic and commercial development led to a concomitant political evolution as diversified, complex societies emerged in which states and clan-based chiefdoms coex-

isted. The Soninke kingdom in Ghana (3rd–11th centuries) fell under the Almoravids, who were later supplanted by the Malinke empire of Mali, which dominated most of western Africa, displaced in turn by the Shongay empire, which fell in the 16th century under Moroccan muskets and cannons. In the meantime, Portuguese ships were docking in the Gulf of Guinea and moving the center of commerce southward.

In the triangle between Ke Macina, Mopti, and Djenné, archaeological research has uncovered clay statuettes dated from the 9th to the 15th centuries in artificial mounds called toguere, *to which the population retreated during the overflowing of the Niger River.*

In addition to statuettes of men and women, the Djenné cache also includes figures of animals, such as hippopotami or elephants or figures of half-human, half-animal beings, perhaps mythological characters from an unknown pantheon.

▲ Anthropomorphic statue, Djenné (Mali), 14th–16th century. Private Collection.

The alluvial plain of the middle Niger's inside delta played a central role in the history of western Africa: while the abundant waterways made navigation possible and gave an exceptional impulse to agriculture and animal husbandry, the plain's position near the desert made it an ideal transit and exchange point of trans-Saharan trade. The city of Djenné, founded around 250 BC, was a cornerstone of this trade.

The Malian empire reached its splendor in the 14th century when its fame spread to Europe, where it was rumored to be a mythical El Dorado. This map of the world drawn in 1375 for Charles V, depicts the king of Mali sitting on a throne, legs crossed, with scepter and crown, holding a golden globe in his right hand.

The fame enjoyed by the Malian empire in the Mediterranean and the Middle East arose when King Mansa Musa I (1307–1332) made a pilgrimage to Mecca. It is reported that his retinue included sixty thousand bearers and five hundred servants with gilt-decorated dresses. The king's gifts of gold were so generous that they caused a devaluation of the precious metal.

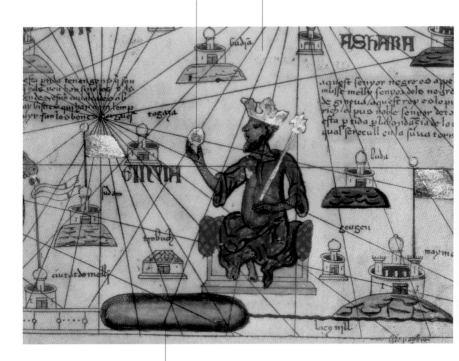

The Malian empire was decentralized, a sort of federation of kingdoms, chiefdoms, and city-states. It was founded by Sunjata Keita around 1230, when he led the Malinke Mande population into battle against the Ghanaian Soninke kingdom, founding a ruling dynasty where the succession was from brother to brother. The oral tradition attributed magical powers to him, and written Arabic sources stressed his faith in Islam.

▲ 1375 geographic map depicting the king of Mali. London, British Museum.

Because these statues were found in homes, they probably sat on family altars, as offerings in the propitiatory rites that oversaw construction of a new home, or perhaps they were offered to the deities in times of illness.

Although they come in a variety of poses – over sixty have been noted – most of these statues are in a kneeling position, with the bust upright and the hands on the knees. This uniformity is probably due to their ritual nature, which accentuates a strict formal language more than artistic freedom.

▲ Clay statue, Djenné (Mali).
Geneva, Musée Barbier-Müller.

In addition to richly attired aristocrats, Djenné artists also portrayed modestly dressed figures, often wearing only a loincloth, sometimes kneeling, with arms crossed on the chest or in more relaxed poses. Instead of frontal poses, limbs placed symmetrically, and the composition of the body in geometric volumes, which are so frequent in African art, these statuettes exhibit a strong, organic fluidity. This is partially due to the pliability of clay, which, being formless, encourages experimentation.

The head is turned upward, perhaps to look at the sky or as a sign of dignified detachment. Nose, mouth, and ears and the face overall are triangular. The beard is prominent and is likely a sign of authority and wisdom: by framing the face from ear to ear, it projects it forward, elongating it and emphasizing the man's importance.

The profusion of ornaments, such as a helmet, jewelry, and a harness, denote the figure's high social status. The attention to detail is concentrated on the upper part of the body, the head in particular, of both horse and rider. The lower limbs of both are barely shaped cylinders. This different treatment corresponds to the different importance attributed to the different parts of the body.

The parts of this sculpture are linked by the linear motifs carved on the headdress, nose, ears, beard, and especially around the eyes. Similarly, the crisscross pattern on the dress is repeated on the horse's harness, and the red-painted stripes on the man's body also appear on the horse's.

▲ Horseman, Djenné (Mali).
London, Entwistle Gallery.

The rider is on a larger scale than the horse because the latter is seen as an attribute of the human being rather than as an autonomous figure. The horse is a mark of status, especially in sub-Saharan Africa, where only the notables could afford them, due to their rarity and difficulty of survival.

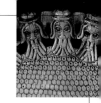

"When the king's palace burns, it will be replaced by one surpassing it in beauty" (Yoruba proverb, Nigeria)

Kingdoms of the Niger

The Nigerian forest was home to many interconnected kingdoms that left important artistic artifacts, principally the Ife (10th–15th centuries), Benin (14th–19th centuries), and Oyo (17th–19th centuries) kingdoms. All had their mythical-religious origin in Ife, the city containing the "world navel," the spot where the divine Obatala (or, according to another version, his younger brother Oduduwa, the usurper who was the first king of Ife and the progenitor of humankind) descended to earth, sent by Olorun, the sky god, to create dry land from the primeval marshes. Oduduwa's sixteen sons left from that same spot to found sixteen Yoruba cities. In all probability, the city of Ife owed its power to its role of commercial broker between the southern forests, the Middle Niger, and the trans-Saharan routes. It was gradually ousted from this circuit by the kingdoms of Benin and Oyo, and probably as a result began to decline. The city of Benin was the kingdom of the Edo people, ruled by a divinized king (*oba*) whose tribe came from afar, for the first king of this dynasty was believed to have come from Ife, invited to rule Benin by the elders who were tired of the abusive government of the previous dynasty. His foreignness heightened the sacredness of his powers, which included the legislative, executive, and judicial branches. He could impose capital punishment, owned all of the kingdom's lands, and held the monopoly on foreign trade.

Kingdoms
Ife, Benin, Oyo

Geographic locations
Nigeria, western Africa

Chronology
10th–15th centuries:
kingdom of Ife
14th–19th centuries:
kingdom of Benin
17th–19th centuries:
kingdom of Oyo

Related entries
Nigerian region,
blacksmiths, Shango
the thunder god,
Ogboni cult,
traditional artists

◄ King Obu Adekola Ogunoye, Olowo of Iwo (Nigeria).

This statue, 19 inches high, represents Oni, the king of Ife, dressed for his coronation ceremony.

The crowns may differ for each Ife ruler, but they all have a crest in the center.

The importance of the figure is underscored by the multiple strands of beads he wears around the neck, on the chest, and as anklets.

In the right hand the king holds a wood insignia lined with beaded fabric.

In the left hand the king holds a buffalo horn full of magic substances.

▲ Statue of Oni, Ife (Nigeria), 14th–15th century. Ife, National Museum.

Starting in 1910, about thirty "bronze" statues made with an alloy of copper, tin, and zinc were found near the royal palace and one of the ancient city gates. The metal-casting lost-wax technique could have reached Ife from the north, by way of the trans-Saharan trade.

The conical crown consists of rows of cylindrical beads that encircle the hair plaited into small braids falling to the nape.

The features of this portrait are of a naturalized idealism, typical of Ife art. The forms are full, the facial features relaxed, the mouth is fleshy, the eyes almond-shaped and without pupils. All these characteristics would also be present in the later bronze art.

In the center of the forehead is the mark where an ornament, now lost, had been attached; it was probably much like what we see on other, similar sculptures.

In the 1957 excavation of the Ife site, four clay heads and fragments of statues were found near an altar. Two heads were crowned, probably portraying queens, and were almost life-size; the other two probably represented servants and were smaller in scale to mark their lower status.

▲ Head with crown, Ife (Nigeria), 12th–15th century. Ife, National Museum.

The serpent, believed to be a messenger of Olokun, the god of the seas, is a recurring motif in Benin sculpture. It was customary to place pythons on the roof of the royal palace to guard it and to mediate between the oba's *earthly power and the heavenly power of the God Osanobua.*

"Portuguese head" motifs, a constant in Benin art starting in the 16th century, appear on palace posts. The trade with Portuguese merchants was a main source of Benin's wealth, and probably these figures had a propitiatory or apotropaic function.

*Most of these plaques portray kings, chiefs, and their attendants in ritual poses. This plaque represents the entrance to the palace of the Benin king (*oba*).*

▲ Brass plaque, kingdom of Benin (Nigeria), 17th century. Berlin, Museum für Volkerkunde.

These brass plaques, about nine hundred of which have been found, once decorated the posts of the Benin palace. Their rectangular shape and the presence of several characters in coordinated, sometimes interacting poses composing veritable life scenes, evoke Western book illustrations, though they seem to lack a narrative content.

The hole at the top of the head held a richly carved ivory tusk. Because the elephant was attributed with strength and wisdom, it was a symbol of royal power, and ivory objects were the exclusive prerogative of rulers.

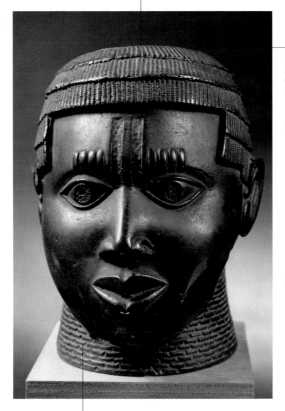

As was the case for the Ife tribe, a central element of power symbolism was the bronze heads lined on royal altars. They was presumably commemorative, or war trophies: the likeness of the heads of the most dangerous enemies killed in war were cast in brass and placed on the war altars or sent to the successors of the defeated chiefs as a warning against further rebellion.

These memorial heads, as well as the brass plaques, first appeared in the 15th and 16th centuries, a period of great expansion of the kingdom of Benin, contemporaneous with the arrival of the Portuguese. Their stylistic diversity has been read chronologically as a passage from a naturalism perhaps influenced by Ife art, to an increasing stylization (stiffer facial features, larger gorget, and multiple ornaments).

▲ Memorial head, kingdom of Benin (Nigeria), 15th–16th century. Lagos, National Museum.

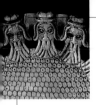

"Huge huts with well-combed thatched roofs, like heads dressed by a London wig-maker" (John Speke)

Kingdoms of the Great Lakes

Kingdoms
Buganda, Rwanda

Geographic locations
Edward, Kivu, Tanganyika, Kloga, and Victoria lakes (Rwanda, Burundi, Uganda, and Tanzania)

Chronology
16th century: Rwanda separates from the small kingdom of Bugesera and begins to expand
18th century: Buganda becomes the largest Great Lakes kingdom
1856–1884: Mutesa I reigns in Buganda
1896: the kingdom of Rwanda becomes a German protectorate
1919: Rwanda and Burundi become Belgian protectorates

Related entry
Swahili

According to a long-standing European theory, the centralized kingdoms of the region bordered by the Edward, Kivu, Tanganyika, Kloga, and Victoria lakes (between Rwanda, Burundi, Uganda, and Tanzania) were born when the aboriginal tribes were conquered by Semitic groups such as Ethiopians, Nilotics or Gallans, who established a feudal-type monarchy founded on a foreign aristocracy of herder-warriors and a subjected mass of aboriginal farmers. More recently, this interaction between herders and farming populations has been interpreted as a centuries-old dynamic of different cultural and linguistic groups that is typical of these lands and that led the states to try to control small communities and pastoralist clans that had slowly migrated to the area over the centuries. The attempts to achieve integration and to control the clans' livestock included cooptation and marriage alliances. The king exercised his authority on the local communities, absorbing their cults and converting them into legitimizing tools of his power. This region, isolated until the mid-18th century, was gradually integrated into the Swahili trading network.

▶ Ronald Muwenda Mutebi II, king of Buganda, Uganda, 1993.

The economy of the kingdom of Buganda rested on farming and its control of the Swahili trading network that in the 19th century linked the hinterland to the coast. The state's power rested on a hierarchy of functionaries appointed by the king, an efficient fiscal system, and the ability to secure the borders against foreign attackers.

With the death of the king, the capital was moved, a symbolic act of regeneration of the kingdom, while continuity was ensured by preserving the jaws of the deceased kings as a visible aid to the historic memory of the dynasty.

At the end of the 19th century, Mutesa I established a national army and the post of mujasi, *an officer in charge of the royal arsenal who, unlike the other chiefs, extended his military power over most of the kingdom, recruiting directly the best warriors instead of delegating the task to the local chiefs. Thus Mutesa cemented his power. He risked being overthrown when the royal army rebelled and the local chiefs refused to come to his defense.*

Dorothy Tennant Stanley, *King Mutesa of Buganda*, 19th century. Private Collection.

Starting in the 18th century, a Tutsi aristocracy gradually took power in Rwanda and ousted the Hutu. In about the same period, in Burundi, the Baganwa dynasty was mediating between the Tutsi and the Hutu. The incoming Belgians took the Rwandan situation as a model of racial hierarchy and extended it to Burundi. The local population, as a result, interiorized this colonial view.

These baskets made of coiled, sewn vegetable fibers complete with conical covers, were made by the women of the Tutsi aristocracy. The traditional colors are natural dried vegetable fibers; red is extracted from seeds and roots, and black from boiling bananas. These objects later entered the tourist market.

▲ Plates and baskets, Tutsi (Rwanda). Private Collection.

The Hutu and Tutsi tribes share a language, a history, and a territory. Their "ethnic" opposition results from 19th century Western racial ideology and colonial policy. The Europeans saw the Tutsi as an intermediate race between blacks and whites, the product of intermarriage with Aryan populations from the north. This racial fantasy, and the feudal system, were implicit in the colonial arrangement of Rwanda and Burundi, where a distinction was made between "Tutsi chiefs" and "Hutu masses."

"As a child said: my mother is my chief, my father is my mother's chief, and the king my father's chief" (Bamileke proverb, Cameroon)

Grassland Chiefdoms

The French word *chefferie* (chiefdom, chieftaincy) denotes in anthropology a sort of intermediate political entity between chiefless societies and states. The concept is somewhat ambiguous, for "chiefs" or "chieftains" in Africa were often a colonial creation, middlemen between the European administration and the natives. Similarly today, with the introduction of the multi-party system in many African states, "traditional chiefs" have been used as efficient vote getters. Still, the difficulties met by the post-colonial states in creating a strong national identity have contributed to a revival of local authority and affiliation. Starting in the 15th century, on the plateaus of western Cameroon, a mosaic of small kingdoms (Bamun, Bamileke, Tikar) emerged, almost one hundred of them, the result of adding to the native populations others who were moving there from neighboring lands. These kingdoms had no homogeneous ethnic base, but were unified in their acceptance of the political and religious power of the king (*fo*). Among the Bamileke, the *fo* oversaw the land, which he distributed among the various families; although not a divine figure, he had a sacral power derived from the founding ancestor, for the fertility of the soil and of women depended on him, thus also the continuation of life and the welfare of the community at large.

Kingdoms
Bamun, Bamileke, Tikar

Geographic locations
Cameroon, western Africa

Chronology
15th century: rise of chiefdoms and small kingdoms
18th century: demographic crisis caused by the slave trade
19th century: apogee of the Bamileke chiefdoms
1902: the Germans enter the Grassland

Related entries
Colonialism, post-colonialism, skull worship

◀ Buffalo mask, Bamileke (Cameroon). Private Collection.

The figure of the king is sacred: his body is a great container of the vital force that resides in the blood received from the ancestors, in the saliva and the sperm. Many emblems of power are "containers" and allude to these beliefs, such as the pipe and the horn for drinking palm wine. The horn is handed down from king to king and in it dwells the strength of all those who drank from it before and left saliva and their words in it (when one speaks on a horn, he can speak only the truth).

The son chosen by his father to succeed him inherits all his goods, including his wives, his titles, his name, and his authority over the children (who until then were his brothers).

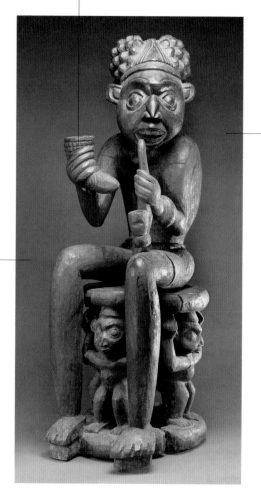

The king does not have absolute authority, which is mitigated and counterbalanced by court advisors, by the authority of the local chiefs, and by more or less secret associations that often use masks. The power of the king (fo) rests on religion, which in turn revolves around the ideas of a mystical energy, of strength (kè), of the god Si, and of the cult of spirits and ancestors. Kè is one and multiple, the source of all forms of life, and dwells in God as well as in man and in all existing things.

▲ Wooden sculpture of a ruler (fo), Bamileke (Cameroon). Private Collection.

Kuo fo, *the royal throne, has a back in the shape of two male figures, perhaps the king's guardians and protectors (*'ngwala e tabue*). Their pose, with one hand supporting the opposite arm's elbow and the other hand supporting the chin, is the respectful greeting owed to the king when addressing him.*

*In the background is the locale (*nemo) *where the king meets with the Council of Nine (*mkamvu'u), *the political-religious board whose members are the descendants of the comrades of the first king of Bandjoun (a hunter who had come from the north) and of the local chiefs he had subdued.*

The gourds covered with glass beads are among the holiest of objects: they allude to the king and his fertility, and are symbolically associated with water. The water that the fo *pours from these "bottomless" gourds never ceases to flow, ensuring that the rains, on which the fertility of the fields depends, will fall. With their presence, the sacred gourds mark the ritual space.*

A leopard skin and an elephant tusk, the symbols of royal power, are laid out before the king. The fo *has the power of turning into a panther, an elephant, a buffalo, or a boa constrictor. Thus, like other African kings, his figure has a dark, frightful side: like all things sacred, the king is at once beneficent and dangerous.*

▲ King Ngnie Kamga of Bandjoun (1934–2003), Bamileke (Cameroon).

Doors consist of raffia sliding panels: the ribs of the raffia leaves resemble bamboo and are used to build walls. The buildings have a square plan and a conical straw roof. Beginning in the 1930s, straw began to be replaced with metal sheeting and the roofs changed from conical to pyramidal.

The carved figures either recall historical events, such as military victories, or are iterations of lines of warriors, heads of executed enemies, or the like.

▲ Carved door-jambs, Bandjoun, Bamileke (Cameroon), 19th–20th century. Berlin, Museum für Volkerkunde.

In the past, not everyone could use carved door-jambs and posts in their home or in shrines. Their use was severely restricted to the king, who alone could own a limitless number of them, and to the nobles, whose ownership of these architectural elements was proportional to their title and the wealth they were ready to disburse. Only the king could decorate with anthropomorphic figures; the nobles were only allowed to use posts carved with non-figurative elements and, more rarely, animals.

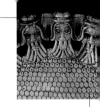

"We fight against the Rengyang, but when one of our two groups fights against a third enemy, we join and fight together"
(member of the Bor Nuer tribe)

Chiefless Societies

Chiefless societies are not constituted as states, that is, they have no central authority. Political decisions are made by the various lineages (groups of either matrilineal or patrilineal descent who share a common ancestor and live in the same area) and clans (exogamous groups of relatives who share a mythical ancestor and could inhabit different parts of a territory). Social life revolves around changing alliances and conflicts between clans and lineages, resulting in a constant break-up and merging of groups. The opposition between chiefless or segmentary societies and state-based ones is not clear-cut: anthropologists have identified "segmentary states," such as ancient Buganda, where a centralized power coexisted with local authorities who were linked to it but still autonomous. The existence of segmentary societies in Africa might be easier to understand if we treated it as a by-product of state societies, the result of pressure applied by large, overarching institutions, such as empires, on weaker societies, instead of trying to see in them the starting point of an evolutionary trajectory that ends in the state as the final political form.

Geographic locations
Western, central, eastern, southern Africa

Related entries
Kingdoms of the Great Lakes, age-sets and initiation

◀ A Nuer man (Sudan).

When the anthropologist Evans-Pritchard studied the Nuer in the 1930s, they numbered about two hundred thousand people, divided into several patrilineal tribes of nomadic herders with no central authority.

The feud was a social institution that helped to manage conflict, changing opposition into cooperation, for blood revenge could be suspended by paying a compensation, the "blood price." Thus the very meaning of "debt" and "credit" that subtends the concept of "feud" made it into a factor of social cohesion.

In addition to being the foundation of the Nuer's economy, cattle is also a "language" that expresses social relations. The Nuer despise the neighboring tribes that do not own cattle, they wage war against other herders, and they use cattle as compensation for murder. Finally, cattle determine the tribes' distribution over the territory, based on available pasture land and water sources.

▲ A Nuer camp (Sudan).

The tribe is the largest political unit: "the larger group whose members believe that they ought to join for the purpose of carrying out raids and for defense." The member of a tribe sees the members of a different tribe as an undifferentiated group, while he sees himself as "a member of a segment of his own tribe." A tribe is a military unit.

Tribes entered into alliances with other Nuer tribes for the purpose of raiding strangers, but only for short periods of time. War among Nuer tribes was subject to restrictions, such as the ban on molesting women or destroying homes and stables. These restrictions did not apply to wars against the Dinka, a foreign people.

Concentric arcs labeled from outer to inner:

THE GOVERNMENT OPERATES FROM MULTIPLE CENTERS

THE DINKA TERRITORY AND OTHER FOREIGN LANDS

THE NUER TERRITORY

THE EASTERN AND WESTERN NUER TERRITORY

OTHER NUER TRIBES

TRIBE

PRIMARY TRIBAL SECTION

SECONDARY TRIBAL SECTION

TERTIARY TRIBAL SECTION

VILLAGE

HAMLET

CATTLE FIELDS

COMPOUND

HUT

A cattle field is formed in the dry season by a village with other neighboring villages.

A hut houses a woman and her children; sometimes, also, the polygamous husband.

The village is the political unit, the smallest of the groups that are linked by blood ties. A village is a community founded on residence, blood ties, and affinities, as well as cooperation in several activities. Villagers feel a strong sense of solidarity with each other, developed in opposition to other villages.

A compound consists of a stable and several huts, where a simple or polygamous family lives.

A hamlet is inhabited by relatives with patrilineal ties, often brothers and their families.

▲ Diagram of Nuer socio-spatial categories, Sudan (from Evans-Pritchard, 1991).

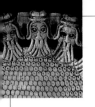

"The calf cannot decide for the leg" (Mongo proverb, Democratic Republic of the Congo)

Age-sets and Initiation

Geographic locations
Western, central, eastern, southern Africa

Related entries
Mande, Maasai, chiefless societies, farmers

In African culture children are not full-fledged human beings but fragile potential lives: though already born, they are not yet living. Access to full humanity is given only upon admittance into society through an initiatory path that gradually leads to knowledge and adulthood. Hence, being an adult is not a biological as much as a "social" age: it means having a set of skills and the rank required to become a full-fledged member of the community. One way of achieving this is to group the males (and, more rarely, the females) who were initiated in a certain time period into the same age-set. Age-sets or age-classes are deeply socializing, for they cut across family and residence, fostering solidarity and cooperation among the members. The youngest engage in community work and provide defense, while the elders conduct the group's business. The age-class organization of chiefless societies means a potentially egalitarian form of government, since in due time all groups, proceeding from rank to rank through the initiation rites, participate fully in the privileges of authority and prestige conferred upon each age-set.

▼ A group of Maasai children awaiting initiation, Kenya.

Horns are a symbol of fertility and vary in number from mask to mask, according to a specific sexual symbolism: three and six denote maleness, desire, and the drive for knowledge; four and eight denote femaleness or passivity, materiality, and life; two, five, and seven denote androgyny or the coexistence of activity and passivity, the duality of intelligence and animality, the need to work, and the fusion of male and female in married life, in society, and in the very unity of the person.

These masks are used by the N'tomo society, which provides the first step in the Bamana initiation, when preadolescent children are grouped and led to the rite of circumcision. The masks associated with each level have the task of transmitting knowledge to the initiates. The N'tomo mask is an image of man just as he left the hand of God. Its symbolism denotes the complementarity of male and female.

Each initiatory level is associated with different degrees of acquisition of knowledge and specific sensorial perception: in the N'tomo society, the nose is an important organ of feeling and of sociality.

▲ N'tomo society mask, Bamana (Mali). London, British Museum.

The Chi Wara society prepares young men for adulthood and its attendant roles of husband and farmer: the members of this initiatory and cult society are in the age-set that already underwent circumcision.

The upper shape is that of a pangolin: both an earth and a plant creature, it joins the roots to the upper part of the sorghum stem (the antelope horns).

The elements of different animals are assembled on several registers in this mask, expressing a plant symbolism associated with farm work: the bottom figure is an aardvark, a burrowing mammal that alludes to sorghum roots.

The curved shape in the middle evokes field stalks bending under the wind, the growth of the cereal, and the peasant's labor.

▲ Chi Wara mask, Bamana (Mali).
Paris, Musée du Quai Branly.

The Kore society is the last step in the initiatory path begun in the N'tomo phase: while the latter represents man as issued from the hand of God, the former elevates the same man to immortality.

The lion mask stands for the justice and serenity that accompany divine knowledge, in contrast to another Kore mask, the hyena, which stands for profane knowledge.

The members of the Kore society try to reach the contemplative, mystical state in which one no longer "speaks" but only "sees." To the initiates who query them about the meaning of symbols, the great teachers reply, "I do not know ... it seems to me that ...," leaving the initiates to find the answers on their own.

▲ Kore mask, Bamana (Mali).
Seattle, Seattle Art Museum.

"The lion that hunts to kill does not roar" (Toucouleur proverb, Senegal)

Secret Societies

Geographic locations
Western, central,
eastern, southern
Africa

Related entries
Western Guinea's
Coast, Nigerian region,
Grassland chiefdoms,
age-sets and initiation,
male and female

Secret societies are often not as secret as one might think. Perhaps, in some instances at least, it would be more appropriate to call them "closed societies," because although membership is restricted and highly regulated by initiatory rites, its members are known to all. These associations are selective and are interested in fostering their own social group, but do form alliances with other groups. The secret lies more in what is done at the meetings and in the magical and sacred sources of the association's power. Here as well, though, we must stress that the potency of the secret as a source of power lies precisely in the fact that the secrecy is a known condition, for often the secret itself is banal, or simply consists in the fact of knowing that there are no secrets. Masks are often used by secret or initiatory societies to wield power, approve transgressive behavior, or exercise social control. In particular, it is one way for men to lord it over women and children, by claiming a super-human reason for their power. But here also, everyone knows who hides behind the mask, and the "secret" is a game shared by all, where everyone "plays" his or her role.

▼ *Waniugo* mask, Senufo
(Ivory Coast). Geneva,
Museum Barbier-Müller.

Masks play an important role in the Poro initiatory society, which is popular with several tribes – such as the Mende, Kpelle, Senufo, Mano, and Vai – in Sierra Leone, Guinea, Liberia, and the Ivory Coast.

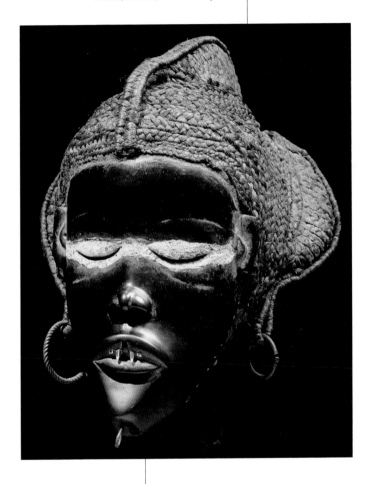

▲ Poro mask, Mano (Ivory Coast). Private Collection.

This society is charged with the initiation and education of young men, preparing them to become responsible adults ready to fulfill their social duties. The masks participate in all the key events of community life, and in addition to the initiation rites, they also attend funerals, end-of-mourning celebrations, and agrarian rites.

This mask is a helmet worn on top of the head, with the wearer's face and body hidden by a costume. These masks were mainly produced, and also perhaps originated, in the Bamileke kingdom of Bandjoun, where the members of Msop, a secret society, use them to hold sway over the community. They rarely perform in public, mostly at rituals such as royal coronations or the funeral of a king or a high dignitary.

In the art of the Cameroon Grassland, the cheeks are frequently swollen and prominent, and the mouth is open to reveal a great row of teeth.

The pupil-less eyes give this mask a ghostly appearance; its expressivity, the fact that the mask is nevertheless looking, is produced by the threatening movement of the concave, jutting surface of the eyebrows.

This mask represents the head of a hippopotamus rising from the water: this animal is the "double" of a high dignitary. The mask is in two parts: a lower, horizontal part and an upper, vertical one formed by enormous projecting eyebrows. The power of this figure is given by the rhythmic play of light and volume that maintains an overall unity, even in the analytical decomposition of the face into geometric shapes.

▲ *Tsesah* mask, Bamileke (Cameroon). Zurich, Rietberg Museum.

These helmets consist of a wood head covered with antelope skin and rest on a wicker disk tied to a dancer's costume. The effect increases the overall size of the mask, projecting an imposing quality. Because some masks are covered with human skin, some theorize that originally the dancer carried on his head the actual head of the slain enemy.

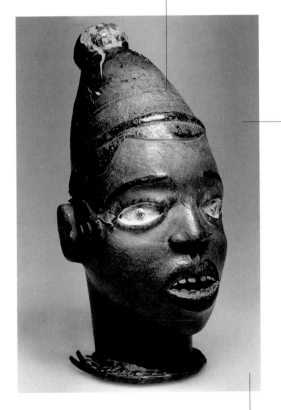

Ngbe is the leopard, whose spirit is evoked to protect the community in the dances that imitate its movements. The Ngbe society conducts the village's business and has both legislative and judicial powers.

For the Cross River Ejagham tribe, the Ngbe society is a secret warrior association that also engages in trade and in political activity. Membership is built through a set of shared symbols including masks and the symbolism of the nsibidi script, whose signs are mimed during the society's ceremonies.

▲ Mask, Ejagham Ekoi (Nigeria).
Private Collection.

141

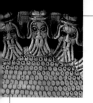

"If you forge a hoe, be sure to make a tip for the handle"
(Kongo proverb, Democratic Republic of the Congo)

Blacksmiths

Geographic locations
Western, central,
eastern, southern
Africa

Chronology
15th century BC: iron-
working sites in the
Niger region
9th century BC: iron-
working sites in
Nigeria
9th–3rd centuries BC:
copper-working sites
in Niger and
Mauritania
7th century BC: iron-
working sites in the
Great Lakes region
5th century BC: iron-
working sites in Gabon

Related entries
Women potters, male
and female

In the Mande region the blacksmiths, organized in endogamous "castes," live and work outside the villages and beyond the farmed fields, in the dangerous, wild savannah. The craft is handed down from one generation to another; it rests upon a mastery of the materials achieved by controlling the vital force (*nyama*) and by alliances with the woodland spirits where the blacksmiths gather firewood and iron ore. Thus they are also knowledgeable about healing herbs. One power attributed to blacksmiths is the ability to conjure rain or prevent it. Thus they are ambiguous men, at once needed and feared, but also despised. Their craft (making iron tools but also carving wood into masks and statues) is linked to their sacred functions. For example, they have a crucial role in the rites of circumcision that initiate the young into adulthood. They also practice divination by interpreting birdsong and the movement of snakes, or by throwing cowrie shells in the air and reading where they fall. Because of its malleability, the Bamana consider iron a symbol of education, while fire, because of the difficulty in taming it, is a symbol of knowledge. These skills in shaping a "trainable" material and taming a dangerous element give the blacksmith a knowledge whose breadth is surpassed only by God's.

▶ Iron horseman, Dogon (Mali). London, Entwistle Gallery.

In many parts of Africa, the art of smelting iron and casting it into objects is symbolized by blacksmiths, who have metaphorically appropriated a woman's reproductive power. Among the Shona tribe of Zimbabwe, this analogy is explicated and visualized by the female shape of the furnace, on which breasts, female scarifications, and sometimes belts for marking, preserving, and enhancing fertility appear. The "fruit" of the furnace emerges from the "belly," an opening between two leg-like projections.

The bellows to stir up the furnace fire (which will melt the ore, generating the iron objects) is often shaped like a penis with two testicles acting like side pistons (two air chambers made of animal skin that are expanded and contracted by two sticks tied to them).

When blacksmiths are busy smelting, they abstain from sexual relations with their wives because, as Malawi's Chewa believe, they are temporarily "married" to the furnace and must devote all their energies to it. Misshapen objects are believed to be caused by the blacksmith's adultery, perhaps with his own human wife.

▲ Bellows (Senegal). Paris,
Musée du Quai Branly.

The iron used in Africa today is not produced from local ore but from European car scraps.

Although the prevailing theory about the origin of iron metallurgy in sub-Saharan Africa is that the technique spread from Carthage or Meroë, archaeological research conducted in the 1980s has yielded dates that might possibly point to an independent discovery in the region: metallurgical sites dating to the 15th century BC have been discovered in the Niger area; in Nigeria, the sites date to the 9th century BC; in the Great Lakes region, to the 7th century BC; and in Gabon, to the 5th century BC.

While most weapons and everyday objects are made of iron because of its malleability and strength, symbolic or ostentatious objects are also made of copper and copper alloys, which although more malleable and brighter in color, are weaker than iron.

Copper metallurgy appeared relatively late in Africa: findings in Niger and Mauritania date its first appearance to between the 9th and 3rd centuries BC, suggesting that paleo-Berber populations – the ancestors of the present-day Tuareg – may have introduced it.

▲ Forge in Njaluahan (Sierra Leone).

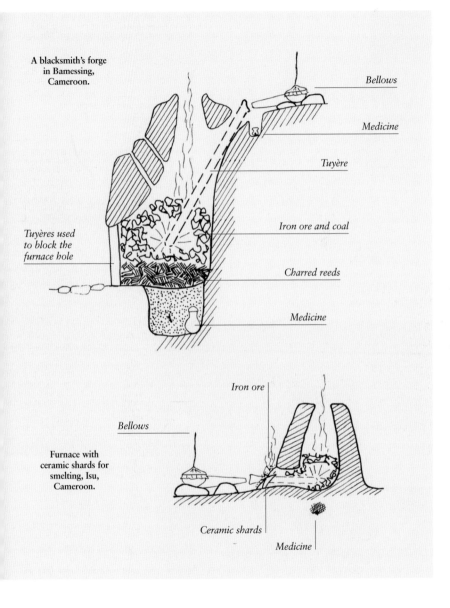

A blacksmith's forge in Bamessing, Cameroon.

Bellows

Medicine

Tuyère

Tuyères used to block the furnace hole

Iron ore and coal

Charred reeds

Medicine

Furnace with ceramic shards for smelting, Isu, Cameroon.

Iron ore

Bellows

Ceramic shards

Medicine

▲ Cross section of a forge, Bamessing (Cameroon) (from Arnoldi, Geary, and Hardin, 1996).

"Alaja, the divine potter, shapes the heads of men, but sometimes they come out flawed when he forgets them on the fire" (Yoruba myth)

Women Potters

Geographic locations
Western, central, eastern, southern Africa

Related entries
Nguni, blacksmiths, male and female

▼ Women making vases, Kassena (Burkina Faso).

In Africa, pottery making is mostly women's work. Only in a few cases, such as the Hausa of Nigeria, are there men potters, and sometimes they create only terracotta figures, leaving the production of utilitarian crockery to women. Knowing how to work clay is often a required female chore but can also become a specialized profession. In the savannahs of western Africa, women potters are the blacksmiths' wives. Often, the connection between woman and clay is conceptualized by drawing an explicit link between shaping and cooking ceramic, cooking food, and conceiving and giving birth to children. In western Cameroon, blackening a vase is akin to giving it a "skin" and wetting the surface with substances to giving it "blood." Another frequent association, perhaps linked to the previous one, is between crockery and funerals: it is visible in the figured Akan vases of Ghana and the Ivory Coast and in excavated pottery of Bura in Mali.

African pottery is made entirely by hand, not on the wheel. The round bottom of the vase is shaped first, or sometimes the bottom of a broken vase is used, then coils of clay are added to throw the sides.

The vase is smoothed inside and out and decorated with relief appliqués; once dry, it is fired on an open wood fire and then, in some cases, burnished or blackened with a second firing.

In Africa there is generally no theoretical distinction between clay sculpture and crockery; sometimes they appear together in the same object, as when the statue has a vase for the base and a figure for the cover, stopper, or opening. This has led anthropologists to theorize that perhaps even ancient African sculpture was made by women.

Sometimes soil is used from river or lake shores, where it is softer. After being left out to dry and beaten to make it uniform, it is mixed with water to make it suitable for shaping; sometimes ground clay shards are added.

▲ Woman making a vase (Benin).

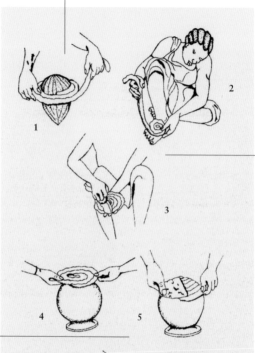

Sometimes the bottom of the vase is made by throwing coils of clay around a palm nut.

Sometimes the support for the coil of clay that is shaped into the bottom of the vase is a foot or the palm of the hand.

A coil of clay is placed on the bottom of an upturned vase and trimmed into a regular shape.

The upper part of the vase, including neck and rim, is made by pulling and trimming coils of clay around the bottom.

The base of the vase is placed on a small hole in the ground to keep it steady as coils of clay are added to complete the vase.

▲ Vase making following the coil technique (from Arnoldi, Geary, and Hardin, 1996).

The relief motifs recall women's ritual scars and also cattle, the primary source of wealth for the Zulu nation.

Zulu women of South Africa make spherical vases used to serve sorghum beer and drink from them: the opening on top usually has a cover of plaited fibers decorated with beads.

Not just the living, but the ancestors as well drink from the same vase and pay tribute to the owner, who has made offerings to them at the ritual time.

The vases to be used for food or drink are given a second firing with dried cow dung that gives it the distinctive black coloring. Finally, the surface is burnished with gooseberry leaves and animal fat.

▲ Vase, Zulu (South Africa). Indianapolis, Indianapolis Museum of Art.

Because women were usually forbidden to make anthropomorphic sculptures, on penalty of losing their fertility, vases such as these were made by men.

The ban on anthropomorphic and, more generally, figured sculpture made by women is common in many parts of Africa, such as the Cameroonian Grassland, where the human figure was the king's monopoly.

These water pitchers were probably made by the Lurangu tribe at the end of the 19th century to fill the request of Europeans for objects with anthropomorphic decorations.

▲ Vase, Lurangu (Sudan).
London, British Museum.

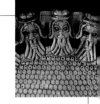

"A world without griots would be flavorless, like rice without sauce" (Fulani proverb, Mali)

Griots

The art of the griot is the word. Their presence at the court of the 14th century emperor of Mali is documented by Ibn Battuta, the Arabic geographer. These bards and singers were found among many western African populations, especially in the Mande region. Only the members of some endogamous families were permitted to learn this art. As was the case for practitioners of other crafts, such as blacksmithing, the griots were both feared and despised, for the power of the word can make a person's good fortune but also cause his disgrace, drawing evil spirits to him. This marginal status allowed a modicum of freedom of expression (not unlike that of the court jesters of Europe) to the griots, including transgressive behavior, such as undressing in public. They were free to ply their trade in villages and cities, or offer their services to noblemen, whose praises and genealogy they would sing. They thus filled an important social, educational, and political role in handing down oral history and in bringing the community together. The sweeping social changes wrought by colonialism, with the demise of the traditional patrons, forced (or allowed) the griots to look for other sources of income, and today some of them have become international musicians.

Geographic location
Western Africa

Related entries
Mande, kingdoms and empires of the Sudan, blacksmiths, traditional music, contemporary music

◀ A griot playing the traditional horn, Republic of Mali.

151

The Bamana of Mali believe that the power of a griot's word rests on his musicianship, which morally and physically reinforces the person to whom the words are addressed, intensifying his nyama, the energy that is present in all organic and inorganic beings.

Poets and musicians tell stories, offer advice, translate and interpret other people's speeches, report and spread news, perform diplomatic missions and mediate conflict, and encourage warriors and participants in sports competitions or elections.

Griot music has a unique sonority because, unlike the music of neighboring tribes founded on a pentatonic scale, it uses a heptatonic one (a seven-note scale), which is different from Western music.

The griot's musical instruments are the kora, a 21-chord harp used by the Mande; the balafon, a wooden-keyboard xylophone; and the ngoni, a small, three- or four-chord lute. Only men are allowed to play these instruments, while women (griottes) can play the bells or karinya. The griots also play drums known as dunun and small talking drums, but not the dejimbe, the most popular drum in the region, which is restricted to the blacksmith caste.

▲ A griot playing the kora (Ivory Coast).

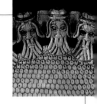

"An unjust war is a war against God" (Bamileke proverb, Cameroon)

Hunters and Warriors

For most African populations, hunting complements agriculture. Only a few societies, such as the Pygmies of equatorial Africa and the San of the Kalahari Desert, subsist entirely on hunting and gathering. In any case, hunting has a highly symbolic value, and many tribes have a hunter as their founding ancestor. In particular, big-game hunting was a specialized activity practiced by men who were often organized in professional associations or endogamous groups. Hunting followed set rituals, with propitiatory ceremonies and reparation rites that sought to gain the consent and forgiveness of the slain animal. Even war, in the past, followed strict rituals: in chiefless societies it did not seek to destroy the enemy or to conquer territory, but merely to capture prisoners and plunder; thus it was short and limited in scope. Even the establishment of new, small states, sometimes by immigrant groups that subjected the aboriginals, was achieved more through political maneuvering than the use of military force. Still, the military was an important constituent of states such as the Lunda and Rwanda, where being a warrior was a privilege of the aristocracy and every new king created his own army, or in South Africa, where the Zulu, a military state, expanded in the 19th century.

Geographic locations
Western, central, eastern, southern Africa

Related entries
Mbuti, San, Nguni, male and female, Abomey

▼ A hunter (Mali).

Hunting is a cooperative effort done with slings, bows, or nets. It is never a solitary activity, and the game is shared by all. When hunting with nets and dogs, the women and the children cry and clap their hands to help the animal run towards the men who set the trap by pulling the net in a semicircle hundreds of feet wide.

The forest is the great uterus that contains all ("Like our fathers and mothers, the forest gives us food, shelter, clothing, warmth, and affection") and contacts with it are spoken of as sexual relations.

The good outcome of the hunt is propitiated with dances and chants that imitate the hunted animal and by lighting the "sacred hunting fire" to bless the forest: this fire is lit under a tree at the camp border or inside the camp, and is marked off by sticks that point in the direction to be taken by the hunting party. The fire is a gift from the forest, and the ritual is a sort of acknowledgment of man's debt to nature and of restitution.

▲ A Mbuti hunter in the Ituri forest (Democratic Republic of the Congo).

*In western Africa, hunters and warriors get the
protection they need to venture into the bush by
sewing to their tunic amulets bearing Koranic
inscriptions or containing "medicine." The tunic
changes with each of the wearer's new exploits,
thus concretely representing his biography and
propitiating his fate.*

*While village residents wear white or colored
cottons, a sign of civilization, the hunter wears
a dark tunic covered with leather, horn, fur,
and tooth amulets that recall the bush
creatures and the hunter's power over them.
Whenever an animal is killed, the hunter adds
a small piece of it to his tunic, which thus
becomes more and more a likeness of the bush,
highlighting the hunter's ambiguity, suspended
between the world of men and the wilderness.*

▲ Hunter's tunic, Bamana (Mali).

The light-colored figures around the lion are the king's warriors slaughtering the dark-colored enemy. In the 18th century, the Fon king in Dahomey had a military corps of "Amazons" in his army, an exception to the widespread ban on women, the life-givers, shedding blood in the hunt or in war or sacrifices.

"No animal displays its rage like the lion." The lion devouring an enemy represents King Glele (1858–1889) battling the neighboring Yoruba to consolidate his independence after his father, Guezo (1818–1858), had freed the Fon from their subjection by Oyo's Yoruba kingdom.

▲ Fabric, Fon (Benin). Paris, Musée du Quai Branly.

Fabrics such as these hung as banners in the royal palace of Abomey. The figure appliqués are also made of fabric; the scenes, as in a puzzle, evoke the "strong names" of the Fon king, which are bestowed on him in the fa divination rite, and which express his powers.

The size of the head and its careful craftsmanship underscore its importance. The elaborate face scarifications identify the man's membership in local groups: those on the forehead mark the point where wisdom enters his head. On the face are traces of cosmetic powder containing cam wood and oil.

This statue portrays a chief who has undergone the highest initiatory rite, that of the "leopard" (nkashama), as evidenced by the leopard-skin apron, the plaited hairdo shaped like a helmet, the ceremonial sword, the necklace, and the armlets.

The concentric circles around the protruding navel recall the generation of life and the ties that bind the living to their ancestors.

▲ Statue of a warrior, Bena-Lulua (Democratic Republic of the Congo). Berlin, Museum für Volkerkunde.

These statuettes probably warded off evil from the chief and ensured the kingdom's well-being; for this reason, they were possibly carried on the battlefield.

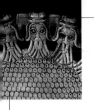

"Men are chiefs during the day, but women become chiefs at night" – an allusion to witchcraft (Luba proverb, Democratic Republic of the Congo)

Male and Female

Geographic locations
Western, central, eastern, southern Africa

Related entries
Blacksmiths, women potters, hunters and warriors, farmers, body arts

The gender difference is part of a cosmological order that opposes the complementary male and female principles, the building blocks from which culture draws rules that define social ties, forbid incest, define a legitimate sexual union, and regulate the division of labor. Thus one becomes a man or a woman and acquires a socially approved identity through the rituals of puberty (circumcision and excision), marriage, and the procreation of legitimate children. In many African societies, particularly agrarian ones in the west, polygyny was practiced, mainly for the purpose of building alliances with other groups by exchanging women. Because there was a scarcity of women, this practice allowed the first-born to exercise power over their younger brothers, forcing them to emigrate and marry later. Even under colonial rule, as the missionaries were pressuring for monogamy, the heavy farm work drove the heads of household to have multiple wives who could work in the fields. The importance attributed to fertility

► Clay statues of a man and a woman, Djenné-Mopti (Mali). London, Entwistle Gallery.

highlights two types of interconnected relations: between men and women, and between ancestors and descendants. Procreation requires not simply the mating of the sexes, but also the protection of the forefathers and the ability to draw from the sources of life and take one's place along a line of descendants.

If these statues project an impression of "coldness," it is because we isolate them from the emotions that went into their fashioning, the hopes and fears of real-life women, for these statues do not simply represent experience, they are part of it: by propitiating maternity, they help realize it.

Begetting a child is not just an event in a couple's life, but one that straddles two worlds and needs the support and participation of the ancestors. Normally, maternity figures depict a woman ancestor or a female deity whose protection is indispensable for impregnation to occur.

The apparent stiffness of African maternity figures may be explained by the different stylistic conventions and the fact that they do not portray an individual story, but the features common to maternity as such.

▲ Maternity figure, Congo (DRC). Tervuren, Musée Royal de l'Afrique Centrale.

The real and symbolic centrality of human fertility and generation makes maternity a central theme in sculpture. African families are extended, sometimes polygamous; they include several generations and not just the living but also the spirits of the dead ancestors and of the children yet to be born.

159

The face, marked by the overarching eyebrows, is shaped like a reclining disc on a slender, bejeweled neck. This style is a local variation on minimalism: the body is a cylinder with short arms stretched to form a cross, and only the navel and breasts are marked; other styles have more realistic anatomies.

In Africa, women supply about eighty percent of the family food and do most of the farm work. Many are also small retail merchants, a business that gives them a modicum of autonomy and, in some cases, wealth: when they are successful, they are nicknamed "Nana-Benz," because they favor Mercedes-Benzes to show off their success.

Sterility is suspect. Often it is thought to be a mark of witches that have cut off all contacts with the community, preferring to live in anti-social isolation. Rather than a biological dysfunction, it is perceived as a social threat and a fault, and whereas the woman is thought to be the culprit, male sterility is not usually recognized.

▲ Fertility doll (akua ba), Ashanti (Ghana), early 20th century. London, British Museum.

According to lore, the first woman to use this figurine was Akua, a childless woman who was mocked because she always carried this wooden doll with her. Since then, women longing to become pregnant carry these dolls on their back, like infants.

It is customary for the men of the Gola tribe to belong to the Poro society and women to the Sande society. Both associations educate the youth and teach them about politics and economics; opposed but complementary, they mark the rhythms of social time, alternating in government. Part of their authority rests on the control they exercise over the spirit world through their masks.

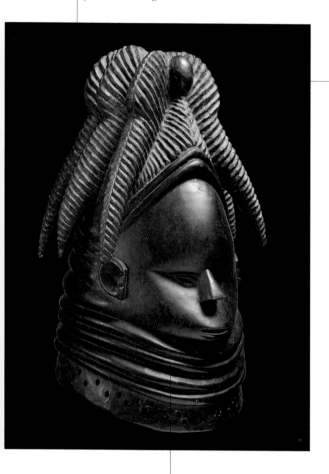

Women must give the artist suggestions for making the mask but without unveiling their secrets, in a give-and-take of jokes and sexual innuendos that masks a serious struggle about the supernatural. The artist is privileged to share in the affairs of the Sande society in a way not allowed to other men, except for some elders.

▲ Zo Ghe mask, Gola (Liberia). Private Collection.

While the mask is a male prerogative, in Liberia and Sierra Leone, some women's associations also use them. The delicate facial features, the polished skin, the fatty folds around the neck, and the headdress all signify health, beauty, and status. When these masks represent spirits, the neck folds suggest the rippling of the waters from which they rise.

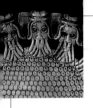

"Above the Ancient and the New World is Africa crucified. Her right arm lies over my country, and her left side casts a shadow on America" (L. S. Senghor)

Slavery

Geographic locations
Western, central, eastern, southern Africa

Chronology
9th–19th centuries: Arab slave trade
15th–19th centuries: Western slave trade
18th century: thousands of slaves in Haiti (*maroons*) flee to the mountains and set up independent communities
1791: the Haitian revolution breaks out ending slavery there; recognized three years later by the French Convention
1807: the British Parliament votes to abolish slave trade

Related entries
Akan peoples, Nigerian region, Swahili, Grassland chiefdoms, colonialism, Black Islam, Abomey

The manpower supplied by the African slaves was a key factor in the accumulation of capital that spurred the European and North American industrial revolution. It is estimated that twelve to fifteen million Africans were victims of the European slave trade between the 15th and 19th centuries. The growth of this trafficking was one leg of a triangle that joined Europe, Africa, and America: textiles, firearms, liquor, metal objects, beads, and other goods were bartered in Africa for slaves, who were shipped to the New World; and the sugar cane, tobacco, and cotton grown on the slave plantations were shipped back to Europe. Still, slave trafficking predated the arrival of the Europeans in Africa, being already practiced in the ninth century by the Arabs, who sold slaves in north Africa and in Zanzibar, and by the Africans themselves, who sold their prisoners of war into slavery. The results of this trade were devastating for many tribes and peoples; still, new cultural and political forms developed out of it, in Africa and across the Atlantic. Western African kingdoms such as the Mossi, Ashanti, Fon, Oyo, Segou, and Kaarta built their fortunes on the slave trade, subduing other black tribes and reselling them on the coast to European traffickers. In these cases, slavery contributed to state centralization.

▶ Theodore de Bry (1528–1598), color engraving of Spaniards repressing an African slave uprising. Berlin, Kunstbibliothek.

These handles brought to Africa by the Portuguese in the 15th century served as the main form of currency along the western African coast. They were used in commercial transactions, in funeral ceremonies, and to set the price of brides. Perhaps because they evoked the shape of local jewelry, women wore them as armlets to show off their family's wealth. In the 16th century they were the main currency of the slave trade.

In 1948, the English colonial government launched "Operation Handle" to replace this type of currency, which still evoked the slave trade, with the official currency of British West Africa. The handles were taken out of circulation in 1949.

In the late 18th century, with the evolution of African demand, brass replaced copper and, in Birmingham especially, handles of different shapes, finish, and size were produced for this market. The price in handles of a slave varied considerably depending on the time and place and type of handle. Their use shrunk in the 19th century with the end of the slave trade, but they continued to be used as payment in palm-oil export transactions.

▲ European-made handles used as currency (western Africa), 16th century. Vienna, Private Collection.

The heads lined up on top of the panel represent dead slaves. The first of these panels was probably made for King Amakiri, perhaps a former slave, who therefore could not use the local funeral insignia and so developed a new funerary tradition to celebrate himself and his progeny.

The panel, used in funeral ceremonies, represents the deceased wearing the mask he wore in his youth, surrounded by his children. This montage, unusual in African sculpture, could be explained by the carpentry skills the artist learned from the native steersmen who worked on European boats along the coast.

The city-state of New Kalabar was founded in the Niger delta at the end of the 18th century by the new king Amakiri, probably a former slave, who had profited greatly from the slave trade.

▲ Funeral panel, Kalabari (Nigeria), 19th century. London, British Museum.

This Ashanti-style drum is similar to those found in Ghana and is part of the London British Museum collection, though its provenance is the United States (Virginia), where Sir Hans Sloane found it in 1730. It was probably carried to America on slave ships and belonged to a British officer who had picked it up in Africa.

The drum is made of wood, with antelope hide stretched on top, pulled by plant fibers tied to pegs hammered into the wood.

In the 18th century, between sixty and eighty thousand people a year were deported to America. The abolition of the trade in the early 19th century did not put an end to slavery: in the U.S., the country with the largest number of slaves, cheap labor was ensured by their natural reproduction; there was also a brisk domestic trade from one corner of the U.S. to the other.

▲ Ashanti-style drum (United States), 18th century. London, British Museum.

Although the process of cultural transmission was greatly damaged by the slave trade, religious beliefs and aesthetic concepts survived and were preserved in the New World. Without their looms, the slaves lost traditional skills, but they creatively adapted their aesthetic sensibility to the new misery, and the patchwork was born.

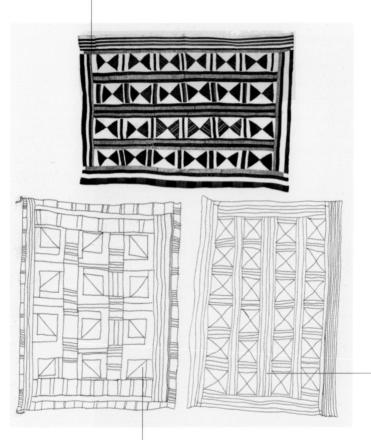

These cloths, made by assembling different scraps and pieces of different shapes, suggest a taste for the unexpected and for approximation, for the rhythmic repetition and sudden asymmetrical variations that are typical of African textiles.

These compositions, born of need, were also a conscious design choice. In fact, when in the 20th century conditions improved and families could afford to buy new fabric, the women cut it into stripes and sewed it into contrasting color patterns that revived the aesthetic of the striped textiles of the Mande and Akan peoples.

▲ Saramacca cloth in a patchwork pattern.

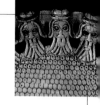

"The best way to learn how to be an independent sovereign nation is to be an independent sovereign nation" (Kwame Nkrumah, first president of Ghana)

Colonialism

At the 1885 Berlin Conference, Africa was divided among the European powers, and artificial borders were created that split tribes and peoples and forced foreign groups to live side by side. The richest lands were assigned to the whites, and the natives who had lived there from time immemorial were expelled. The economy and the infrastructure of a continent were modified to fit the export of raw materials to the benefit of the colonial powers. Thus single-crop plantations of coffee, cacao, cotton, and oil palm were born. Elsewhere, farmers were forced to plant the new crops and reduce the acreage set aside for growing vegetables and staples for local consumption. The raw materials were sent to Europe, where they were processed into finished products, some of which were shipped back to Africa, so that the natives ended up producing goods they did not consume, and consuming goods they did not produce. The English preferred to rule indirectly, granting the natives a modicum of autonomy while retaining full control for themselves. The French aimed to assimilate their subjects, in the name of the universal nature of the French Republic. Still, both powers used "traditional authorities" (often appointed by them) to keep the peace, collect taxes, and recruit manpower. One effect of this policy was tribalization and a deepening rift between chiefs, notables, and the masses.

Geographic locations
Western, central, eastern, southern Africa

Chronology
1855: the Berlin Conference divides Africa among the European powers
1900: first Pan-African congress held in London
1957: the Gold Coast is the first African country to gain independence; it renames itself Ghana
1960: "the year of Africa," when seventeen African countries become independent
1963: the African Unity Organization is born
1994: end of apartheid in South Africa

Related entries
Post-colonialism, literature, filmmaking

◄ Kasongo, *Les parachutistes l'assaut.* Tervuren, Musée Royal de l'Afrique Centrale.

Often these threatening-looking statuettes carry a spear and are used to pursue thieves, to heal, or to seduce women. What matters most is its hidden part, the "medicine" concealed in the belly and the "soul" that animates it.

The shaman has stuck nails in the figure to activate it; the soul inside could be that of an ancestor come back to earth to help the nkisi's owner, or it could be a wandering spirit undone by witchcraft, who is captured and made to serve the community or an individual's whim.

▲ Nkisi figure, Kongo (Democratic Republic of the Congo), 19th century. Berlin, Museum für Volkerkunde.

In the colonial period, these statuettes were a symbolic form of resistance, of ritual opposition. Because the staggering power imbalance did not permit an open struggle, the opposition became more subtle and included the preservation of an imaginary space where the native could believe that he was different from what the colonial powers wanted him to be. Aware of these statues' potential danger, the Belgian colonial administration tried to confiscate as many of them as possible.

Colonial art expresses power relations, compromise, and resistance. Behind the reverence might lurk dissent, for example in the "Africanization" of this portrait, exemplified by the disproportionate size of the head, or the use of a Western portrait to "magically" capture the person depicted.

The queen's face is younger than her real age, a touch typical of the ephebism of Yoruba aesthetics that pays homage to the elders by representing them at the height of their vigor. Elsewhere (on Ghanaian drum decorations, for example), Queen Victoria appears bare breasted.

Colonial Nigeria was governed by indirect rule: public officials were drawn from the educated Yoruba and Igbo classes, a practice that helped develop a feeling of ethnic belonging that had not been known before.

▲ Wood statue of Queen Victoria, Yoruba (Nigeria), 19th century. London, British Museum.

The artist probably used as a model one of the many photographs of the queen that circulated in Nigeria.

The French and English empires disintegrated after World War II under pressure from their winning allies, the U.S. and the U.S.S.R., and the democratic expectations of public opinion and of African soldiers. This group had lived the conflict as a war of liberation and expected the liberation of Europe from Nazism to be followed by the end of colonialism in Africa.

The first country to achieve independence was the Gold Coast, under Kwame Nkrumah: in 1957, it took the name of Ghana in a symbolic gesture toward the ancient Ghanaian kingdom. The independence movement gained speed in 1960 when seventeen African countries became independent, some of them peacefully, others through armed struggle.

Anti-colonial nationalist claims were cemented in the Pan-African movement that promoted the union of all African and diaspora populations. The movement had its first congress in London in 1900; it flourished under the leadership of Kwame Nkrumah.

The last colonial bulwark to fall was the South African regime. Formed in 1910, it was reinforced in 1948 under the National Party government, a party of white Boers, with a parliament of whites elected by whites only. In the 1970s, the first strikes that joined labor demands to anti-apartheid protest broke out. The regime fell at the end of the Cold War: in 1990, after twenty-six years in jail, Nelson Mandela regained his freedom.

▲ A woman wearing a dress with Nelson Mandela's picture, Cape Town (South Africa).

▶ Child walking in front of an anti-apartheid slogan, Johannesburg (South Africa), 1985.

"When a state begins to fall, it starts from the belly" (Akan proverb, Ghana)

Post-colonialism

After gaining independence, the African states fell into the clutches of the Cold War and of dictatorships. The adoption of the Western industrial, urban model of development, to be pursued with the revenues from the export of raw materials and with international aid, was a failure. The African states have remained economically dependent agricultural countries; political colonialism has been supplanted by an economic colonialism that mostly benefits local elites and the countries of the Northern Hemisphere. In the 1990s, with the end of the Cold War, democratic movements arose that drove many single-party regimes to allow multi-party systems, as was the case in Benin, Togo, the Ivory Coast, and Cameroon. The new pluralism brought with it some freedom of the press and private radio and television. Often, however, the changes have been only skin-deep, and the old hegemonic groups have retained power. With elections becoming increasingly important, issues such as citizenship and the distinction between "autochthonous" and "allochthonous" people have come to the fore; thus democracy has intensified "tribalism" and patronage, and the collapse of the state increases the risk of both government-sanctioned and private violence.

Geographic locations
Western, central, eastern, southern Africa

Chronology
1989: multi-party system introduced in Benin
1991–2002: civil war in Sierra Leone
1995: the Tutsi are massacred by the Hutu militia in Rwanda
1995: South Africa sets up a Truth and Reconciliation Commission to investigate the apartheid years
1997: dictator Mobutu is overthrown by Kabila's rebel forces; Zaire renames itself the Democratic Republic of the Congo (DRC)
1999: after years of military rule, a civil government is restored in Nigeria

Related entries
Colonialism, images of power, contemporary visual arts, contemporary music, African cities

African wars are often caused by conflicting interests in mining precious raw materials. In the civil wars that ravaged Sierra Leone, Liberia, Nigeria, Angola, what was then Congo, and Uganda, Western multinationals fought for control of the mining licenses by arming the different warring factions. In Congo in 1960, Belgium fomented the secession of Katanga and civil war to secure control of the region. Congo's prime minister Patrice Lumumba was murdered in 1961, and a U.S.-aided coup ushered in Mobutu's dictatorship.

Diamond trafficking is one cause of the recent wars that have devastated the Democratic Republic of the Congo, Liberia, and Sierra Leone. In the 1980s, the predominance of large corporations such as De Beer's was threatened by traffickers who bought diamonds with arms and drugs and tried to control politics with mercenary armies.

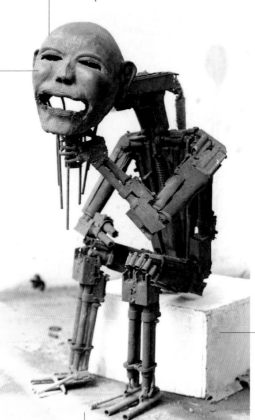

This throne is made with weapons from the Mozambican civil war fomented by Rhodesia and South Africa that ended in 1992.

▲ G. A. Mabunda and E. D. Santos, sculpture made with weapons.

The oil fields discovered by Royal Dutch Shell in Nigeria in 1958, just before independence, ignited coups d'état and civil wars. In 1967, war erupted in Biafra, where the modernist Igbo elites tried to wrest power from the northern traditionalist Hausa in order to seize control of the oil revenues from Hausa land. Since the 1980s the Ogoni have been fighting against oil-related injustice and pollution.

An urban folk school of painting developed in what is now the DRC. Well-known abroad, its themes are colonial violence, corrupt African governments, the war between the sexes, and post-colonial social injustices. Among the best-known artists of this school are Moke, Cheri Samba, and Thsibumba Kanda, who find inspiration in local news and politics. Their ironic style can be quite effective in conveying moral criticism.

The preacher towers among the faithful, whom he tramples unknowingly under his lion-paw-shaped shoes. Post-colonial Africa has seen a strong growth of independent churches and messianic movements.

The style is borrowed from the West, and might include cartoon-like written messages. The images have a narrative tone, evoking anecdotes and events well known by the local buyers, who are mostly drawn from the Kinshasa urban middle class.

▲ Moke, *The Preacher*, 1995.

Post-colonial African economies are fragile, burdened by debt interest and limited to exporting just a few types of raw materials, whose prices are set by the multinationals of the Northern Hemisphere. Single-crop export farming threatens economic stability when prices fall; it also limits the acreage farmed for the local markets.

Trapped in "shipwrecks of economic development" (Latouche, 1991), Africans survive thanks to an "informal" economy not reflected in official statistics. It thrives in clan-type solidarity networks that only partially follow market logic. Thus "friends' societies" are born, and credit associations exist side by side with official banks, handling large flows of money that could even imperil the official economy.

▲ Cheri Samba, *Le monde à l'envers*, 2000.

Forty percent of Africans live below the poverty line. One-third of sub-Saharan Africans are undernourished, an effect not so much of lack of food as of poverty. Poverty, demographic growth, and pollution create a self-perpetuating vicious circle. This situation has worsened after the structural changes imposed by the International Monetary Fund cut social expenditure funds, thus worsening people's lives.

"Like a lion's or a leopard's skin, authority is full of holes"
(Fang proverb, Gabon)

Images of Power

One popular African custom is the printing of fabrics for celebrations and commemorative purposes, to remember the deceased or a head of state, or for special events such as funerals, state visits, or national holidays. The high visibility of these fabrics is one way of committing to new generations the memory of a dear departed or the consolidation of a regime. The fabrics are made in Europe, but for the local taste; they became popular in the 1920s as a reasonably priced substitute ("fancy cloth") for the "Dutch wax" fabrics printed industrially in the 19th century by the English and the Dutch to imitate Indonesian batik, which was popular in Africa at the time. One reason for the popularity of fancy cloth is that it can reproduce portraits. Its use as propaganda began during the African wars of independence and continued in the post-colonial period. The heads of state use it to reinforce their networks of clients: the cloths are given away as gifts or distributed in the local markets at low prices.

Geographic locations
Western, central, eastern, southern Africa

Chronology
19th century: "Dutch wax" fabric trade by the English and the Dutch
20th century: "fancy cloth" fabric trade

Related entries
Colonialism, post-colonialism, body arts, weaving and clothing

◄ Woman wearing a dress with the portrait of President Idi Amin (Uganda).

More than any other medium, fabric can guarantee a long life for and widespread diffusion of political portraits, even if the wearer does not necessarily approve of the politician portrayed. Sometimes the wearer simply wants to show his or her powerful connections or wear a free garment.

Armando E. Guebuza, a leader of Mozambique's war of liberation, secretary of Frelimo, and a businessman, became president of Mozambique in 2005.

Using these garments or commenting on them could be a way of criticizing the politician portrayed, and irony and double entendres abound that reverse the original meaning. For example, one could sit on a politician's face, or call a fabric celebrating the fight against inflation "recession cloth" (as happened in the Ivory Coast).

▲ Fabric with portrait of President Guebuza (Mozambique).

General Mobutu seized power in the former Belgian Congo in 1965 with a coup, during the civil war that ravaged the country after independence and the murder of Prime Minister Lumumba. Born during the Cold War, his despotic regime was supported by the West and by Belgian mining interests. The end of the Cold War and the kleptocratic regime that raped the country finally alienated foreign and domestic support from Mobutu, who fled to Morocco and died there in 1997.

Mobutu's regime fostered a personality cult and an ideology of "authenticity" that led him to change his French name to Sese Seko and impose the use of African geographical and personal names throughout the country. He even changed the colonial name of "Congo" to "Zaïre."

▲ Fabric with portrait of President Mobutu (Sese Seko), Zaïre (now the Democratic Republic of the Congo).

Political use of textiles is part of a broader social use of clothing in Africa: printed fabrics are given names, sometimes arbitrarily, and associated with proverbs. Many fabrics become popular because they interpret desires or dissatisfaction, offering a means of expression to the wearer but avoiding political repression or open family strife.

Divinities and Religion

African Religions
Divination
Granary of the Pure Earth
Nommo Genies
Water Spirits
Twin Worship
Shango, the Thunder God
Eshu, the Rogue God
Voodoo
Mami Wata
Black Islam
African Christianity

◄ Ritual mace of *oshe* Shango, the
god of thunder, Yoruba (Nigeria).
Seattle, Seattle Art Museum.

"Is there anything after death? / Your fear is childish! / Is there anything after death? / Intones the zither player / What does the empire of the dead hold for us?" (Fon chant, Benin)

African Religions

Geographic locations
Western, central, eastern, southern Africa

Central beliefs
Creator God, lesser spirits and deities, representation of divinity, Yoruba pantheon

Related entries
Divination, Granary of the Pure Earth, *nommo* genies, water spirits, twin worship, Shango the thunder god, Eshu the rogue god, voodoo, Mami Wata, Black Islam, African Christianity

Traditional African religions have been called animistic, fetishistic, polytheistic, and primitive monotheistic. It is not clear, however, how much of this diversity is to be attributed to the African beliefs themselves, and how much to their interpretation or to the super-imposition of Islam and Christianity. While Bantu-speaking peoples address the Creator as a provident father who supports his creatures even after Creation, for others God seems to have created the world out of boredom or by chance and then forgotten it. For some, the Creator God is at the center, and spirits and other deities are his manifestations; for others, He is little more than a marginal figure. For some, God is close to men and resorts to intermediaries; for others, He is distant, outside of men's lives and cares, and has withdrawn from his Creation. Still others believe that the lesser deities are simply reflections of God, or that there is no Supreme Being, opting for a pantheistic or polytheistic conception of the world, or even that there is no God at all. Thus, the image worship of many cultures notwithstanding, the fact

that there is no representation of the Supreme Being is for some an indication of His transcendence; others believe that since God is everywhere, there is no need to give Him an image, and we can turn directly to any of his creatures.

▶ Street altar (eastern Nigeria).

Ikenga *are altars dedicated to an Igbo man's* chi *– his personal spirit and the most unique part of his person. They do not simply represent the moral order of family relations, but also the man's success. Periodic sacrifices are made to the* ikenga *to ensure a good outcome for ventures. Christian missionaries tried to assimilate this personal spirit into the figure of the guardian angel.*

The horns are those of a ram and symbolize strength and fertility; sometimes they crown the heads of other animals, such as snakes or leopards, which are associated with warriors.

The knife and the head of the slain enemy express the warrior's aggressiveness.

▲ *Ikenga* wood statue, Igbo (Nigeria). Private Collection.

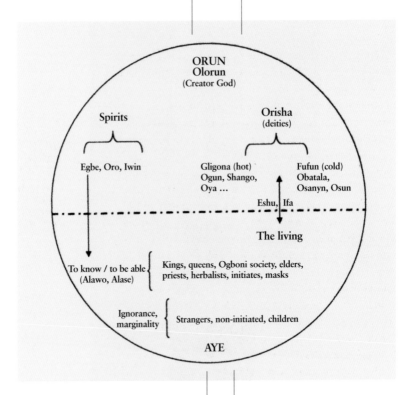

The deities that rule over divination, Ifa and Eshu (the former guarantees order in the world, while the latter is responsible for the chaos introduced by change), stand at the threshold of the two worlds (of the living and the dead) and carry messages across the divide.

Deities (orisha) are deified ancestors or personified forces of nature; they are seen as "hot" (voluble and unpredictable, like Shango, the thunder god, or Ogun, god of iron and war), or "cold" (calm and thoughtful, like Osanyn, god of medicine).

ORUN
Olorun
(Creator God)

Spirits

Orisha
(deities)

Egbe, Oro, Iwin

Gligona (hot)
Ogun, Shango,
Oya ...

Fufun (cold)
Obatala,
Osanyn, Osun

Eshu, Ifa

The living

To know / to be able
(Alawo, Alase)

Kings, queens, Ogboni society, elders,
priests, herbalists, initiates, masks

Ignorance,
marginality

Strangers, non-initiated, children

AYE

The political system is also based on the cosmic order: the king derives his powers from Olorun, king of the sky; from the Ogboni secret society, which brings together the elders devoted to Onile, the earth goddess (or to the ancestors who inhabit the earth); and from the state council (Oyo Misi), whose members represent the people and, on a different plane, humankind.

Nigeria's Yoruba believe that the world is like a pumpkin cut in half, with one half, Aye (the earth), acting as a container, and the other (Olorun, the sky) as a cover. The possibility of life runs along the cut that both separates and unites.

▲ Diagram of the Yoruba pantheon (Nigeria) (from Drewal, Pemberton, and Abiodun, 1989).

"A man asked to have his neighbor's wife; the soothsayer consulted the spider and said: 'Take whichever you want.' And so the man took the soothsayer's wife" (Bamileke tale, Cameroon)

Divination

What happens in the lives of men and women, and the uncertainty of their future, needs interpretation so that situations may be dealt with and choices made: the visible world draws its meaning from the invisible, from relationships – harmonious or conflicting – with deities, spirits, and ancestors. Among the more common divination techniques is throwing objects such as nuts, pebbles, and bones, and reading where and how they fall. Among the Yoruba of Nigeria and the Fon of Benin, divination (*italfa*) is done by throwing kola nuts: depending on the results, lines are traced on a plate creating 256 possible combinations that correspond to all of man's destinies. Sometimes animals are part of divination practices. Mali's Dogon use the jackal, an animal born from the union of the sky god and the earth and the repository of God's first word. The soothsayer attracts the animal with bait left on the divination tablet on which sand has been scattered and where the jackal will leave traces of his passage. The Bamileke of Cameroon use a spider (*migala*). Lines are drawn at the entrance of its den, representing both maternal and paternal ancestors, and objects such as flowers, leaves, pieces of kola nuts, twigs, and small pebbles are placed in the den: when the spider comes out at night, it will push some of the objects along the traced lines, where an answer will be found.

Geographic locations
Western, central, eastern, southern Africa

Central beliefs
Ifa divination, interrogating the jackal, spider divination, divination tools

Related entries
African religions, sickness and healing, witchcraft

◀ Divination mask, Vili (Democratic Republic of the Congo), 19th century. Berlin, Museum für Volkerkunde.

The facial features are in typical Senufo style: strong, protruding jaws, long nose dividing the plane of the face, jutting eyebrows that build the eye through shadow, and a crest-like headdress. The harmony of the composition is in the skillful balance of rounded volumes and sharp edges that projects a sense of mastery and self-contained strength.

The Senufo diviners of the Ivory Coast are mostly women; their statuettes are inhabited by bush spirits with whom they maintain contact, provided that certain rituals are observed and sacrifices are regularly made.

▲ Divination statuette, Senufo (Ivory Coast). Private Collection.

These sitting figures are coupled with female figures on horseback and are some of the vast array of objects that the soothsayer questions to help her supplicant client. Sometimes she instructs her client to keep simpler versions of these statuettes at home.

According to Igbo beliefs, each person has a moral quality that ties him to the group, arising from a prenatal pact between the person's own deity (the chi) and his ancestors. In each person is also a non-predestined sphere linked to the pact he made with the peer group. The ikenga (the altar he erects to his own chi) is the visual expression of that pact.

The horns refer to the ram's strength, fertility, growth, and aggressiveness.

On the forehead are the scarifications that mark the notables (ozo).

▲ *Ikenga* divination statuette, Igbo (Nigeria). Private Collection.

In addition to the personal and the group ikenga, *there are smaller ones, such as this, used in foretelling the future. Here the body follows the shape of the ritual object, the* ofo – *a bundle of sticks that evokes the group's cohesion.*

Kuba divinatory practices use wood objects (itoom) in the shape of crocodiles, lizards, warthogs, or dogs. The animal's back is moistened and rubbed with a small wooden cylinder; if the cylinder remains attached to the surface, it means that the question asked is the right one.

▲ Divination tool, Kuba (Democratic Republic of the Congo). Private Collection.

Oracles are used to identify witches,
thieves, or unfaithful wives. The animals
evoked are associated with divination on
account of their nose or sight, or their
ability to track and catch prey.

The diviner draws opportune signs about her client's problems by looking at the arrangement of the small sticks moved by a mouse inside the vase.

The sculpture depicts a client of a diviner. The diviners carry these containers on their back as they move from village to village. The statuette identifies their trade.

Divination with mice yields less explicit answers than those obtained in a trance. In the latter case, the state of trance is induced by the sound of a small hammer struck rhythmically on a gong. The diviner's body is seized by a bush spirit or by divinities that are tied to a specific family from generation to generation. Possession can be violent, endangering the very life of the possessed.

▲ Divination vessel, Baoulé (Ivory Coast). Paris, Musée du Quai Branly.

"Genies fall from the sky only when they are angry or when pushed" (Ogotemmeli, a Dogon elder, Mali)

Granary of the Pure Earth

Ogotemmeli, the Dogon elder, told the anthropologist Marcel Griaule that when the eight ancestors of humankind climbed to heaven and reached the two primordial genies (*nommo*), they transmuted into *nommo* themselves, beings with the upper body of a man and the lower one of a snake. Thus from two, the *nommo* became eight, and this large number created chaos. The eight, who had broken God's (Amma's) ban by mating, thus became impure and descended to earth, taking with them anything that could be useful for life among men and women. They lowered themselves on an ark shaped like an upside-down basket that the ancestor Blacksmith had thrown against the heavenly vault like a spindle: it was the Granary of the Pure Earth. On the terrace, the Blacksmith placed both fire, in the form of a piece of sun that he had stolen, and the forging tools that men would need to make farming implements. The shape of the granary recalled an anvil. When, at the end of its run along the rainbow, the granary touched down, the crash scattered men, animals, and plants and broke the Blacksmith's legs and arms, creating the knee and elbow joints. Thus his limbs, now flexible like a snake's, became useful for his work.

People
Dogon

Geographic locations
Mali, western Africa

Central beliefs
Descent of the *nommo* genies, the granary as world system, man's work, agriculture, architecture

Related entries
Blacksmiths, *nommo* genies, farmers, food, Dogon

◀ Dogon granary (Mali).

From the center of each square rises a ten-step stairway; the horizontal part of each step is female and the vertical part male. Together, all the stairs represent the eighty families born from the primeval ancestors.

The basket in which the ancestors rode down to earth to build the world was the model for today's granaries: the square bottom was the roof and the opening rested on the ground; the square terrace symbolized the sky and the circular base, the sun.

An opening in the northern stairway leads to the interior, which is partitioned into eight rooms arrayed on two floors.

The circle at the center of the terrace represents the moon.

On the sixth step is the opening to the granary: inside is the belly, or the inside of the world. "To poke one's head in a granary door" means to penetrate a womb, to put a family on edge, to bare one's entrails.

On each step, linked to a constellation, stood a class of creatures: on the western stair (the "large-tailed star") were fierce animals, plants, and insects; men and fish were on the northern stair (the Pleiades); on the southern stair (Orion) were domesticated animals; and on the eastern one, (Venus) the birds.

GROUND FLOOR PLAN **UPPER FLOOR PLAN**

On the eight sections arrayed on two floors were the grains that God bequeathed to the ancestors: little millet, white millet, pearl millet, finger millet, beans, wood sorrel, rice, and fonio.

The eight sections also symbolized the eight organs of the Water Genie: stomach, gizzard, heart, small liver, spleen, intestine, large liver, and bile sac. In the center, a spherical vase stood for the uterus. The skeleton acted as walls and partitions to support the organs. Thus the granary was the image of a woman, and the stair opening was its sexual organ.

▲ Map of the ground and upper floor of the Granary of the Pure Earth (from Griaule, 2002).

The small granary doors are often carved in geometric patterns and with figures of ancestors, lizards, birds, or breasts. The figure or the couple on the lock usually represents the founders of the clan; the other figures are twin couples, a symbol of fertility. A zigzag design evokes the falling rain and the spiraling movement of the sun's rays.

Doors consist of one, two, or three wooden panels joined together with iron staples.

Granaries have a wood frame resting on stones, a thatched conical roof, and thin walls made with mixed clay, millet straw, and manure. Granaries reserved for men differ from those for women.

▲ Granary door, Dogon (Mali).
Private Collection.

In addition to their function, the carved locks of granaries and other buildings are also symbols of the owner and his social status.

Locks may be classified into different groups, depending on the form of the upper part (decorative), central (the lock proper), and lower.

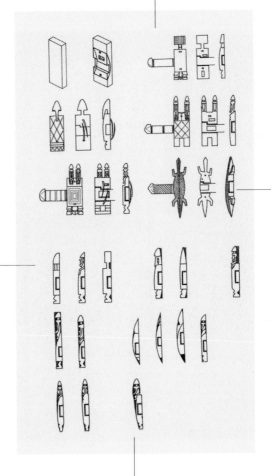

In some cases, the lock is one single piece.

These locks, originating from Arabia, were uniquely adapted in Africa with symbolic and aesthetic details.

▲ Door locks, Dogon, Mali (from Bedaux and Van der Waals, 2003).

"God created them like water. They were green, in human and snake form: human from the head to the kidneys; snake-like below" (Ogotemmeli, a Dogon elder, Mali)

Nommo Genies

For the Dogon of Mali, the *nommo* are genies with a human upper body and a snake's lower body. Made of water, they have no joints (unlike man, whose joints make him fit for farm work). The male and female *nommo* twins were born from the mating of Amma, the Creator God, with the earth, which was fertilized by the god's semen. *Nommo* live in every kind of water and are also in the sun's rays, which are made of copper and are their excrement: thus the earth owes its fertility to them. Men are indebted to *nommo* for language, for weaving, and for the art of the forge. The twin couple is a symbol of perfection contrasted with Ogu, the jackal, who cannot reproduce because it lacks its female twin, having been born from Amma's stormy relationship with the earth, whose termites' nest (the clitoris) he excised when it rose against him like a penis. To cleanse the earth's impurity, Amma sacrificed a male *nommo* still in the egg, breaking it into sixty-six parts. He then recomposed him into a human shape, using the earth's placenta, and resurrected him with the pure lymph of a tree. This sacrifice purified the earth and prepared it for the landing of the ark that carried the eight ancestors of the human race.

People
Dogon

Geographic locations
Mali, western Africa

Central beliefs
A male and female couple of twins, the jackal, *nommo*'s sacrifice and its resurrection

Related entries
Blacksmiths, divination, Granary of the Pure Earth, Dogon

◀ Male wood statue, Dogon (Mali). Private Collection.

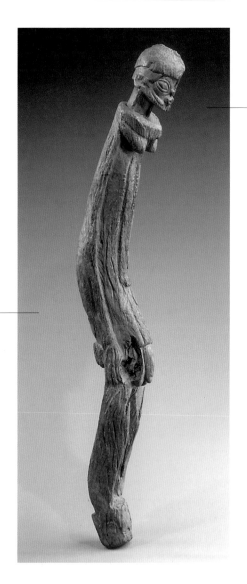

*Articulated limbs
pertain to human
beings, but the
nommo are genies
with a human head
and torso and
lower snake-like
body. The
litheness could be
appropriately
explained by the
lack of joints
and the wavy
movement by their
watery body. In
following the
wood's natural
curve, the sculptor
has captured the
essence of the
nommo*

*Perhaps this
statue with
breasts and a
penis represents
a mythological
nommo.*

▲ Hermaphrodite statue,
Dogon (Mali). Paris, Musée
du Quai Branly.

In the Dogon shrines that dot the village of Sanga, a number of figures depict the nommo's resurrection and his role as "father" of humankind, guardian of the universe, and dispenser of rain.

This drawing is a diagram of the nommo, the plan from which it is created. It is analogous to the cornerstones of a new house, which become boundaries for its walls. The diagram is the direct expression of the thoughts of Amma, the Creator God.

The vertical line dividing the head recalls the upright position of the resurging nommo.

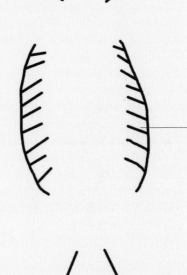

The nine ribs allude to the nommo's female twin and the eight ancestors of mankind, who are its sons: these ten "people" were sent by Amma to populate the earth.

This drawing is also the "diagram" of the resurrected nommo. The three parts (three is a male number) are placed under the main altars of the Sanga village (the head faces east, the torso is at the center, and the feet face west), ensuring its protection. The founding ritual includes a human sacrifice: the victim will be the nommo's deputy, and the altar will be "planted" on his head.

Drawing: the resurrected nommo (from Griaule and Dieterlen, 1965).

195

"Sons of the sea with shells on their head / Rulers today, tomorrow, and always / Fire on their head, extinguished by water" (Ijo prayer to the water spirits)

Water Spirits

People
Ijo

Geographic locations
Nigeria, Niger delta, western Africa

Central beliefs
nature spirits, masks

Related entries
Post-colonialism, African religions

The Ijo have no images of their Creator God, but they carv masks and statues of ancestors, woodland spirits, and wate deities. Although most of them today call themselves Christian they still follow their traditional beliefs. According to the Ijo o Niger's central delta region, before birth human beings mak contact with nature spirits that sometimes follow them on earth Thus, in the other world everyone chooses, more or less pru dently, their life on earth, so that being rich or poor, fertile o sterile, are not chance happenings but the outcome of thei choices. The spirits are prone to human passions and weak nesses, and often problems and misfortunes may be explained b a person's difficult relationship with the spirits that come to hir in dreams or during possessions, or that spontaneously materia ize, perhaps as a boat that suddenly appears on and then disap pears from the water's surface. To find solutions to thei predicaments, people turn to soothsayers, who can track dow the cause of the problem in their prenatal life and suggest how t calm the spirits.

▼ *Abua* helmet, Ijo (Nigeria). Indianapolis, Indianapolis Museum of Art.

These masks of the Ijo Kalabari people embody the water spirits and are the exclusive property of men. Still, Ekine, the mask society, bears the name of a mythical woman who took the masks from the water spirits' world and brought them to earth.

These large masks worn horizontally on the head represent water spirits who have become embodied as sharks, dolphins, or sawfish; they may also be composites of different animals, such as fish or crocodiles. These shapes, however strange, are those of the spirits when they appear at the water line. Masked dances are festive events when the villagers make fun of each other with tall fishermen's tales.

While the dark-skinned jungle spirits are ugly and dangerous, the generally light-skinned water spirits are attractive and benevolent deities, even if sometimes they raise destructive storms. Although their beliefs preceded the arrival of Europeans on the continent, the natives linked the white man to the water spirits, as both came from the sea carrying riches.

▲ *Agbo* Ekine helmet, Ijo (Nigeria). Seattle, Seattle Art Museum.

Instead of being recycled, the gas produced by the oil refinery is burned, wasting resources and creating greenhouse gases: this situation is especially critical in the Niger delta, which has the highest such pollution in Africa.

The Ijo believe that the oil companies offer human sacrifices to the water spirits to secure their assent to drill oil wells.

▲ Fishing in the Niger River delta.

The author Ken Saro Wiwa, an Ogoni human rights activist, was hanged by the Nigerian government in 1995 for denouncing the pollution, social injustice, and corruption that revolve around the oil industry.

In recent years, several multinational companies have built oil refineries in the Niger delta, but this great wealth does not trickle down to the natives, who bear the consequences of environmental pollution. This is fueling violent unrest and crime, including attacks on the oil rigs.

This spirit is half-man, half-hippopotamus. The helmet is worn horizontally, with the face facing the sky.

The masked festivals are a time when the Ijo renew their ties to the water spirits, who are invited to come ashore and mix with human beings. They return the hospitality by providing abundant fishing.

In addition to being fishermen, the Ijo were once also warriors, pirates, and slave traffickers. There was also violence in their initiation rites: one trial to which a youth had to submit to become a warrior was to kill a hippopotamus. In some areas the link between masks and violence is explicit, and masked dances are one way of defusing tension.

▲ *Otobo* mask, Ijo (Nigeria). Paris, Musée du Quai Branly.

The statues of ancestors are painted brown to signal their humanity, in contrast with heroes and water spirits, whose statues are painted white or other colors. The only distinguishing feature of hero statues is their headdress (sansum).

According to the Kalabari, the world was created by a god from whom three types of spirits descend: ancestors, water spirits, and village heroes. This cosmology reflects a society based on the opposition between clan autonomy and village unity.

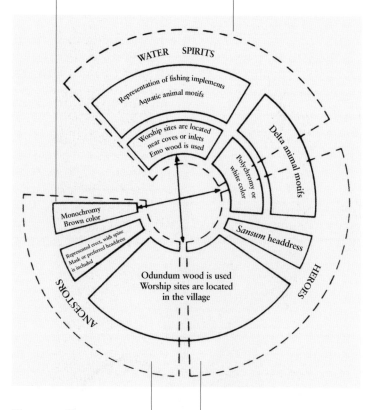

WATER SPIRITS

Representation of fishing implements
Aquatic animal motifs

Worship sites are located near coves or inlets
Emo wood is used

Delta animal motifs

Polychromy or white color

Monochromy
Brown color

Represented erect, with spine
Mask or preferred headdress is included

Sansum headdress

Odundum wood is used
Worship sites are located in the village

ANCESTORS

HEROES

The statues of heroes or ancestors never include fishing gear or aquatic animals, which appear on the statues of water spirits. And while ancestors are depicted upright, with a spine, heroes are sinuous, just like the water spirits.

The heroes who came from the sea taught man how to maintain unity in the village among the various clans, for they occupy a midway position between ancestors and water spirits. The statues of heroes are made from the wood of village trees, unlike the statues of water spirits, for which mangrove wood is used.

▲ Iconography of the Ijo Kalabari, Nigeria (from Layton, 1983).

"Because there is palm oil and beans / I am not afraid / No, I am not afraid of giving birth to twins / Because there is palm oil and beans" (Yoruba song, Nigeria)

Twin Worship

Peoples
Dogon, Bamana, Gourmantché, Malinke, Ewe, Fon, Yoruba, Igbo, Bantu

Geographic locations
Mali, Burkina Faso, Togo, Benin, Nigeria, Republic of the Congo, western Africa, central Africa

Central beliefs
Ambiguity of twins, perfection and monstrosity, cult figures

Related entries
Divination, *nommo* genies, Shango the thunder god

In many African cultures children are ambiguous figures, poised between the spirit world, from which they have just been released, and the human world, where they do not as yet have a defined role. In his early years, it is not a given that the child will remain on earth, for his ties with the other world are still strong, and there is a high probability that he will return there. The fact that a child walks on all fours, or does not speak clearly, is a sign of her connivance with the forest spirits. This suspicion is even stronger in the case of twins. If for the Dogon, Bamana, and Malinke, twins represent the principle of original perfection, for the Gourmantché, Ewe, Yoruba, Igbo, and Bantu populations, a twin birth is a bad omen. It may be seen as erasing the distance between opposites, as an intrusion of animality, or, for those tribes who believe that twins are children of the sky or the moon, as a threat to the cosmic order, which is founded on the separation of sky and earth. No wonder then, that twins used to be killed or were left to die in the forest, whence it was believed they came. More recently, the Yoruba, Ewe, and Fon have reworked their ancient aversion and founded a cult of twins that uses wood figurines. The birth of twins is now considered propitious, although their dark powers and monkey-like origins are still feared.

▶ Statuette of a twin (*ibeji*), Yoruba (Nigeria). Private Collection.

When one or both twins die, the mother asks the advice of a soothsayer (babalawo) and commissions dolls of the same sex. She ritually feeds, washes, and dresses them because they are repositories of the children's spirits, and neglecting the dolls could trigger the spirits' destructive anger.

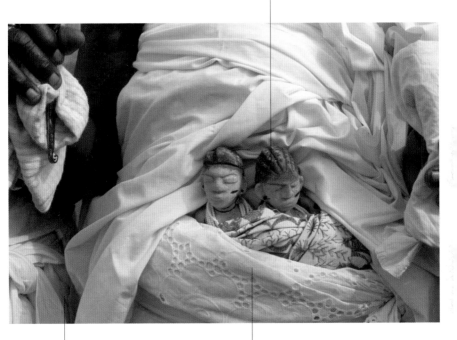

When one twin survives, he, instead of the mother, may be the custodian of the doll representing his brother.

Women carry these dolls in their skirts and go around dancing and singing their praises, collecting offerings from the bystanders, whom they bless.

▲ Twin figures carried in the skirt, Ouidah (Benin).

The exceptional status of being a twin is expressed by the simultaneous presence of contrary elements: although portrayed as children, these figures have sexual organs, face scarifications, and adult hairdos. The fact that they were carved without the mother increases their exceptional status.

The arms stand symmetrically apart from the body; the palms face inward, touching the hips, and suggest a quiet, inner composure.

Twins are known as the Thunder Children, and their statuettes are associated with the worship of Shango, the thunder god, with whom they share a symbolic color, red. Shango was the father of twins; in the Oyo region he is considered their protector and the source of their power.

▲ Twin figures (*ibeji*), Yoruba (Nigeria). Private Collection.

"Living with Shango is not easy" (Yoruba saying, Nigeria)

Shango, the Thunder God

The myths of the Yoruba people of Nigeria about Shango, the god of thunder, address the beneficial but also dangerous power of kings. Shango was the fourth king (*alafin*) of the Oyo dynasty, hailed as a god by his subjects. A ruthless tyrant endowed with magical powers he could barely control, he was expelled and took his own life. But the king took revenge by hurling thunderbolts at his subjects. The Shango myth teaches that to be beneficial, strength must be harnessed, and in fact, the Yoruba concept of energy (*ashe*) implies character (*iwa*) and mystical composure (*ititu*). All of this is visibly expressed in the objects associated with Shango; his power, restored to balance through the cult, is so much greater and worthy of respect because it is harnessed and used wisely. It is also true, however, that power is not something one possesses, but a state to be achieved. The god seizes the dancing worshipers, and they fall into a trance: the women violently shake Shango's sticks above their head towards the surrounding faithful, while they sing of the unpredictable, quick-tempered nature of the god. After witnessing these dances, our experience of Shango sculptures is more complex and contradictory than it would be if we just looked at them as objects in a museum.

People
Yoruba

Geographic locations
Nigeria, western Africa

Central beliefs
Kingdom of Oyo, ambiguity of power, representation of the deity, male and female

Related entries
Nigerian region, Kingdoms of Niger, male and female, African religions, twin worship, oral tradition and writing

◄ Ritual vessel for the Shango cult (*arugba* Shango), Yoruba (Nigeria). Private Collection.

Shango's staffs are sealed at each end with the god's "fiery stones." The axe that the god hurls down to earth to produce thunder during a storm symbolizes his power and virility. The prehistoric flint stones that peasants find while hoeing the fields are believed to be signs left by the thunderbolts thrown by the god.

Women devotee to Shango twir this staff in dances tha alternate orderl movements with convulsive ones to express th ambivalent powe of this god tha can bless as we as harm

▲ Ritual staff of the god of thunder (*oshe* Shango), Yoruba (Nigeria). Seattle, Seattle Art Museum.

Shango is never represented directly. His terrifying power is translated into the beauty, composure, and sobriety of the female figure. Its symbolic dimension is adequately expressed in this carving. Everything works to stress the centrality of a balance, at once ethical and aesthetic: the carrying-pole shape, the symmetry of the form and the carved decorations, the dignity of the posture and the facial expression.

Only women devotees of Shango can carry on their head the two fiery stones of the thunder axe, symbol of divinity. They support the stones not so much with their physique, since the muscles and the facial features do not appear contracted with effort, as with their inner strength.

The head, seat of intelligence, is central to Yoruba symbolism and aesthetics: its importance is underscored by the exaggerated size of the elongated hairdo, understood as a visible representation of the size of the inner head (ori inu).

Ambiguity and double-dealing do not pertain to Shango alone, but also to women, who can be fearsome witches. The positive aspect of femaleness lies in motherhood, which guarantees the continuation of life, and brings with it the affirmation of the community. Shango increases fertility, which explains why women worship him.

▲ Female statuette with child, Yoruba (Nigeria). Seattle, Seattle Art Museum.

Shango is represented only indirectly, through the likeness of his priestesses and women worshipers.

The iconography of Shango's staffs always includes the two stones that evoke thunder, the expression of the god's power, though the shape may change.

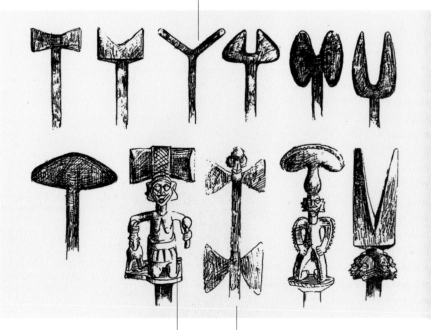

On the basic diagram of the divinity may be grafted a number of variants that refer to humankind, such as the figure of a priestess. The variations range from adding a head to including the entire body.

In societies that have no writing proper, plastic forms become a permanent support for words, acting as repositories of knowledge and ensuring its transmission. This function limits but doesn't deny a margin of variance to artistic forms, which must always be comprehensible.

▲ Iconographic variants of Shango's staff (*oshe* Shango) (from Williams, 1974).

"Where you fetch evil things, there you also fetch the good ones" (Yoruba priest, Nigeria)

Eshu, the Rogue God

The Yoruba divination ritual (*ifa*) uses the mediation of the gods Eshu and Ifa, who stand at the threshold of the invisible kingdom of the spirits and deities (*orisha*) and carry their messages back to the human race. While Ifa stands for order, Eshu is chaos and change. Both elements are equally necessary "because without a storm there can be neither crop nor harvest." According to the myth, after a contest with other deities, Olorun, the supreme god, awarded Eshu the power (*ashe*) of causing things to happen and multiply. Thus he personifies the vital force and the principles of action and individuality that stir men to make choices about what is true or false, right or wrong. For this reason, points of passage are crucial to this god and consecrated to him, for at crossroads and in market squares or at the threshold of homes, opposites clash and fuse, making choice a difficult and morally binding act. But appearance does not always reflect truth, and so Eshu is an ambiguous god who will dispense heaven's gifts but, if neglected, will also deceive, leading man to make catastrophic choices.

People
Yoruba

Geographic locations
Benin, Nigeria,
western Africa

Central beliefs
Order and chaos,
change, divination,
divination tools

Related entries
Nigerian region,
African religions,
divination

◀ Ritual staff of Eshu,
Yoruba (Nigeria). Private
Collection.

Often the god's headdress is phallic or resembles a knife blade: whenever he performs an extraordinary act or is sexually aroused, the blade stands up. (The same word, abe, means both knife and penis.) Both the blade that prevents the carrying of loads balanced on the head (a symbol of labor) and unchecked sexuality express the irresponsible, voluble nature of the god.

The ridges on the crest refer to the pumpkins that contain Eshu's magic potions.

Cowrie strands (cowries are white Indian Ocean shells), like bells, imply noise, movement; because they were traditionally used as currency, they are also a tribute to Eshu, who always demands his share of the offerings to other deities, an allusion to the riches he can send your way.

The disorder at the heart of Eshu's personality is also expressed sexually: because of his ambiguity and ambivalence, he is portrayed as either a man or a woman, or even as a couple.

▲ Ritual staff of Eshu, Yoruba (Nigeria). Seattle, Seattle Art Museum.

The container holds sixteen palm-tree nuts used in divination. The diviner turns them in his hands and tries to catch as many as he can with his right. The number of nuts remaining in the left hand determines the signs traced on the dish and the Odu Ifa passage that the diviner will recite in answer to the query. Because the diviner does not know the problem that prompted the query, it is the client himself who must find the connection.

Palm-tree nuts symbolize the tie that binds human beings to the god Ifa, given to them at the inception of time, to help them face life's hardships.

Central to this artifact is the horseback figure whose elevated social status is marked by his central position, the beard, the horse that he owns, and the soldiers flanking him. This composition could refer to the identity of the fortune-teller's clients.

By practicing ifa divination, which is part of Odu Ifa, an oral body of literature, the Yoruba learn which forces shape their lives and how to order them to their advantage. They turn to fortune-tellers for problems such as an illness, a relative's premature death, sterility, or witchcraft, or for guidance before making a decision.

▲ Divination vessel, Yoruba (Nigeria).

This wood dish can be round, rectangular, or in the shape of a half-moon. Around the border are carved geometric patterns and figures, which allude to the order of the universe and to the ifa ritual's ability to restore primal order, eliminating disturbances.

The center of the dish (ita orun, "the seat of paradise") must be left empty, without decoration; the fortune-teller (babalawo) spreads cam tree powder on it, in which he traces signs.

The figures and shapes carved along the borders are a sort of praise to Ifa, to soothsayers, and to those who turn to them.

The fortune-teller sits before Eshu's face, the focus of the representation: his presence and vital energy are needed to realize the ifa's predictions.

▲ *Ifa* divination plate, Yoruba (Nigeria). Private Collection.

"When someone falls under the spell of a spirit, his eyes dilate to make space for the inner eyes, those of the god" (Araba Eko, Yoruba priest)

Voodoo

When speaking of voodoo (or *vodun*), we usually refer to Haitians and their syncretic beliefs, born from Catholicism and the traditional Fon, Ewe, Yoruba, and Kongo religions brought to Haiti by the slaves. This Haitian Creole religion has two parts: Rada, from the name by which the slaves from Arada, on the Benin coast, were known; and Petro-Lemba, from the messianic figure of the Haitian Don Pedro and the Congolese society of Lemba healers and merchants. The Haitian voodoo pantheon has its roots in the beliefs of the Yoruba (whose gods are called *orisha*) and the Fon (who call their gods *vodun*, or "mysteries"). From the Kongo tribes, the Haitians took their belief in the powers of the dead and the use of statuettes (*nkisi*) to heal or intimidate. Rada is the calm face of voodoo, while Petro-Lemba is its impetuous side. In the Gulf of Guinea, the Ewe, Fon, and Yoruba religions have come to share common beliefs and divinities as a result of the wars and the trade that mingled their lives together. In the early 18th century, the Fon kingdom of Abomey extended its rule to the coast and was active in the slave trade. As a result, the deities of conquered populations, such as the Ketu and the Anago Yoruba, were assimilated into the Fon pantheon. Deities such as the god of iron and war, or the god of thunder, are found with similar names in Benin, Nigeria, and Haiti.

Peoples
Ewe, Fon, Yoruba, Kongo

Geographic locations
Togo, Benin, Nigeria, western Africa

Central beliefs
Haitian voodoo, possession, cult figures

Related entries
Nigerian region, African religions, sickness and healing, Abomey

▼ Initiation to a voodoo cult during a ceremony (Togo).

In the Ouatchi tongue, the term vo *means "hole" or "cavity," signifying not so much emptiness as the invisibility of a secret. The sacred enclosure (*vodukpame*) containing the initiates is also a cavity. The term* du *means "sign" or "message" (*du *are the objects used in Afa divination). Therefore,* vodu *means "the messenger hidden in the hole," or "the messenger of the invisible law."*

▲ A woman in a trance,
Lomé (Togo).

The acolyte who is initiated into a cult puts herself under the protection of the god and gives up her body in exchange, which the deity will ride during the trance. One chooses voodoo either because one is driven to it or because a soothsayer suggested it. Lore has it that some children were begotten by a certain voodoo, to whom they therefore belong; one may also consecrate a child to a certain cult, to repay the deity or exact a favor from him.

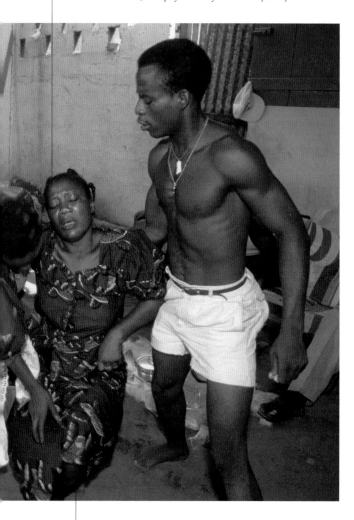

A voodoo can assume a physical form as a vaguely anthropomorphic "fetish," layered with disparate materials as a result of the many sacrifices that "nourish" it. Thus the voodoo reenters the visible world and is made more accessible, allowing human beings more control over it.

The voodoo of the Fon people of Benin are either hennovodun (deities tied to family worship) or tovodun, whose worship is not family related. Other distinctions are between "earthly voodoo" and "heavenly voodoo," and between "head voodoo" (ta vodun) and "shoulder voodoo" (achinan). The "head voodoo" possess the acolyte's body, while the other voodoo are "carried on the shoulders."

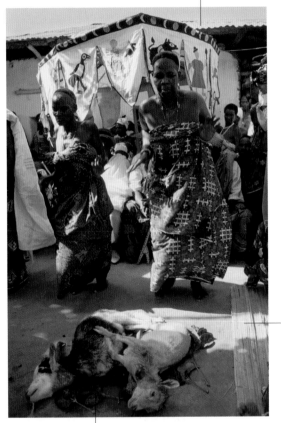

In the city of Ouidah the high priests are Danbenon, great dignitary of the sea voodoo; Huessinon, the priest of the smallpox god Sapkata; and Zonon, the priest of the great lord of the fire. The first leads in rank, partly because of his ties to the king of Abomey.

▲ A sacrifice at a Ouidah temple (Benin).

After Benin's Marxist regime banned the voodoo cult in 1972, the practice is again publicly recognized. Promoted by UNESCO in 1992, in Ouidah, the first international festival of voodoo art and culture was held. Thus a sacred forest that the Marxist government had almost destroyed has become a tourist site, though it is still the site where the voodoo powers, embodied into animals, meet and where religious celebrations are held.

"Many girls and women put on make-up because of Mami Wata, because Mami Wata has a lovely face" (Sim Simaro, Congolese artist)

Mami Wata

The Mami Wata cult is transnational, being practiced in both western Africa and the Congo region. Depending on the location, she is known as the Queen of Women, the Queen of Waters, or the Mermaid. Although closely linked to femaleness, this deity has an ambiguous sexual identity because it is not a human being but a spirit embodied in a human form. When embodied in a male form, it is usually depicted as a three-headed, six-armed Hindu divinity, called Densu in Togo. Everything about this deity is excessive, including beauty and wealth. Its devotees aspire to receive these same gifts: uniting sexually with Mami Wata can cause a man to succeed in business. The Mami Wata cult allows the devotee to build an individual identity outside of the clan, for his wealth is acquired, not inherited. Mami Wata iconography is derived from late 19th century European color lithographs that became popular in India as well as in Africa, especially in the 1940s and 1950s: they portray a woman with long black hair holding a snake coiled around her neck. While Westerners read in it the image of a woman snake charmer, a symbol of the voluptuous Orient, the Africans saw in it a water spirit of European origin.

Geographic locations
Western and central Africa

Central elements
Modernity, exoticism, seduction, wealth, individualism

Related entry
African religions

◄ Agbagli Kossi, *Mami Wata*, 1990.

Mami Wata is rendered as a light-skinned, seductive woman with long black hair, fashionably dressed and bejeweled. Her nudity is clearly erotic, her sexuality for pleasure. The well-being that she promises is akin to Western consumerism. For this reason, she is considered a white woman who is comfortable with technology. She travels on ships and speaks on the telephone, and cult sites dedicated to her can be found even on the Internet.

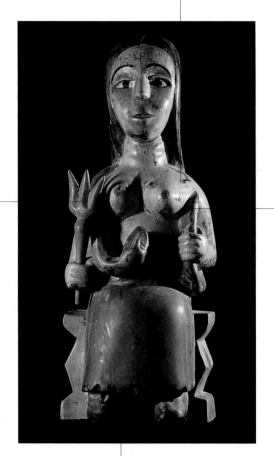

The trident Mami Wata holds in her right hand is a Hindu detail that is often associated with Shiva.

In one hand she holds the s nake that coils around her neck, confirming her association with water: in fact, she represents the rainbow that appears after the rain and joins the earth to the sky, which is called, appropriately, "python-in-the-sky."

▲ Altar figure of Mami Wata.
Private Collection.

Mami Wata is a mischievous, wild spirit who reflects the uncertainty and precariousness of life: she gives favors only to take them back, or grants them at a high price, for those possessed by her often fall sick, become sterile, or succumb to venereal disease. In women particularly, uncommon beauty is paid with sterility, like the deity herself suffers.

Mami Wata has become a common theme in urban folk African art. She was popular in Zaïre in the 1960s and 1970s, during Mobutu's regime and when the country's economy flourished, then began a slow decline. In a period of relative well-being and plentiful consumer goods, Mami Wata celebrated the golden age when the gods dispense their favors.

The work of John Goba (1944–), a Sierra Leone artist, is known internationally. His art reflects the themes of the Ode-lay society, which in Freetown in the 1970s adapted traditional masks for their street theater. This group of young people mixed amusement with harsh competition for popularity, and affirmed their own modernity. Sometimes they broke vinyl records as sacrificial offerings.

▲ John Goba, *Untitled Sculpture*, ca. 1990.

Often Mami Wata holds a mirror, again recalling water surfaces and the horizon line that separates water and earth. The mirror symbolizes the boundary that the deity crosses to enter the body of her mediums and the boundaries that the possessed cross in their dreams. The mirror attracts spirits and is also a sign of Mami Wata's vanity.

Mami Wata is often portrayed as a siren, perhaps a recollection of the figureheads of European sailing ships.

The deity's ambiguous nature is expressed in white and red, the colors that are symbolically associated with her in western Africa, signifying creativity and destruction.

The layering of elements from disparate cultural sources is also visible in the altars dedicated to Mami Wata, whose "table" (a piece of furniture that is not part of African tradition) evokes a vanity covered with the cosmetics of European ladies, a dinner table for ritual meals (again, a Western practice), and a Christian altar. Finally, it recalls altars in general, with their incense and images.

▲ Altar to Mami Wata. London, Hornimam Museum.

"What they long for and seek far away exists on their own land" (Mouride saying, Senegal)

Black Islam

By the seventh century, Islam had reached Africa by way of Nubia and the Red Sea. In the following three hundred years, it spread to the East African coast and then to the western part of the continent. In the tenth century the Soninke, black Mande-speaking tribes who had converted to Islam, reached the Senegal River and Niger River Valleys. Here they founded the savannah kingdoms that thrived on the trans-Saharan trade that stretched from the Mediterranean to the forest. Starting in the 17th century, the Hausa, Diula, and Ligbi – black Muslim merchant tribes – set up a vast network that extended from Liberia to Cameroon. Through both orthodox practice and pragmatic adaptations, this expansion gave rise to an African Islam that varies from area to area and coexists with earlier cults, for while the Prophet's religion looks to salvation in the afterlife, traditions tied to the local spirits help to cope with everyday issues like the richness of the soil and good harvests. The Islamization process did not just mean a new faith, but also a new way of life, ushering in urbanization and changes in architecture, funeral customs, diet, material goods, writing, political institutions, and relations between men and women. The Arab slave trade that had devastated many regions expanded greatly in the 19th century, as the West was shutting it down. Sometimes Islam's advance was accompanied by a forced "Arabization," as was the case in southern Sudan.

Geographic locations
Western, eastern, southern Africa

Central elements
African Islam, jihad, trade, architecture, writing

Related entries
Fulani, Nigerian region, Swahili, kingdoms and empires Sudan, African religions, trade, oral tradition and writing

▼ Hausa horsemen celebrate the end of Ramadan, Kano (Nigeria).

The sticks (toro) projecting horizontally from the walls of this mosque are unique to Islamic architecture in western Africa: they buttress the structure of the building, allow repairmen to climb the walls, and symbolically evoke the branches of a tree, with budding leaves and associations of rebirth.

▲ Mosque, Kan-komboli (Mali).

The architecture in cities is clearly differentiated from that in villages and the countryside: city buildings are rectangular, whereas village huts are round with thatched, conical roofs. Above all, the mosque or its inner garden (and private homes as well) must be square, to imitate the Ka'ba in Mecca.

As Islam penetrated the area, villages and towns were built around two different religious, cosmological, social, and urban centers. One center is the ancestral altar, surrounded by the homes of family and clan; the other is the Ka'ba prayer room, with the direction and layout of the buildings developed around it. The sacred tree is replaced or flanked by the minaret.

The 1907 restoration of this mosque, carried out by the French colonial government, modified the size, interior spaces, and style of the pre-existing building in an effort to reconcile the Sudanese-Islamic tradition with the needs to develop tourism and make the site more secure.

The mosque is built with sun-baked bricks; half of the building is covered by a roof supported by ninety wood posts, while the other half is an open interior garden.

The Djenné Mosque is one of the best examples of Sudanese-Islamic architecture. First built in the 13th century, it was destroyed in 1834 by Seku Ahmadu (Ahmad Lobbo), whose jihad had defeated the kingdom of Segou and founded the caliphate of Macina. Seku Ahmadu thought the building excessive and not reflective of Islam's original spirit. The mosque as it appears today was rebuilt in1907. In 1988 UNESCO added it to its list of world heritage sites.

▲ The Great Mosque
of Djenné (Mali).

Between the 18th and 19th centuries, a vast reform movement in West Africa led to numerous jihads; as a result, Islam became deeply rooted in this region. The intense preaching and military conquests were supported by the merchant class, which was trying to regain control of the trade routes, and by the peasants, who were victimized by the high taxes and the slave trade. Reformist Fulani preachers were especially active.

In the background are burning villages. Samori became a myth of the African resistance and an icon of the anti-colonial movements, even though the Islamic sultanates that resulted from the jihads also practiced slavery with prisoners of war.

Some major 19th century jihad leaders were Uthman da Fodio, in the Hausa states, in 1804; Seku Ahmadu, in the Macina region, in 1918; and Umar Tal, who fought the Bamana kingdoms in 1852. In the 1850s, Umar Tal founded the Toucouleur empire; at his death, it was torn apart by civil war.

▲ Pierre Castagnez, *Portrait of Samori Touré*, early 20th century. Paris, Musée du Quai Branly.

Born in Mali in 1835, in 1861 Samori led his group, the Kamara, in a policy of conquest that alternated war and diplomacy, finally subjecting the Mandingo states. His social base was the Diula merchants. Starting in 1881, as the Europeans invaded the continent, his feats took on the character of a jihad against the foreign infidels. As troubles mounted, in 1892 Samori went east to found a new empire, today's Ivory Coast. There he fought the French, who captured him in 1898 and deported him to Gabon, where he died in 1900.

"The Son of Man came to accomplish, not to destroy"
(Engelbert Mveng, a Cameroonian Jesuit)

African Christianity

Geographic locations
Western, central,
eastern, southern
Africa

Central elements
African Christianity,
missions, colonialism,
independent churches

Related entries
Colonialism, African
religions, Black Islam

Christianity has existed in sub-Saharan Africa, Ethiopia, and Nubia since the first centuries after Christ. It reached western and central Africa later, but was already in Kongo and Angola in the 1500s. Christianization followed the expansion of Portugal's commercial depots along the continent's coast. The Jesuits reached the coast of Mozambique in East Africa in 1590. Here, as in the western countries of Senegal, Gambia, and Guinea, the new religion had to contend with the native polytheism and with an already deeply rooted Islam. In the slave-trading 17th and 18th centuries, evangelization stagnated; in 1665, the Portuguese were expelled from the Kongo. By the early 1800s Christianity had almost disappeared from the continent (with the exception of Ethiopia), its presence having been limited to the coastal areas. When the 1884 Congress of Berlin divided up Africa among the European powers, Christianization followed colonization, with Catholicism taking root in the French, Belgian, and Portuguese colonies and Protestantism in the English, Dutch, and German territories. Still, the Gospel message of equality was a powerful social detonator for oppressed groups such as slaves, women, the young, and the poor, who found a way to social emancipation through the education they had received in missionary school.

► Archbishop
Desmond Tutu in
Soweto (South
Africa), 1990.

In 1491 the Kongo king Nzinga a Nkuwu converted, changing his name to John I. It was a mass conversion that included, at least formally, the entire population, including the nobility. In reality, most people did not discard their pre-existing beliefs, and often the missionaries just baptized the converts.

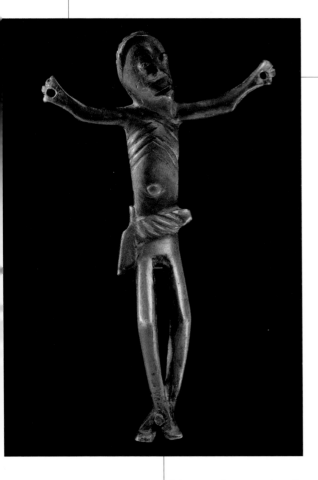

The sign of the Cross was superimposed on local traditions, and the latter continued to thrive. In fact, before it symbolized the Passion of the Christ, for the Bakongo people the cross symbolized the cosmos, the movement of the sun, and the cycle of reincarnation. The horizontal arm evokes the water line that separates the world of the living and that of the dead, while the vertical line is the path that moves from one to the other.

▲ Bakongo bronze crucifix (Democratic Republic of the Congo). Berlin, Museum für Volkerkunde.

Religion can be a cause of conflict, and so the Christian message is negotiated, "misinterpreted" or "Africanized." This is not simply a matter of insufficient doctrinal knowledge, but of a local appropriation of the new religion. Shorn of their meaning, crucifixes have been used to seek favor for the hunt, after being bundled in medicine packages, just like fetishes.

African religious pluralism is evident in the mushrooming of local and transnational "independent churches" such as Harrism, Kibangism, Zionist churches, etc., that try to unmoor Christianity from its colonial heritage and find deliverance from current misery. Faced with the bankruptcy of the modernizing nation states, these churches – veritable new communities – fill a crucial role in helping to build one's identity.

Since the 1980s Pentecostalism has made great inroads, perhaps because it stresses the emotional and bodily aspects and personal and shared experience of faith, faith healing, and a charismatic priesthood. Born in the United States, this church has spread worldwide, also thanks to its effective use of televangelism, advertising, and happenings.

The 1990s "democratization" of Africa put an end to the state monopoly of the media, allowing more access to religious movements. In Nigeria, this has led to competition between Muslims and Pentecostals for the control of mass media. In Ghana, the Pentecostal vision of a "Christian nation" rising against occult forces has reconfigured the language of politics.

▲ Poster advertising a Gospel Faith church, Port Harcourt (Nigeria), 2004.

*In the "House of Happiness" (*nemo*) in Bandjoun (Cameroon), ancestor figures and symbols of local traditional religion coexist with figures and symbols of Islam and of the Catholic and Protestant religions. There is nothing unusual in this, since the subjects of the king of Bandjoun practice all these religions.*

Friction between Christian missionaries and traditional chiefs revolved particularly around the role of the king as God's intermediary (Si), polygamy, secret societies, and the schooling of women and the lower classes.

Although traditional power was emasculated by the colonial and post-colonial governments, it still maintains a modicum of importance among the masses as it helps to define their identity and because of the religious and sacral importance that, at least partially, still surrounds the figure of the king. Historically, the acceptance of the religions of the Book was not without tension and strife, precisely because they could undermine the king's power base.

▲ House of Happiness, Bandjoun (Cameroon), 2002.

Ancestor Worship

Funerals in Ghana
Asen
Egungun Masks
Ogboni Cult
Skull Worship
Fang and Kota Reliquaries

◀Ancestor statue, Hemba
(Democratic Republic of the
Congo). Private Collection.

"A coffin is the only thing that a dead person owns" (Kane Kwei, a carpenter and coffin maker, Ghana)

Funerals in Ghana

Geographic locations
Ghana, western Africa

Related entries
African religions,
African Christianity

Funerals in Ghana are not usually the work of undertakers but of the entire community and are customarily held on Fridays and Saturdays. It is a necessary ritual that sends the dead on to their ancestors and then reincarnates them in newborns in the same family. About a year after the first burial, which marks the death and the taking leave of the human world, a second funeral is held that signals the deceased's arrival in the realm of the ancestors. A lot of money is spent on funerals, signifying their importance, and people often fall into debt. Traditional funerary sculpture consisted of memorial terracottas, but starting in the 1950s, the carpenter Kane Kwei (1927–1992) began to build figured coffins that visualized the life and personality of the deceased: a parrot with a pen in its beak became a favorite coffin of college professors, while the cocoa bean pod, the onion, and ears of corn were adopted by wealthy farmers and land owners to signify their success. Another symbol of success is the coffin shaped like a Mercedes-Benz, often complete with the plate number of the deceased's car, which follows the funeral procession. Orders from Western art galleries also began to arrive, and coffins began to be displayed in museums as works of art.

▼ Coffin in the shape of a beer bottle (Ghana).

Although they have only generic features, these terracottas served as "portraits" of the deceased; individualization was accomplished through details such as hairdo or scarifications, which identified the deceased's gender, social role, and status.

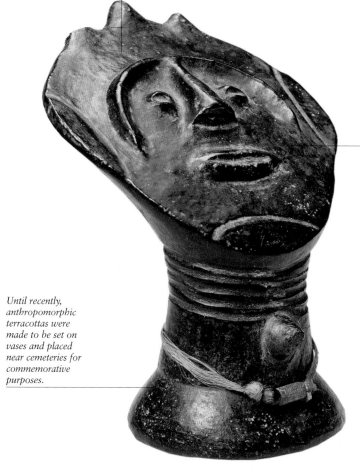

The dignified, composed expression is that of the Akan aristocracy: these generic terracotta heads varied in style from region to region, but all had the round head on an inclined plane and the bejeweled neck typical of the Akan style.

Until recently, anthropomorphic terracottas were made to be set on vases and placed near cemeteries for commemorative purposes.

▲ Terracotta funeral portrait,
Akan (Ghana). Private Collection.

The cow-shaped coffin is a favorite of wealthy herders or wholesale meat distributors.

The airplane-shaped coffin was first built by two carpenter brothers, Adjetei and Kane Kwei, for their mother's funeral, because although she never set foot on a plane, she dreamed of it from the day that an airport was built near her home. It was so successful that they decided to build personalized coffins as a full-time business.

▲ Workshop with coffins shaped like airplanes and cows (Ghana).

People do not discriminate between shapes of animals, plants, or Western machines, for whether "traditional" or "modern," they are all part of their everyday life, both real and imagined.

The bird-shaped coffin was copied from a palanquin that the sculptor Ata Owoo (1904–1976) had built for a local chief. Eagle-shaped coffins are usually reserved for chiefs; hen-shaped ones are chosen by offspring in grateful recognition of their mother's solicitude.

The Catholic and Protestant churches discourage use of these coffins, which they see as a return to "fetishism."

After the wake in the funeral home, the bier is escorted by relatives and friends to the burial site.

▲ Funeral procession with a bird-shaped coffin (Ghana).

"Asen are pumpkins inside which we place food offerings for the dead" (Fon saying, Benin)

Asen

Asen are metal altars stuck in the ground, often made with recycled materials, by the Fon people of Benin. They honor the important dead and contribute to a family's reputation, since the skill with which they are crafted is a sign of the family's socioeconomic status. The worshipers place before them sacrificial offerings to the deceased and the gods. These altars associate the concepts of revelation and hiding, for while the visible part is the most apparent, the hidden part – the ground on which they rise, readied with leaves, food, and other materials and consecrated to the deceased – is the most meaningful. The offerings are not made to the *asen*, but to the ground where it is planted. *Asen* figures are symbolic and recall proverbs whose meaning is somehow related to the deceased person, making it a sort of "portrait." These altars already existed at the court of the Fon rulers of Dahomey in the late 18th century, and until the early 1900s it seems that they were for the sole use of the royal family. The custom spread to the masses after the French conquest put an end to the kingdom, thus wiping out, among other things, the obligation that had restricted the artists to work for the dynasty alone.

People
Fon

Geographic locations
Benin, western Africa

Related entries
Funerals in Ghana, Abomey

◄ Portable *asen* altar, Fon (Benin). Paris, Musée du Quai Branly.

The meaning of an asen *cannot be inferred by abstracting it from its context to analyze its imagery, for only those who knew the deceased intimately can reconstruct his life story from it; this would not even be possible for the next generation of his family. Still, the* asen *that populate the family altar continue to give meaning, even if just as a material expression of the continuity of the family over time.*

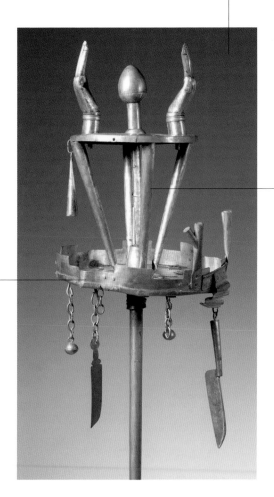

The pendants are also made with recycled tin cans and might include old French francs, which help in dating the asen.

The altar consists of an iron pole ending in an upside-down cone structure, to which symbolic objects or animal and human figures are attached.

▲ *Asen* altar (detail), Fon (Benin).
Paris, Musée du Quai Branly.

"The essence of communication passes through the eyes"
(Yoruba proverb, Nigeria)

Egungun Masks

The Egungun cult, which originated in the Yoruba Oyo kingdom, spread to other areas as people migrated after the fall of the kingdom. In olden days, one task of the more powerful Egungun masks was to kill witches; they also attended the execution of the kings who had been sentenced to death. Each year, festivals honoring the ancestors are held, both inside the family compounds and in public places. Each lineage has a mask of the founding ancestor, though there can be other masks as well for branches of the clan or for individuals, whose stories are thus represented and incorporated into the group's. An individual might learn from a diviner that a deceased relative requests to have a mask made; the choice about the look and shape of the mask is made jointly by the person commissioning it, the soothsayer, and the artist. After the medicine man fills the inside with "medicine,"

People
Yoruba

Geographic locations
Nigeria, western Africa

Related entries
Nigerian region,
kingdoms of Niger,
Shango the thunder
god, Ogboni cult,
dance

the mask is carried by the cult chief, who consecrates it; then, escorted by women, it visits all the married women who live outside the compound. Because it is a collective endeavor, making an Egungun mask expresses the socializing power of the ancestor within the blood group, reinforcing its members' unity.

◄ Upper part of an
Egungun mask,
Yoruba (Nigeria).
Private Collection.

239

The double-faced, sack-like costume of the Egungun masks allows the dancer dramatic transformations, thus highlighting the truism that "things are never what they appear to be."

▲ Dancing Egungun mask, Yoruba (Nigeria).

The costume billows with each swirling movement of the dancer, proof that the mask's aesthetics cannot be separated from the performance, for it is only in the dance movements that new, unexpected forms appear and we can fully experience the event. And because the aesthetics of the mask are multi-sensorial, it cannot be separated from the song and music that accompany the dance.

Egungun masks reveal the power of the ancestors and the gratitude of their descendants for keeping them alive.

This costume is supported by a wooden lath that rests on the dancer's head; sometimes magical substances are sewn into the headdress.

Every year new fabric strips are added by the family in honor of and gratitude to the ancestor; thus their number can help date the mask.

The costume is made by human being, but since it hides the dancer's body, highlights the liminal state of the ancestor who was at one time also a man; the same can be said for the mix of anthro- and zoomorphic elements that characterize ancestor figures and are meant to highlight the ancestor's humanity but also his otherness and his distance.

Egungun masks come in varying shapes and are made of fabric or of wood with anthropomorphic or animal figures.

▲ Egungun mask costume, Yoruba (Nigeria). Newark, Newark Museum.

"The right hand belongs to men, the left to the gods" (Ogboni society saying, Yoruba, Nigeria)

Ogboni Cult

Ogboni is a secret society whose members are influential elders dedicated to worshiping the ancestors who rest underground and from whose spirits they draw energy. The society has a leading role in safeguarding ancestral law and overseeing the king's actions. This activity is part of the broader goal of reordering the cosmos, restoring unity to the universe, which was split between the opposing principles of the earth's femaleness and the sky's maleness. The mysterious power of the Ogboni society is expressed in a symbolism that inverts the norms of Yoruba society in order to highlight its closeness to the sacred: members use their left hand instead of their right for greetings; they dance on the left side of the floor; they prefer the number three (the sign of mystery) to the number four (sign of harmony), and they wear their clothes inside out as if offering the inside of their body for view. In the past, the Ogboni society acted like a court: when the chiefs could not resolve a dispute, the warring parties were referred to the society, whose members, to guarantee an impartial verdict, listened and voiced their opinions hidden behind a screen of branches. Sometimes they resorted to an ordeal, by driving into the soil the emblems of the society (*edan*), which would fall only before the guilty party.

People
Yoruba

Geographic locations
Nigeria, western Africa

Related entries
Nigerian region,
kingdoms of Niger,
twin worship, Shango
the thunder god

◀ Statue of Onile, Yoruba (Nigeria). Paris, Musée du Quai Branly.

The chain that joins the figures by the head marks the symbolic unity underlying the man-woman opposition and the Ogboni intervention that makes this unity possible.

The bulging eyes, typical of Yoruba art, allude to the devotee's state of divine possession.

This couple of founding ancestors alludes to the single Ogboni member depicted in the ancestral hermaphroditic form, and to his obligations to everyone in the clan, of any gender. This may be inferred from the similarity of the figures, which are differentiated only by their sexual organs.

The iron tip was used to stick the edan into the ground, thus establishing contact with the ancestors' dwelling. Lore has it that the edan were also used to execute those sentenced to die, by driving them through the nose to pierce the brain.

▲ Emblems of the Ogboni cult society, Yoruba (Nigeria), 19th century. Private Collection.

Each member of the Ogboni society owns these figures (edan) as a sign of his membership and carries them as he dances. As conduits of the ancestors' activity, the edan have multiple tasks: they point out and punish the guilty in ordeal ceremonies; in initiatory rites, they heal and protect the owner and reveal his life span.

We are all just one mouth" (Bamileke proverb, Cameroon)

Skull Worship

he Bamileke of Cameroon raise their dead to the rank of
ncestors, worthy of worship and sacrifice, in a ritual that calls,
wo years after death, for unearthing the corpse and detaching
he skull. To propitiate the deceased, the skull is rubbed with
alm oil and kaolin and placed in a vase with some soil, so that
nly the top is visible; the vase is stored in the heir's home,
nder his bed or in a specially made cabinet. The skulls are wor-
hiped, especially in times of misfortune or personal bad luck,
when the relative consults a soothsayer, who questions the spi-
er (the *migala*) and tells the client which ancestor must be
rought food offerings. Then the heir (the skull's guardian) sac-
ifices a goat or a cock and roasts the meat, some morsels of
which are placed on the vase to invoke the ancestor's protection;
he rest is eaten by the family, who attend the ceremony. Special
ttention is reserved for the ancestors-in-law and the maternal
randfather and great-grandfather. Through the sacrificial
fferings, the descendant acknowledges his debt and symboli-
ally reenacts the giving of the marriage dowry that the father
ad paid to the mother's family.

People
Bamileke

Geographic locations
Cameroon,
western Africa

Related entries
Grassland chiefdoms,
male and female,
divination, witchcraft

◀ Entrance to the
concession of a Bamileke
notable, Bangangte
(Cameroon).

At one time the dead were buried in the fetal position (now they are preferably laid out) on the day of their death. After the funeral, the dwelling of the deceased is emptied of furniture and the floor strewn with dry leaves, the "ground of the dead," on which the mourning relatives sleep, with no outside contact for four days.

On the morni of the fifth d the floor is swep the furniture brought back, t mourning cease and the relatio change cloth and return their usual li Mourning replaced by party, where t family ea drinks, dance and jokes. The after the ritu separatio the fam is reintegrat into socie

▲ Memorial portrait of a notable, Bamileke (Cameroon).

A widow must banish the suspicion that she has caused her husband's death. Following custom, her own children accuse her of murder, shave her head, and store all the hair in a pumpkin. They lead her to the river, where she enters the water and drops the pumpkin. If it disappears with the current, the widow is declared innocent, but if it is caught in an eddy or moves upstream, she is proved guilty.

"You don't teach the way to an old gorilla" (Fang proverb, Cameroon)

Fang and Kota Reliquaries

The Fang people live between southern Cameroon and the Ogooue watershed in Gabon, where they settled after a number of migrations in the jungle to the northeast and southwest, starting in the 18th century. Instead of building altars to their ancestors, the Fang kept the skull and bones in bark containers that they carried with them in their frequent migrations. On top of the reliquaries they placed wood figurines or heads – not portraits of the ancestor, but guardians to ward off strangers. In other circumstances, they could represent the ancestors, who were consulted before every important decision. These figures were used to communicate with the ancestors to obtain protection and in initiation rituals, when

Peoples
Fang, Kota

Geographic locations
Gabon, central Africa

Related entries
Age-sets and
initiation, theater

they would be detached from the reliquary and moved about like puppets: thus the ancestors were brought back to life and introduced to the young initiates. In the 1920s, when the Fang were colonized and experienced the occupation like a defeat of their ancestors at the hand of witchcraft, they adopted the *bwiti* cult, which added Christian elements to ancestor worship.

◀ Reliquary head,
Fang (Gabon).
Private Collection.

The surface is burnished and darkened with repeated applications of resin and palm oil, substances that the wood will slowly release, even after many years.

The eyes are made with metal inserts.

The proportions of the various parts of the body are childlike, symbolically recalling the continuity between the ancestor and his progeny.

These figures are found in two basic styles: in the north they are elongated; not so in the south, where forms and volumes are concentrated by shortening the limbs so that the powerful muscles appear contracted. Many intermediate forms exist between these two extremes.

▲ Reliquary figure, Fang (Gabon). London, Entwistle Gallery.

The mouthless face is framed by a large, sickle-shaped headdress with side locks.

This reliquary guard is made of wood overlaid with brass and copper plates.

The diamond-shaped lower part was used to set the figure in the reliquary basket and probably also as a handle during ritual ceremonies.

The Kota, who live in Gabon, gradually moved south over time, driven out by the Kwele and Fang tribes, who also worship ancestor relics. The baskets were placed in appropriate shelters on the outskirts of the village.

▲ Reliquary guard, Kota (Gabon). Private Collection.

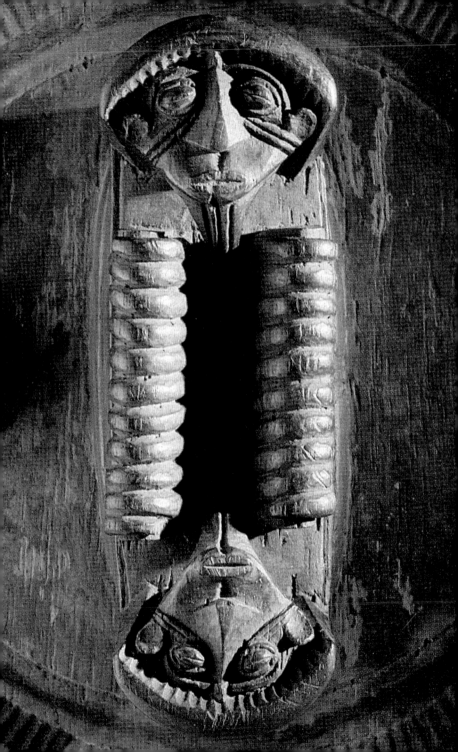

Everyday Life

Farmers
Herders
Trade
Food
Sickness and Healing
Witchcraft
Body Arts
Weaving and Clothing
Beads
Oral Tradition and Writing
Literature
Traditional Artists
Contemporary Visual Arts
Filmmaking
Traditional Music
Contemporary Music
Dance
Theater

"When the earth is rich, even the remote corners are farmed"
(Bamileke proverb, Cameroon)

Farmers

Geographic locations
Western, central,
eastern, southern
Africa

Related entries
Age-sets and
initiation, male and
female, colonialism,
herders, food

The myths speak of agriculture as a gift from either the gods or a civilizing hero. The ritual gesture of marking the earth is as important as the technical one: before settling in a place and making it suitable for farming, the group must have permission from the spirits inhabiting it. For this reason, the descendants of a place's "first" inhabitants maintain religious power over it even after political rule has shifted to the populations that settled it later. In building settlements, the farming tribes follow a layout that starts from the village and extends in concentric circles towards the wild bush, passing through farmed orchards and fields. Agriculture seems to have developed in somewhat parallel fashion in ecologically different habitats. The savannahs of western Africa have been agricultural for at least three thousand years; their principal crops are cereals, such as sorghum, millet, and fonio, and rice (in alluvial areas). The main forest crops are

oil palm, tubers (yam, cassava, taro), and legumes. Two agricultural revolutions deeply marked African history: the introduction of plants from the Far East, such as the banana and the taro tree in the first millennium AD, and the introduction of American crops such as corn, sweet potatoes, cassava, tobacco, peanuts, Phaseolus beans, and capsicum to central and eastern Africa by the Portuguese, between the late 15th and the early 18th century.

▶ Woman sifting rice,
Bidjogo Islands (Guinea-
Bissau).

Colonial cacao plantations contributed to changing the ownership status of the land from communal to private property, and introduced the salary system. Among the Yoruba, for example, the land was owned by the clan and subject to redistribution: each member was assigned a lot depending on his needs, and his heirs would inherit the plants. But because the cultivation of the cacao tree does not allow other plants to grow on the same soil, the owner of the plants became the de facto owner of the land.

Traditionally, Africans do not use a cattle-drawn plow, but hoe the fields by hand. Low-lying vegetation is burned to free up the soil and fertilize it with ashes.

▲ Farmed fields near Virunga Park (Democratic Republic of the Congo).

A diversified agriculture yields different crops throughout the year (reducing the danger of famine) and protects the fields from erosion. Modern single-crop farming disregards the fragile nature of some soil and sudden changes in climate. Thus, while reducing hunger by, among other things, improving transportation, the introduction of single-crop export farming has worsened the quality of available food.

Millet, fonio, and sorghum are the staple cereals of savannah people, eaten in soups or baked into "loaves." Sorghum and millet are also brewed to make beer, which is always part of the offerings to ancestors. According to the local calendar, the millet harvest in October marks the beginning of the new year.

In Dogon symbolism, the growth of cereal plants recalls speech, for "as the word is like the germination of man's vital principles, so is the germination of the seed a word." Thus, to farm means to drive the ancestor's words into the ground, colonizing it. And because weaving, too, is "speech," the peasant's coming and going as he works his fields is analogous to the shuttle moving through the web, so that working the land is akin to weaving a great blanket filled with words.

All the children and grandchildren of the field owner harvest the millet. Men cut the stalks, which can reach several meters in height, with a knife and lay them on the ground to cut the spikes. Behind them, women and children gather the spikes in baskets and bring them back to the village. The cereal is ground whenever needed in large wood mortars. Leftover ground millet is stored with ash to preserve it.

▲ Woman husking millet, Dogon (Mali), 16th–17th century. Private Collection.

The man in the center holds an ivory tusk and a fan: these objects, with the hat and the bead necklace, identify his high social rank; at his side are his wives, one of whom is nursing, the other pregnant. Because the yam is a very important staple in Igbo society, it is also a symbol of masculinity.

The centrality of the family is the iconographic theme of the Igbo clay altars of Nigeria, which are consecrated to the yam divinity. The well-being and reputation of the family group and the awarding of prestige titles all depend on the quantity and quality of the yam crop.

A specific deity, Ahaiajoku, is deemed to concern himself with yam crops. From this god come the soil's fertility and the crops' vitality. Before yams from the new crop are eaten, an animal is usually sacrificed to the god.

▲ Altar for the yam feast, Igbo (Nigeria). London, British Museum.

Thrust skyward, horns are the symbol of growing plants and therefore of fertility, like the calf that the antelope carries on its back.

The vertical thrust of antelope sculptures is a metaphor for the growing fonio and millet plants.

The fretwork on the back could be a sun symbol, while the back's curve could allude to the heavenly vault along which the sun rises and sets daily. The back recalls not only hard labor (working with a bent back) but also the children that one leaves behind.

The shape of the antelope recalls a horse, the only domesticated animal that is associated with the sky and therefore with the earth-fertilizing rain.

▲ Chi Wara helmet, Bamana (Mali). London, British Museum.

Chi Wara masks bring forth the ritual elements needed for the crops to grow and to spur peasants to work. They create a communion between men, wild beasts, and cultivated plants. Through the mask, the animal, whose land men are turning into farmed fields, is made closer to man; and humankind and the vegetable world share the labor of the growing plants and the toiling man. Millet makes the man, it is man, and a myth recounts how the first progenitors materialized from millet seeds.

"'Look for the cow' is the best advice one can give to those wishing to understand Nuer behavior" (E. E. Evans-Pritchard)

Herders

Livestock breeding is believed to have originated in southwest Asia and to have spread from there to Africa, though the domestication of horned cattle might also have developed independently in the Sahara about eight thousand years ago. Horned cattle breeding in the savannahs is restricted by the natural environment, since pastureland and watering places become scarce towards the north and the tsetse fly tends to inhabit the south. Lacking stables and pastures, the cattle and the nomadic people who tend them migrate seasonally; thus this type of livelihood is associated with low population density. The animals yield food such as meat, milk, and blood, and raw materials such as hides, wool, horns, and bones for manufacturing garments, objects, and tools. In many cases, herding populations, such as the Fulani in western Africa or the Nuer and Dinka in Sudan, do not farm land. Sometimes, as in the Great Lakes areas, the difference between herders and farmers also marks a social distinction between the aristocracy and the lower classes. In any case, the two groups exchange complementary goods, and the distinction is not fixed but tied to changes in climate or the environment: for example, the drought that struck the Sahel in the 1970s drove many herders to become sedentary and take up farming, while waiting to rebuild their herds.

Geographic locations
Western, central, eastern, southern Africa

Related entries
Fulani, Maasai, Nguni, Great Lakes kingdoms, chiefless societies, farmers, food

▼ Milking cows, Dinka (Sudan).

Today, about three million people in Africa still lead a pastoralist life. Their migration follows seasonal rains as they search for available grass and water. In particular, transhumance paths have water wells as their hub points, and the paths may change according to the weather.

Ownership of herds and flocks is increasingly being transferred to farmers and to city people, and the herders are becoming salaried employees. There is less cattle breeding now, in favor of sheep and goats, which are more resistant to thirst.

In the dry savannah, the traditional herding methods must cope with the effects of desertification caused by drought, the excessive use of land for pasture and for agriculture, and the cutting of trees for firewood. The expansion of farming, driven by demographic growth, is shrinking the acreage used for pasture and hampering seasonal migration. The use of cereal crop residues as animal feed is growing, as is the shift to a sedentary life and to a mixed farming and herding economy.

▲ Aerial view of a cattle herder's camp (Kenya).

Oxen may also be identified by their horns, whose shape is modified at will by the herders, or by the shape of their cut ears.

The rich vocabulary related to cattle and sheep suggests their material and symbolic importance: in addition to being useful, they inform poetry and aesthetics.

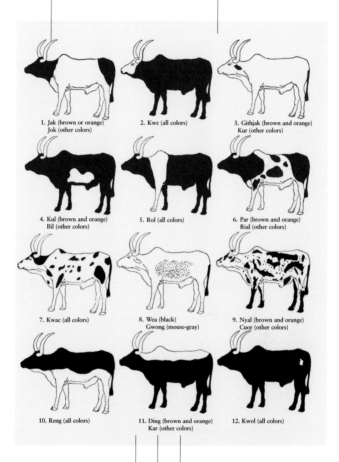

1. Jak (brown or orange)
   Jok (other colors)

2. Kwe (all colors)

3. Githjak (brown and orange)
   Kur (other colors)

4. Kul (brown and orange)
   Bil (other colors)

5. Rol (all colors)

6. Par (brown and orange)
   Rial (other colors)

7. Kwac (all colors)

8. Wea (black)
   Gwong (mouse-gray)

9. Nyal (brown and orange)
   Cuor (other colors)

10. Reng (all colors)

11. Ding (brown and orange)
    Kar (other colors)

12. Kwol (all colors)

Terms referring to oxen relate to the animals' colors and their patterns. There are ten principal colors, and the animals are identified based on a combination of white and a second color.

The names of cattle vary according to their age and sex, such as "young cow who has not yet given birth" or "calf who has not yet gone to pasture." Often men take the name of one of their animals and use it as a theme for their poetic compositions.

▲ Illustration of cattle color classification, Nuer (Sudan) (from Evans-Pritchard, 1991).

Some colors and combinations are named after animals: a brown ox is the "red savannah cobra"; a mouse-gray ox is "the sad jungle shadow."

"Riches are like a child's teeth: they shine but are brittle"
(Bamileke proverb, Cameroon)

Trade

Geographic locations
Western, central,
eastern, southern
Africa

Related entries
Mande, Fulani,
Nigerian region,
Grassland chiefdoms,
farmers, herders

Most products from traditional rural Africa were not sold on the market (although markets did – and do – exist) because the farming economy was primarily one of subsistence. Each family produced for its needs, and the limited surplus was usually confiscated by the chiefs or kings as tribute; later, part of it was redistributed to the people at festival times. Land was inalienable: the king or the chiefs owned it but distributed it for the use of each clan or family. The king, the chiefs, or sometimes specific guilds held a monopoly on the trading of luxury goods that came from afar and on Arab or European trade, and competed against each other by forming alliances through the exchange of prestige items. The circulation of goods in Africa was not effected by barter alone, but also through solidarity networks of families, clans, and societies that required the exchange of gifts, thereby creating long-lasting social ties beyond these multiple exchanges of goods. These restrictions notwithstanding, commerce was important to some populations, kindoms, and city-states, especially in western Africa, where the Dyula, the Hausa, the Igbo, and the Bamileke were and still are known for their entrepreneurship.

▶ View of the market, Lagos (Nigeria).

In Africa "coins" can be of different shapes that may seem odd to the Western eye: fabrics, jewels, shells, handles, weapons, musical instruments, hoes, gold weights, etc., have all been used as currency.

These objects have lost their original function but gained a symbolic one. They resemble tools and ordinary objects, but without their original physical and functional properties (for example, they are either too light or too heavy to be used for their original purpose).

▲ Bronze coin, Dan (Ivory Coast).
Private Collection.

The term coin *is improper when applied to these objects only if we think they must have a precise, fixed value in relation to things they can be traded for, or that there is a price for everything. In effect, they are not part of a unified market, only a conglomerate of separate spheres of exchange.*

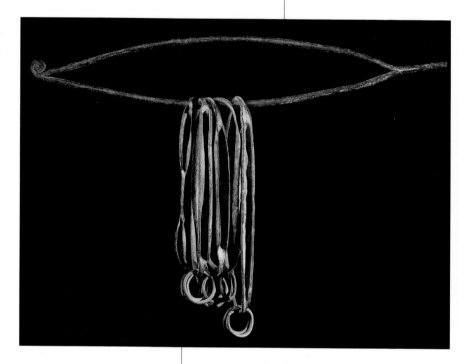

The more aesthetically elaborate "coins" are reserved for important social exchanges and are only secondarily used in commercial transactions. What transforms an object into a "coin" is simply that it is generally recognized and accepted as such within a certain sphere of exchange. These "coins" are traded at important events that change a person's or group's status, such as births, marriages, funerals, alliances, and diplomatic relations between kingdoms.

▲ Iron coin, Mumuye (Nigeria).
Private Collection.

These are not weapons that were later used as "currency," but symbolic objects in the shape of a weapon. These "spears" cannot be used as weapons because they are too light, bend easily, and have no blade.

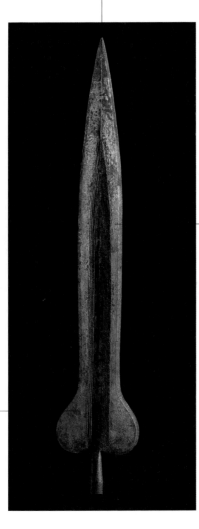

The function of these "coins" is primarily political and for display: owning them is a visible index of the strength and legitimacy of the owner's power, and precisely for this reason they are valuable.

Even materials such as iron (see page 142 for the special role enjoyed by blacksmiths in Africa) are heavy with symbolic and sacral implications that go much beyond their material utility.

▲ Iron coin (*likonga*), Zande (Democratic Republic of the Congo). Private Collection.

"If the meal is ready, all those present are invited" (Wolof proverb, Senegal)

Food

Geographic locations
Western, central, eastern, southern Africa

Related entries
Nigerian region, Kuba, male and female, farmers, herders

The basic distinctions in the African diet are not between ethnic or national cuisines but between the savannah and the forest, herders and farmers. While Europe is a wheat civilization and Asia a rice civilization, the African savannahs are a millet and sorghum civilization. Here the basic dish is *fufu*, which contains millet and sorghum, a vegetable (usually yam), and a fruit (usually *plantin*). Forest people instead survive on tubers and leguminous plants. African cuisine and diet have changed over time: rice, bananas, sweet potatoes, and taro were introduced from Asia; manioc (a tuber that is a staple in humid regions), corn (especially in West Africa's savannahs), tomatoes, and cacao (mostly an export crop) are American plants. Undoubtedly, modern urban life has changed the eating habits of many: for instance, women who work outside the home have replaced sorghum, which requires long cooking times, with rice.

Still, some foods that are no longer part of the daily diet retain their cultural and religious importance; for example, corn, a food originally from the Americas and part of the African daily diet, is not easily accepted for sacrificial offerings, for which more ancient, native cereals are preferred.

▶ A kitchen, Nuba (Sudan).

264

"Eating" is also a metaphor for expressing social relations. It can refer to sexual activity, the greed of the powerful ("belly politics"), or cannibalism linked to witchcraft. In turn, the language of witchcraft is used to explicate tribal or family conflicts.

An unmarried woman cooks outdoors so that everyone can smell the delicious aromas coming from her pot. A married woman cooks inside the house, in the kitchen that her husband built and where only he can taste her food.

Food and drink are always part of social events, be they family activities, sacrificial offerings to the ancestors, a king's visit to his subjects, rituals for the acquisition of aristocratic titles, the payment of membership fees in secret societies, or, last but not least, witchcraft.

African cuisine is essentially home cooking, with preparation and eating taking place in a protected space. There is great mistrust of food prepared by women who are not relatives. It is precisely the fear of poisoning, one of the sorcerers' weapons, that led to the success in Africa of canned food, especially sardines.

▲ A woman cooking, Tamberma (Togo).

The symbolic message of this artifact is the association between woman and spoon based on the idea of "containing" and on the woman-kitchen relationship (and therefore nourishment, growth, life). Sometimes, as in this spoon, the concave part coincides with the head, at other times with the body.

The carved decorations on the handle recall the scarifications of Dan women.

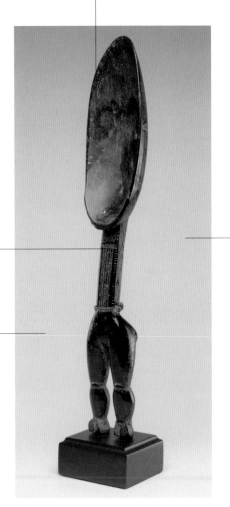

Women display these spoons at dances and celebrations as a sign of their social status; they symbolize a woman's generosity towards her guests. They are especially used when the men return from initiation rituals, or to offer food to the masks visiting from neighboring villages.

While the mask is the symbol of male power, the spoon is a female insignia.

▲ A spoon (*wakemia*), Dan (Ivory Coast), end 19th–early 20th century. Houston, Museum of Fine Arts.

These heavy wooden plates are used to serve kola nuts to guests. This traditionally male ritual is now becoming popular with women and is a way of challenging male authority.

In the center is the elaborate cover carved with geometric or anthropomorphic decorations. Underneath the cover, the wood is hollowed out to house pepper- and peanut-based condiments.

The cylindrical center is the "chopping board" on which the nut is broken into small pieces.

The kola nut is purplish white with a somewhat bitter taste and is rich in caffeine. Africans use it as a stimulant to lighten hard work, promote sexual activity, and help digestion. Shared with guests as a welcoming, friendly gesture, it is also part of many ritual celebrations.

▲ Plate, Igbo (Nigeria).
Private Collection.

Kuba art developed in a highly structured society where the nobility flaunted their status by displaying unusual, rare objects. Thus a demand grew for items such as cosmetic boxes and palm-wine goblets. In the latter case, the goblet was given an anthropomorphic shape, with the opening at the top of the head.

Palm wine is low in alcohol content (three to six percent) and has a somewhat sour taste; it is made with the fermented sap of the palm tree. The sap is tapped drop by drop by climbing the tree and making cuts at the efflorescence points. Because it is highly perishable, it must be drunk within two days of collecting it.

Palm wine is often used in initiation rites, funerals, and marriages, or in sacrificial offerings to one's ancestors and to the gods. It is poured on the ground or on the cult statues. It is also drunk at feasts and offered to visitors as a sign of hospitality.

▲ Drinking cup for palm-tree wine, Kuba (Democratic Republic of the Congo), 19th century. Berlin, Museum für Volkerkunde.

Palm wine is still appreciated today, though consumption is shrinking due to the growing spread of Islam, plantations that were farmed too intensively, and the competition from industrial beverages such as beer, a symbol of modernity. But when the African city dweller visits his native village, he likes to become reacquainted with tradition, which includes beverages such as palm wine, sorghum, or banana beer. Their low price also helps.

"Birth can be delayed, but not death" (Rwandan proverb)

Sickness and Healing

Traditional medicine has remedies for healing the sick but also treats illness as a social phenomenon. When someone falls ill and the illness lingers, it awakens the anxiety of friends and kin and becomes a sign that the ties binding the living, or relations with the ancestors or the gods, have been damaged. Thus the cause of a disease is to be sought in a failed offering to the ancestors, or in a broken taboo that the local spirits had imposed, or in warlocks that had attacked the victim in search of human flesh. The illness is not an accident but the result of negligence or malice; it implies human agency, and may include responsibility on the part of the sick person. Therefore, the diagnosis is to be sought from soothsayers, who will find the cause and suggest how to look for the guilty party and heal the breach. In addition to curing the body, the prescribed therapy will seek to redress the world's balance, resituating the sick person in his or her family, village, or age-set.

Geographic locations
Western, central, eastern, southern Africa

Related entries
Voodoo, food, witchcraft, body arts

In today's world, torn by agonizing changes, "traditional medicine" is aided by Western medicine, possession cults, and a multiplicity of healers (marabouts, prophets, etc.) who try to "tame" modernity by offering cures more in harmony with urban life, as an alternative or complement to traditional village cures.

◀ Street vendor selling medicines, Kinshasa (Democratic Republic of the Congo).

269

"Fetish markets" are also tourist attractions. A Togo Internet tourist site announces that the Lomé fetish market "is the perfect place where animist religion, voodoo, and traditional medicine meet."

Mineral substances, leaves, roots, and bits of animal parts are some of the ingredients that go into making a "fetish," little bundles usually hidden inside a vase, a hollow statuette, or a special container. Fetishes' power depends on the properties of each ingredient and their combination, on the energies and spirits they conjure up, and on the meaning they assume. They are one conduit for contacting the voodoo and can also protect from black magic.

▲ Stall at the "fetish market," Lomé (Togo).

Those who are possessed lose their individuality for a short time in a regulated ritual, as a spirit enters their body. It is one way of dealing with "the other": this "mimicry," the "staging" of what is outside oneself, is an attempt to become an other (being possessed by the god) while still remaining oneself (and increasing one's understanding and control of reality).

The popularity of possession rituals in Africa is linked to colonization: in situations of extreme subjection, the natives tried to symbolically harness modernity, turning it to their advantage and blending it with their own past. The problems that these widespread rituals try to confront cut across local identities and ethnicities.

The clan-based cults of the Hausa people survive side by side with Islam. Bori is a healing cult that treats spirit-induced sickness. The sick person offers a blood sacrifice to the injured spirit and upon being healed is initiated into the cult and "ridden" by the gods. This desire for gratification and personal liberation runs counter to the Islamic values of modesty and self-control.

▲ Men in a state of trance, Kano (Nigeria).

This artifact represents a torfan – *a mythical, multi-headed, snake-shaped animal.* Torfan *are believed to live in honey and to attack those who try to steal it. These metal objects were first made upon the advice of a shaman, to protect against the* torfan *and heal any wounds they might cause.*

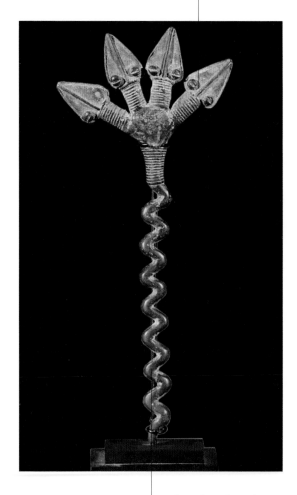

▲ Healing instrument, Gan (Burkina Faso). Private Collection.

In Africa, the snake is often associated with the ancestors because it goes into and comes out from the depths of the earth, and with the rainbow (the python-in-the-sky), which connects heaven and earth.

These figures are believed to embody nature spirits or ancestors that manifest themselves both at home and in public. They are used to promote a common good under the aegis of the ancestors, but also to support individual goals. They may be used for divination, to hunt witches, to pursue wealth, or to satisfy one's thirst for vengeance.

To be effective, the fetish must be "consecrated" by inserting a "medicine" in its hollow inside and inviting the spirit to enter it. Sometimes the "medicine" is wrapped around the fetish, modifying its aspect.

Depending on the substances applied, "fetishes" are used in healing rituals, to seek favor for a hunt, or to secure vengeance, though there is no reliable correlation between the figure's features and its function.

▲ Human-shaped figure, Teke (Democratic Republic of the Congo). Paris, Musée du Quai Branly.

The distortion of this mask is due to a facial paralysis. The two-colored face reflects falling into the fire during an epileptic seizure, or more generally, the health-sickness duality. The left side of the face has suffered (the eyelids are pockmarked), while the right side looks healthy.

The accompanying costume and dance movements strengthen the mask's symbolism: the costume has a hump, in which an arrow is buried, and the dancer moves as though to avoid other arrows, or mimics wobbling on a cane.

The intentional asymmetry of the mask serves to visualize the dark action of witchcraft: by contrast, symmetry expresses traditional aesthetic values and health. The Mbangu mask portrays sickness or the misfortune of a sorcery victim.

▲ Mbangu mask, Pende (Democratic Republic of the Congo). Tervuren, Musée Royal de l'Afrique Centrale.

"The witch doctor doesn't go inside other people's homes"
(Kongo proverb, Democratic Republic of the Congo)

Witchcraft

Christian missionaries have often looked at witchcraft as an expression of the devil, but in reality it is not customarily part of a dualistic opposition of the irreconcilable principles of good and evil, for the same powers can heal as well as hurt, depending on how they are used and on the intention of the manipulator. Sometimes the warlock and the healer are different individuals; sometimes they are one and the same. In Africa, witchcraft is not a vestige of a primitive mentality but is fully immersed in modernity: it is a symbolic system of representation that tries to make sense of suffering and injustice. It does not fade away because the confusion and inequality wrought by modernity keep growing, and so witchcraft as well becomes more widespread, not just among village peasants, but with city people of all classes as well. The language of witchcraft gives expression to the break-up of families and tries to heal them, or it may explain sudden wealth. The poorer classes use it to indict the powerful, who in turn resort to it as an instrument of terror.

Geographic locations
Western, central, eastern, southern Africa

Related entries
Post-colonialism, divination, African Christianity, sickness and healing

▼ A healer (*mganga*) (Kenya).

The disillusion that followed the end of apartheid and the lingering of deep social inequality in South Africa have increased frustration and fueled charges of witchcraft.

*Those struck by sorcery turn to shamans and healers (*sangoma*), who prescribe remedies to undo the spell and protect the injured from further harm. One Zulu* sangoma *told a victim to prick his body with hedgehog quills until bloodied all over; boil and ingest vomit-inducing herbs for fourteen days; "wash" with soil taken from his mother's grave; apply mercury to the wounds; and again drink the herb potion, vomiting for another fourteen days.*

▲ Healers (*sangoma*),
(South Africa).

Only men can wear masks, though "male" and "female" masks exist, based on facial traits and color. Female masks are white with features outlined in black and are associated with fertility and benign spirits. Male masks are much more powerful and aggressive: they are used in war and to guard the enclosures where the circumcision of boys takes place.

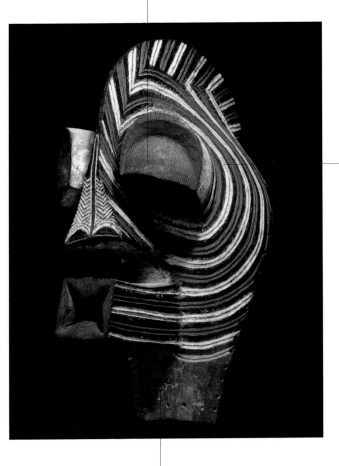

The surface incisions have symbolic significance: they evoke the underground whence the spirits who founded the Kifwebe society came, or, on a different level of meaning, the womb of the caves from which the first men emerged.

These masks belong to the Bwadi ba Bifwebe society, which uses the mystical powers of sorcery to check the power of the village chiefs. They are also used outside the Songye tribe: similar masks, though in a rounded shape, also exist among the Luba people.

▲ Kifwebe mask, Songye (DRC). Private Collection.

"Not even the best hairdresser can cut his own hair" (Kongo proverb, Democratic Republic of the Congo)

Body Arts

Geographic locations
Western, central, eastern, southern Africa

Related entries
Sickness and healing, witchcraft, weaving and clothing, beads

▼ Woman painting her daughter's face, Mbuti (Democratic Republic of the Congo).

The Bafia people of Cameroon claimed that ear piercing and tooth filing were necessary to distinguish them from chimpanzees or swine. For African societies, the body is a metaphorical field on which to paint social relations or make one's own mark by changing appearance. Achieving a new status, whether transitory or lasting, is celebrated with permanent changes such as scarifications, tattoos, mutilations, or bone deformations, or temporary ones such as body paint, garments, and headdresses. The elaborate nature of the garments or headdress, governed by taboos and restrictions, is one way of expressing social rank. But body arts evolve: there is room for fashion, for changes that evolve locally or are introduced from the outside, and for aesthetic appreciation. Going naked or neglecting one's hair is a sign of social marginalization and of a humanity threatened by animality or by disorder, which is synonymous with death. Often nakedness or shaving one's head is used in mourning or for initiations where one dies a symbolic death only to be reborn transformed; they are also marks of children's pre-social status and their not quite yet full humanity. Long, disheveled hair is often a sign of madness, witchcraft, or the apparition of evil spirits.

Color can be the subject of ethical, medical, religious, or aesthetic judgments. Beauty is not a given, but the result of caring for one's body with baths and cosmetics. The Mende of Sierra Leone, for example, prize a shining, polished black skin – the result of frequent oil applications – as a mark of feminine beauty.

The Yoruba of Nigeria practice scarification over their entire body to reach a visual and tactile symmetry (idogba), the result of alternating shiny and opaque, smooth and rough surfaces, all carefully incised and cared for. The black pigment used in scarification lessens the shine and modifies the color of the skin.

The African idea of color revolves around the combination of white, red, and black, with red mediating betwenn the other two. For the Ndembu of the Democratic Republic of the Congo, red stands for blood, white for mother's milk and sperm, and black for feces and urine. White and black express the contrast between goodness and malice, life and death, health and sickness. The white of mother's milk, of sperm, and of flour is associated with nourishment, procreation, truth, and ritual purity.

▲ Man painting his body, Nuba (Sudan).

Hairdos are often elaborate architectural creations achieved by shaping one's hair and adding hair extensions or wigs with the help of combs, butter, oil, soil, and cam-wood powder. Sometimes the hairdo is supported by a wood, bamboo, or wicker frame. The overall effect is perfected by decorations such as little bells, shells, or seeds, or amber, silver, gold, or ivory jewelry.

The significance of hair is also seen in the practice of medicine men who treat the hair to heal the person, and in funeral rites – for example, in the Democratic Republic of the Congo, the Bembe tribe inserts in their ancestor figurines a few hairs of the deceased, as a guarantee that he will continue to be present among the living.

▲ Woman with typical hairdo, Himba (Sudan).

In urban Africa today, hairdressing is a profession. But this was not so in the past. Entrusting one's head to a stranger exposed a woman to a serious risk of sorcery: by working on her hair, the hairdresser could seize her personhood. For this reason, hairdressers were intimate relatives and trusted friends.

The meaning of the concentric-circle motif (ilweeng alweeng, or "the driven stopper") carved on the temples, nape, back, and arms, changes according to the number of circles and the part of the body. On the temples, it preserves clarity; on the nape, it guards the channel of communication with one's ancestors.

The truncated conical hat (lakét) is a mark of power that chiefs and dignitaries receive upon being appointed; it symbolizes wisdom and intelligence.

The zigzag pattern appearing vertically on the torso is the "scorpion's back" (mbish a kot), which stands for the connection between ancestors and descendants. On the right arm (the body's stronger side) and on the left (the weaker side), it balances the contrasting powers that traverse the body.

The hands on the belly stress the shared origin of the chief and the community he leads.

▲ Figure of a chief, Ndengese (DRC). Tervuren, Musée Royal de l'Afrique Centrale.

The torso is elongated to increase the writing space and to stress, through the iteration of the signs, the importance of the message, which is the unity of the king, the people, and the ancestors.

This headdress is a veritable sculpture: to the hair, arranged on a frame, are added combs, hairpins, and amulets. Elaborate hairdos are also achieved by shaping the hair with clay and palm oil. Since carrying loads on the head is impossible with such a hairdo, it is used only for special occasions.

The male and female Igbo masks are opposites: the Mmwo masks painted with white kaolin evoke femininity, youth, and benign spirits, while the dark, distorted masks evoke the night, male power, "bad" spirits, and death.

▲ Mmwo mask, Igbo (Nigeria). Paris, Musée des Arts d'Afrique et d'Océanie.

This white mask, with its delicate features, a gentle smile, face decorations, and elaborate hair, projects the ideal of feminine beauty. The aesthetic canons applied to anthropomorphic images are the same as those applied to a woman's beauty: a mask is beautiful if it has pleasing human features, and a beautiful woman is said to be like a statue.

"A lovely fabric does not dress itself" (Ewe proverb, Togo)

Weaving and Clothing

Textile manufacturing can be divided into two principal areas – western Africa and the Congo region – each with their own distinct materials, technology, and stylistic traditions. The first difference is in the type of loom used: in western Africa a narrow, horizontal loom is preferred, while in central Africa a larger loom, placed vertically or slanted, is used. The two areas also have different designs. Sudanese textiles have horizontal or vertical bands; Congolese ones, slanted gridlines. The raffia fabrics of the Congolese Kuba people, and the kente cloth of Ghana's Ashanti are among the highest achievements of African textile art. Another difference is the use of cotton in western Africa, which spread with the advance of the Muslim conquerors. Cotton gradually supplanted raffia and other types of coverings, such as body paint, tattoos, animal skins, and beaten bark, which, however, survive in rituals that rebind ties with the ancestors. Still, cotton in western Africa preceded the arrival of Islam, having apparently been introduced at the time of Meroë, between 500 BC and 300 AD; it is also possible that the natives domesticated the wild cotton tree that grows in the Upper Niger region.

Geographic locations
Western, central, eastern, southern Africa

Related entries
Mande, Akan peoples, Kuba, Grassland chiefdoms, male and female, traditional artists

◀ Ashanti dignitaries wearing kente cloth (Ghana).

283

Cotton is woven on a narrow, horizontal loom with from two to six heddles. More rarely, wool or silk are woven, and more recently, rayon as well. The heddles and the comb are very narrow and produce strips between three and five inches wide, or as narrow as half an inch.

The weft yarn is pulled by tying it to a stone several yards away, which the weaver pulls closer as he works and as the yarn is used up.

In western Africa, weaving is a male trade; women weavers (in Nigeria and Cameroon) generally use simpler looms to make utilitarian cloths for household use. Men have a monopoly on the more valuable textiles.

▲ A weaver at work, Djenné (Mali).

Heddles are moved with the feet.

The bogolan *cloths of Mali's Bamana people identify and protect the wearer who sheds blood: by absorbing the blood in the weave, they protect the hunter from the vital energy released by the animal as it is killed. They also allow a woman to conserve her energy by collecting the blood she sheds during genital cutting, menstruation, or childbirth: the cloth she wears at crucial moments in her life will later be her burial shroud.*

Bogolan *cloths are made by sewing the cotton strips together in varying numbers, depending on the wearer: for a woman, seven strips are needed.*

▲ *Bogolan* fabric, Bamana (Mali).

Patterns are created with the block printing method: first the fabric is dyed yellow with vegetable dyes, then mud from a pond (a fertile place, like a woman's womb) is used to trace the pattern on one side of the fabric and is left to dry. The yellow sections are then painted with a paste made of ground peanuts, caustic soda, and millet bran, which turns the yellow into brown. When dry, the fabric is rinsed and the mud that preserved the pattern from the dye is washed off.

Originally, a tear on these raffia cloths would be mended by hiding it with a patch, which itself would be hidden by embroidering false patches around it. The composition has no center, and even the real patches – if they exist – are indistinguishable from the "fake" ones, except in that they cover a real tear. The fact that the several panels of this long ceremonial skirt were embroidered separately by different women makes the overall design unpredictable.

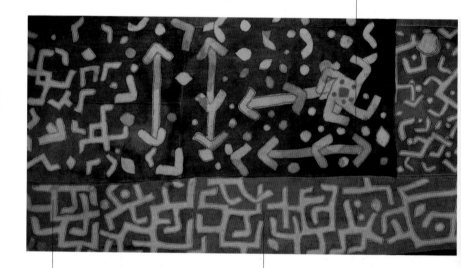

Kuba textiles come in two very different styles: one is based on the repetition and variation of combined or interlaced geometric patterns; the other (illustrated here) juxtaposes distinct geometric motifs. The latter is less popular, and we find it in women's tattoos, in buffalo-horn drinking cups, and in ntshak *ceremonial skirts worn at funerals or in ritual dances.*

In the Congo region, weaving is done by men, but women embroider; thus the more artistic part of the work is theirs. The Congo loom used in weaving raffia yarn extracted from palm leaves has a single heddle moved manually, with a fluctuating warp set on two sticks attached to the loom. Sudanese looms are faster because the weaver uses his feet to raise or lower the warp yarn, leaving his hands free to guide the woof's movement.

▲ *Ntshak* fabric, Kuba (Democratic Republic of the Congo). Private Collection.

A symbol of male power, ndop fabrics were once the monopoly of the Bamileke king (fo), who controlled their production and distribution; towards the end of the 19th century, they were even used as currency. Their high symbolic value is probably found in their origins, in the adjacent, powerful Bamun kingdom of Foumban: they were evidence of good diplomatic relations among the Grassland kingdoms. Their design is a sort of symbolic representation of the royal palace.

The ndop cloth is worn draped around the waist; in recent decades it has become a symbol of Bamileke identity, and its designs are reproduced industrially on fabrics for shirts or dresses, even for women.

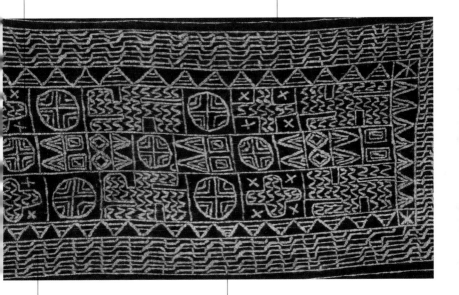

The linear design contrasts with curvy female motifs such as crocodile scales or the cross-shaped design of cowries and kola nuts. All are symbols of royal power.

Starting in the 1920s, ndop textile manufacturing was no longer a royal monopoly. It entered an elaborate commercial network with northern Cameroon: the Bamileke would sell kola nuts to the north and buy cotton fabrics, which they brought back to the Grassland for embroidering; these were sent back north to be dyed with indigo and block-printed, for subsequent return to Bamileke country.

▲ Ndop fabric, Bamileke (Cameroon).

"Those who own beads do not have a neck to wear them, and those with a neck do not have beads" (Kongo proverb, Democratic Republic of the Congo)

Beads

Geographic locations
Western, central, eastern, southern Africa

Related entries
Kingdoms and empires of the Sudan, trade

West African beads are evidence that commercial routes crisscrossed the continent, tying it to the rest of the world. Beads were produced locally and also imported from the Middle East, India, and Europe, and were of many styles and shapes to satisfy the local taste. Styles and production techniques did not change much over time: they followed ancient Roman and Egyptian designs or Arab styles, which in turn revived the ancient Mesopotamian and Meroite glass art. In the area between Timbuktu (Mali), Gao (Niger), and Adrar des Ifoghas, beads made of quartz, carnelian, ostrich eggshells, fossilized shells, and amazonite have been found, dating from 6000 to 1000 BC, that were perhaps used as funerary ornaments. In the tenth century the Soninke, a black population that had converted to Islam, reached the Niger and Senegal River Valleys; as the Muslims began their penetration, so did Syrian, Persian, Egyptian, and Lebanese glass beads and Indian carnelian and agate beads. The most important finds were excavated in the Tegdaoust and Koumbi Saleh necropolises; the latter was

▶ Necklace made of glass beads, Ndebele (South Africa), 19th century. Private Collection.

likely the capital of the kingdom of Ghana in the tenth century. In the 14th century, the Arabs in-troduced the Murano glass beads that the Venetians sold to North Africa; at the end of the 15th century, with the arrival of the Europeans in the Gulf of Guinea, these were traded directly with sub-Saharan Africa, without the Arabs as middlemen.

Fragments of these Middle Eastern or Persian beads dating from the 9th to the 12th centuries were found in archaeological sites, combined in jewelry with small bronze bells, shells, Indo-Pacific beads, and carnelian.

These monochrome white disk beads were imported from India.

Striped beads with eye motifs. The eye motif wards off evil and is also found in Babylonian, Egyptian, Phoenician, Roman, and Arabic cultures.

▲ Necklace, Simbi site (Mali).
Private Collection.

Monochrome Nila or Wind Trade disk beads in different colors, from Ceylon or southern India, were found in large quantities in West African tombs.

These beads were probably made in a Nestorian community already in Mali in the 8th century (the patriarch Nestor was expelled from Constantinople in 430).

▲ Necklace made of monochrome beads. Private Collection.

Glass beads were important trading goods, both during the slave trade and after its abolition; all European merchant companies traded them.

Relief flower beads from early 19th century Venice were made specifically for the African and Middle Eastern trade.

Bead designs varied, depending on the goods they were exchanged for and the buyers' demand: those exchanged for gold in western Africa were yellow with eye designs; those sent to central Africa to be exchanged for ivory were monochrome, usually red or turquoise; the Bohemian beads exchanged for slaves were usually blue.

▲ Necklace made of glass beads. Private Collection.

Starting in the 18th century, the Venetian bead monopoly was weakened by the Bohemians, first with printed beads, and then, in the 19th century, with glass beads imitating agate and Indian carnelian.

The millefiori or "real mosaic" Venetian beads were known as chacaso in West Africa; they were traded in the African colonies in the early 20th century.

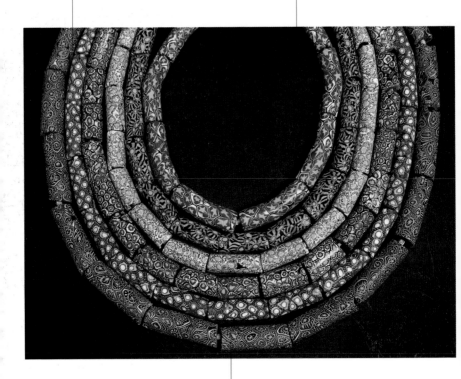

The technique for making these cylindrical beads with rosette mosaic inserts was invented in the 15th century. It calls for the successive fusion of different colored glasses in open, twelve-pointed, star-shaped molds, resulting in multi-layered cylindrical beads.

▲ Necklace made of Venetian beads. Private Collection.

"The poison in a word is the word itself" (Swahili proverb, South Africa)

Oral Tradition and Writing

For a long time, the concepts of "civilization" and "culture" were linked to the appearance of writing, and preliterate societies were considered primitive and inferior. In reality, oral societies have efficient means of creating and transmitting their culture. In cultures that maintain an oral tradition, everything is consigned to memory. However, since there is no awareness of the act of storing memory, the collective memory can be erased, conflicting ideas and perceptions revised, and information discarded if it poses a threat to new rulers. Thus, although historical memory does exist, it is continuously reshaped by the needs of the present. Knowledge is transmitted by recitation of mythical tales, ritual formulas, or family genealogies. It is always part and parcel of discourse, of specific situations, and of the corporeal presence of interlocutors that highlights the emotional aspects of expression. In such performative discourse, words and gestures are presented in an animated, repetitive manner to ensure that the listener understands. Additionally, societies without any form of writing are rare, for alphabet scripts are not the only way to record knowledge. Sculpture, textiles, objects, and tattoos interact with words to fulfill many of the functions associated with phonetic writing in the West: they promote the processing of thought, aid in long-distance communication, and make possible the transmission of ideas over time, giving a concrete, visible support to words.

Geographic locations
Western, central, eastern, southern Africa

Related entries
Guinea's western coast, Akan peoples, Nigerian region, colonialism, Black Islam, traditional music

◀ Koranic script, Djenné (Mali).

King Njoya of Foumban devised the mom *writing system, at the end of the 19th century, from a dream: this syllable-based script took as its model the Arabic alphabet that the Fulani Muslims had brought with them. Numbering at first about a thousand signs, it was repeatedly improved and reduced to eighty.*

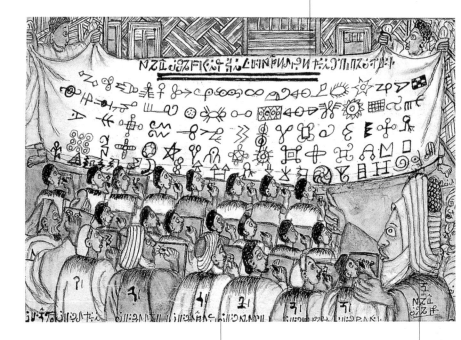

The different versions of mom *(except for the secret one) were taught in the schools of the kingdom until the French exiled Njoya, first to Dschang and then to Yaoundé, where he died in 1933.*

▲ King Njoya teaches writing to the notables, Foumban (Cameroon) (from Nicolas and Sourrieu, 1997).

The mom *script was invented to be used for secret communications between the king and his military chiefs and notables, to escape enemy espionage. Njoya also used it to preserve the kingdom's memory and, to that end, a history of the Bamun people was written, along with a compendium of local medicine. Excerpts from the Bible were also translated, and administrative and legal practices written down.*

Nsibidi is a script used in initiations. It was created about two centuries ago by Ekpe, a secret society of the Ejagham people; it is also used by neighboring tribes. Though it varies from group to group and has evolved over time, it has approximately a thousand signs, about six hundred of which are shared by all the initiation societies.

The signs are traced on the ground, mimed with gestures, and painted on fabric (ukara) and on masks. They may be classified in two major groups: signs that describe human relations and household objects, and signs that are esoteric messages about danger, death, punishment for infractions, and the society's organization.

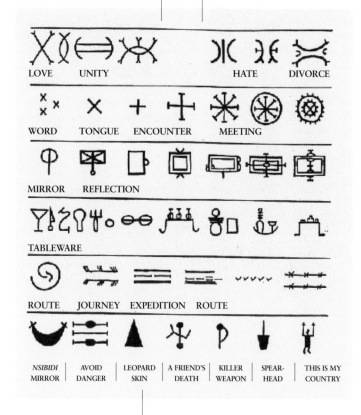

LOVE UNITY HATE DIVORCE

WORD TONGUE ENCOUNTER MEETING

MIRROR REFLECTION

TABLEWARE

ROUTE JOURNEY EXPEDITION ROUTE

| *NSIBIDI* MIRROR | AVOID DANGER | LEOPARD SKIN | A FRIEND'S DEATH | KILLER WEAPON | SPEAR-HEAD | THIS IS MY COUNTRY |

Nsibidi messages were sent using the nervations of palm-tree leaves, on which the signs were carved or painted. The Ejagham devised a duplicate set of gestures, used by the members of the Ngbe society in debating contests on various topics. Apparently, the construction of sequential gestures followed "grammatical" rules.

▲ Nsibidi script, Igbo, Efik, Ejagham (Nigeria, Cameroon).

The ki-ka-ku *script consists of 195 syllabic signs written from right to left. It was somewhat popular in the 1920s and 1930s, but was replaced by the alphabet-based writing introduced by the English.*

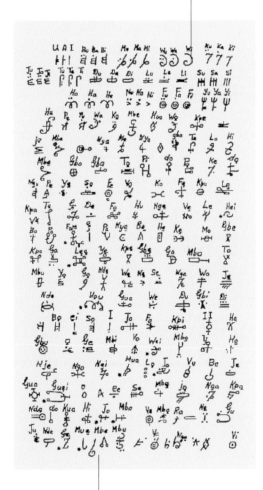

This Mende script was devised in 1921. Its inventor, Kisimi Kamara (ca. 1890–ca. 1962), a tailor, wanted to help his people compete with the English, who used writing and education as powerful tools in ruling the colonies.

▲ *Ki-ka-ku* script, Mende (Sierra Leone).

The designs found on adinkra *fabrics are probably, at least in part, adapted from the Kufic script that Muslim merchants introduced to the Ashanti region in the 19th century; many other motifs have a local origin and are part of a repertory of constantly evolving signs.*

◎	**CONCENTRIC CIRCLES**	Greatness, charisma, leadership
✳	**SPIDER'S WEB**	Wisdom, creativity
✤	**KOLA NUT**	Abundance, unity
⛎	**CROCODILE**	Adaptability
⊞	**TEETH AND TONGUE**	Friendship, interdependence
✺	**YELLOW-FLOWER PLANT**	Jealousy, envy
▦	**BEAUTIFUL BED**	Good marriage
⌗	**HE WHO DOES NOT KNOW CAN LEARN**	Knowledge, education
☾	**MOON AND STAR**	Love, faithfulness, harmony
☰	**STAIRCASE OF DEATH**	Mortality
⌽	**SEED OF THE WAWA TREE**	Strength, perseverance

Adinkra cloths are worn for mourning. The design is made by painting squares on the fabric, then using stencils to insert small drawings inside each square.

▲ *Adinkra* script, Ashanti (Ghana).

"A man who cannot say where the rain hit him doesn't even know where his body has dried. The writer must tell the people where the rain hits" (Chinua Achebe)

Literature

Geographic locations
Western, central, eastern, southern Africa

Related entries
Swahili, griots, colonialism, post-colonialism, Black Islam, African Christianity, oral tradition and writing

▼ The author Mongo Beti.

Africa had an oral as well as a written literature even before the arrival of the Europeans. Ethiopian religious literature in the Ge'ez language, born in the fourth century AD, reached its apogee in the 14th; Swahili literature, of which only 18th-century manuscripts with epic themes survive, is also ancient. Western Africa had an elite Arabic-script literature during the Mali and Shongay empires, of which several 15th-century historical chronicles survive. This varied body of literature would survive the European conquest. Under colonialism, the Latin alphabet, the press, and compulsory schooling were introduced. Against this backdrop, a literature in the local languages (stimulated especially by the Protestant missionaries and their Bible translations), as well as in English, French, and Portuguese, developed in the 1920s, as expressions of the westernized elites and African nationalism. African literature became known abroad during the Second World War with the Negritude movement. The struggles for independence were marked by the passage from poetry to novels with politicized contents that critiqued colonialism and the despotism of the new African leaders.

Born in Joal, Senegal, Léopold Sédar Senghor (1906–2001) is one of the most renowned African literati and politicians. He was president of the Republic of Senegal from 1960 to 1980, when he voluntarily resigned. With Léon Damas and the Caribbean poet Aimé Césaire, he founded the Negritude movement. In 1983 he was inducted into the Académie Française.

*Senghor's poetry ranges from the elegiac and a nostalgic search for lost authenticity (*Chants d'Ombre, *1945) to political, anti-racist works (*Hosties Noires, *1948) to masterpieces such as* Ethiopiques *in 1956.*

With his concept of "negritude," Senghor envisaged a humanism that would integrate Western and African cultures: uniting a mastery of technical-scientific rationality and a sense of animist communion with nature. Hence the key role that art and literature can play, for the magic of the word creates reality, its rhythm shapes form, and creation is a collective endeavor. Some have criticized him for re-proposing racial stereotypes that assign rationality to the white race and emotion to the black race.

▲ The author Léopold Sédar Senghor.

*Born in Nigeria in 1930, the realist author Chinua Achebe wrote four novels between 1958 and 1966 (*Things Fall Apart, No Longer at Ease, Arrow of God, A Man of the People) *in which he analyzed the devastating changes wrought by colonialism: the social and psychological fallout from colonization, Christianity, compulsory schooling, and the corrupt governments put in place by the post-colonial elites.*

The primacy of individual selfishness and material interests – a legacy of European domination – has brought about social fragmentation. As Obierika, a character in Things Fall Apart, *comments: "Now it has conquered our siblings and our clan will never be the same. It has thrust a knife between what kept us one, and we have fallen down."*

The European literary model was adapted by shifting the focus from the individual characters to the community, modulating the rhythms to those of African quotidian life and oral literature. Achebe's characters speak Igbo as well as English, but the author writes in English and wants to be judged by Western standards. Rather than a betrayal of the African cause, he sees his choice as stemming from the same process that led the African nations to independence, for beyond being the language of the colonizers, English is also a major language used throughout the continent.

▲ The author Chinua Achebe.

Wole Soyinka was born in Abeokuta, Nigeria, in 1934. After attending Anglican missionary schools, being directly exposed to Yoruba tradition, and attending college in Abeokuta, Soyinka moved to England, where he studied theater and worked in London as a Royal Court Theatre director, screenwriter, and actor. In 1960 he returned to a newly independent Nigeria, where one of his major plays, A Dance in the Forest, *premiered.*

*Soyinka has written novels (*Season of Anomie, 1973)*, plays (*A Dance in the Forest, 1960; The Road; The Strong Breed; Kongi's Harvest; Death and the King's Horseman, 1975)*, poetry (*Poems from Prison, 1969; A Shuttle in the Crypt, 1972)*, and literary criticism (*Myth, Literature and the African World, 1976). In 1986 he was awarded the Nobel Prize in Literature.*

Soyinka weaves Yoruba myths into his dramas, working them into a symbol of man's universal condition. His work is fraught with pessimism about men's pettiness. It is also highly critical of Nigeria's despotic regimes, which jailed him and sentenced him (in absentia) to death. His critique of Senghor's negritude is condensed in one sentence: "A tiger does not proclaim its 'tigritude,' it pounces."

▲ The author Wole Soyinka.

Taiwo of Ilaro, a Yoruba sculptor who died in 1920, was known as Onipasonobe, which means "he had a knife like a whip," for he called forth forms that obeyed his commands.

Traditional Artists

Geographic locations
Western, central, eastern, southern Africa

Related entries
Body arts, weaving and clothing, traditional music, dance

While Africans appreciate the skills of a good artist, they do not seek his personality in his work, which is not an expression of individual interiority but a medium for visualizing and achieving societal, political, or religious ends. For this reason, African art is not the end-product of the "artist" alone, but the shared output of several individuals, for the patron (a person, association, or family), the diviner, the healer, and the priest can all physically or symbolically affect the work. In fact, ethnographic research has identified many different circumstances in which art is produced. The apprenticeship may be formal or not; the artist's skills may be considered innate or derived from supernatural causes. The craft may be handed down from generation to generation, or it may be a personal choice, sometimes dictated by a premonitory dream. Artists may work alone or organized in guilds or castes; they may work full- or part-time, with much of their time spent in farm work; they may specialize or work in different crafts. Some artists are highly respected; others are despised or treated as regular folk without any special gifts.

▶ Innocent Tzvako, a Bamileke artist in Bandjoun (Cameroon).

Good sculpture must possess jago – *decoration that goes beyond practical usefulness to vivify and beautify the object –* and jayan – *clarity and precision tending to abstraction, which lead to the real meaning of things, seen in their structure.*

The praise of "clarity" goes beyond art to express the contrast between action without measure, typical of the young, and the circumspect wisdom of the elders.

*Among the Bamana people, wood carving is the province of blacksmiths, who often specialize in a genre, such as masks or locks. They alone have mastered "the science of trees" (*daliluw*), a knowledge that endows them with power. Their treatment of wood, disassembling it into elements and recomposing it into a work of art, is analogous to their use of medicinal plants, from which they extract essences that they recombine into new substances. Like wood sculpture, when properly mixed, these substances project* nyama, *the vital, beneficial energy. Mediocre sculptors produce lifeless objects whose parts lack integration.*

▲ A sculptor at work,
Bamana (Mali).

Many Senufo masks are owned by the Poro initiation society to which all men belong, divided into age-sets. The masks perform during the initiation rituals; at the funeral of a Poro man, they drive his hovering soul away from the village.

This sculptor is carving a waniugo *(or* kponungo, *the "Poro chief"), a frightening mask that sometimes spits fire while dancing. Its supernatural character is rendered by combining features from different animals: buffalo horns, crocodile maws, warthog tusks, hyena ears, and human eyes.*

Among the Senufo, the craftsmen who do not farm belong to small ethnic groups within the larger population and have a lower social status than the farmers. Wood carvers belong to the Kulebele group, which moved from Mali to the Ivory Coast in the past century.

The artist has carved two chameleons on the forehead and nape of the masks, for their shifting color is a symbol of change. They move with circumspection because, having been born at the time of creation, when the earth had still not solidified, they could have sunk into the ground as they climbed down the trees. Chameleons are respected for their wisdom but also feared, for they are believed to be capable of killing.

▲ A sculptor at work, Senufo (Ivory Coast).

Hausa indigo dyers, especially active in the cities of Kano and Sokoto, are mostly men. They work in small pits (there were two thousand such pits in Kano alone in the mid-19th century). Production is destined both for the local market and for export to the Tuareg and the Moors, or to the Grassland areas of Cameroon and Benin.

The fabric is dipped in the dyeing bath and soaked in a rubbery solution, then rubbed with an indigo bar made with the dried foam from boiling the indigo plants. Once dry, the fabric is pounded to create the popular metallic effects.

Indigo is used in Africa for cosmetics, as a condiment (Nigeria), and in traditional medicine to cure skin diseases and as a sedative. The wearer of an indigo-dyed cloth is aware of both its medicinal and aesthetic properties.

▲ A textile dyer at work, Hausa (Nigeria).

Indigo dyeing was known in Africa by the 10th century, as evidenced by textile fragments found in the Dogon region of Mali. Undoubtedly, the influence of Indian cottons introduced by the Arab merchants helped spread this technique.

These cloths are for wear, but they also serve as currency and are kept as markers of one's social status. They are part of bridal dowries and are also used to pay off debts or as compensation for adultery or in divorces.

▲ Women embroidering, Kuba (Democratic Republic of the Congo).

Even if the design patterns are drawn from a repertoire of traditional elementary motifs, and common techniques are used to partition the surface (with a division first into squares and rectangles), the final result is always somewhat unpredictable, for the execution is left to the embroiderer's imagination.

Men weave the canvas, and women embroider it with geometric designs. First the pattern is traced with needle embroidery; then small tufts of raffia are stitched in the intersections between the warp and the weft to fill the spaces, after which they are shaved with a blade to create a "velvet" finish.

The cloths pictured here have simplified versions of traditional designs, developed in the 1950s for the tourist trade. The composition is more uniform, the color contrasts are stronger, and the "velvet" finish, which replaces embroidery, is easier and faster to achieve. Instead of multiple patterns, there is now just one, enlarged and repeated over the entire surface. In the older cloths, the overall aesthetic effect was produced by the iteration, variation, and combination of different superimposed or interrupted patterns, shaded tonalities, chromatic contrasts, and variations in the density of the "velvet" filling: everything contributed, sometimes unpredictably, to give dynamism to the composition.

Contemporary Visual Arts

Geographic locations
Western, central, eastern, southern Africa

Contemporary African artists move between two imperatives: they want to be recognized as artists for their work and their unique qualities (like any other artist), but they must also satisfy the international art market that demands that they be identifiable as African artists. While artists try to assert the contemporary nature of their work, the West tries to confine them into the primitive art mold, for an African artist is always expected to express his roots, the uninterrupted thread of tradition. And if these qualities cannot be perceived, he risks disappointing the art world. In reality, contemporary African art presupposes both a break with the past (since the traditional artist neither saw himself as an artist nor was recognized as one) and the creation of an African modernity with its own history. The African artist is also increasingly a citizen of the world, with a composite cultural identity that, more than being just the reflection of a group, expresses his own unique background. Thus a work of art often captures the tension between individual dreams and the world's expectations and demands.

▶ Magdalene Odundo, *Ceramic Vase*. London, British Museum.

Jane Alexander was born in Johannesburg in 1959 and has a fine arts degree from that city; her work has been exhibited at the 1995 Venice Biennale and other international shows.

Her art, imbued with strong realism, creates disturbing part-human, part-animal figures. According to the artist, the realism dispenses her from the need to explicate her work, which is left to the viewer's interpretation. However, it is difficult to escape the impression that perhaps these mutants, apparently calm and sure of their identity, are a sort of mirror in which our quotidian hideousness, and that of our society, are reflected.

▲ Jane Alexander, *Butchers Boys*, 1985. Cape Town, National Gallery.

Born in 1951 in Angola, where he lives and works, António Ole graduated from the American Film Institute; in 2003 he exhibited at the Venice Biennale. His themes are the great social issues of our time and historical memory.

By assembling recycled sheeting, doors, windows, and street signs, Ole carries over into art the makeshift construction of African shantytowns, especially the ghetto-like black districts of South Africa. The walls become the visual representation of social marginalization, but also of an always evolving space, a social laboratory from which a different world vision can evolve.

▲ António Ole, *Township Wall N. 10* (Angola), 2004.

"In 1955 when a small group of Africans and Europeans discussed movies in European cafés, no one heeded them ... but they too were fighting for independence" (P. S. Vieyra)

Filmmaking

African cinema was born just before independence and has the potential, even with little funds and with distribution problems, to project a different image of the continent than that of Hollywood's Tarzan movies. It was born with the didactic, political purpose of building an image and a memory of Africa free of colonial distortions. Recurrent themes are the contrast between modernity and tradition and between community values and individual ambition. The filmmakers tend to favor content over form, for when poverty is denounced there can be no room for aestheticism. Like other types of contemporary art, cinema is also subject to cultural dependency, inherent in the fact that it is a Western art form (and production funds come from the West). In fact, African cinema has remained for the most part an elite phenomenon directed to an international audience. The very few movie theaters in Africa (they cannot compete with home video) usually show genre movies from the U.S. or India, or martial arts pictures. However, these same genres combined with the expressive traditions of Yoruban popular theater are also the basis of the recent busy production of Nigerian and Ghanaian videos made for an African audience, a type of popular movie very different from auteur cinema.

Geographic locations
Western, central, eastern, southern Africa

Related entries
Colonialism, post-colonialism, contemporary visual arts, theater

▼ A scene from *Yaaba* (1987), by Idrissa Ouédrago (Burkina Faso).

Souleymane Cissé was born in 1940 in Bamako and studied cinematography in Moscow. His first full feature, Den Muso (The Girl, 1975) is a story shot in the Bamana language about a young mute woman who is raped by an unemployed man. Pregnant, she is deserted by the man and rejected by her family. The film was censored; it was released only three years later, in Mali.

In Yeelen (The Light, 1987), Cissé narrates a conflict between father and son, with the son stealing his father's sorcery secrets. To neutralize the father's rage, the mother sends the youth to visit his twin brother. He reaches his brother after many misadventures, only to find out that he will still have to face his father's rage. The story takes place in pre-colonial times, but is devoid of neo-traditionalist nostalgia.

Cissé pays great attention to image quality and the aesthetics of the film, the landscape in particular. The warm morning light is the real protagonist of Yeelen, and even the final clash unfolds in a blinding light. Allegorical violence appears in the fights of animals (buffalo, lion, elephant), the magical metamorphoses of the protagonists, drawn from traditional African symbolism.

▲ A scene from Yeelen (1987), by Souleymane Cissé (Mali).

In Camp de Thiaroye *(1987, Senegal), Sembene narrates the violent repression by the French of the Senegalese Riflemen (a corps in which Sembene had fought), who demanded to be paid at the end of World War II. In* Ceddo *(The People, 1977) he criticizes the forced Islamization that took place in 17th-century Senegal. He inaugurated the return of African cinema to its origins with works about pre-colonial times.*

Born in Senegal in 1923, Sembene migrated to France, where he supported himself with odd jobs (mechanic, construction worker, longshoreman) until he achieved notoriety as an author. He then went to Moscow, where he studied at the Gorki Film Studio. His first full feature, Black Girl *(1966), is a story about a woman who follows the family she works for to France and takes her own life.*

Speaking about his preference for close-ups, the director explained that it was in keeping with traditional African sculpture and masks: the emphasis on details heightens the emotions and traits of his characters.

▲ The director
Ousmane Sembene.

*Sembene sees his work as a continuation, in a different medium, of the art of the griots, the traditional storytellers: his films are moralistic stories that produce political effects. They explore colonial violence (*Emitai, the Thunder God, *1975), corruption in the African ruling class (*Xala, *1975), and the rights of women and children (*Moolaadé, *2004). The last, which broaches the subject of female genital mutilation, received a prize at the Cannes Film Festival.*

"Rhythm is at the root of the struggle between Life and Death, being and nothingness, time and eternity" (Engelbert Mveng)

Traditional Music

Geographic locations
Western, central, eastern, southern Africa

Related entries
Griots, contemporary music, dance

Unlike Western classical music, which, since the Baroque period, has been composed around one meter and one melody, traditional African music is polyphonic, with multiple rhythms and counterpoints: the voices and the instruments do not follow the same theme but rather weave together a dialogue. Just as important are pauses, silences between rhythmic beats that leave room for the musicians and the audience to improvise. Musicians' and singers' skills lie in the iteration of the same verse or theme, each time with slight variations in tone or background music. Unlike in Western music, the accent is not so much on melody as on rhythmic structure: the solo voice is not the focus of the composition, but only an interlude between repetitions of the choral theme; the hand clapping that accompanies the singing crosses it without respecting the pauses between words. The overall effect is produced by the blend of different rhythmic combinations: the hand clapping beats different rhythms that have only the starting point in common; and the drums follow different patterns, sometimes changing them as they play. The rhythms cross each other without ever converging in the principal beats, and fade away following their own trajectory without a single, dramatic finale.

► Figure of a king playing the drum, Kuba (Democratic Republic of the Congo), end 18th century. New York, Brooklyn Museum of Art.

For many African populations such as the Yoruba and the Akan, the sound of drums, flutes, whistles, and gongs are a sort of "sound language" that schematically reproduces language's tonal differences, thus allowing the long-distance transmission of messages. Unlike in the written language, it is the sense of hearing, rather than sight, that acts as the transmission channel, and the receiver is not an individual, but the collectivity.

▲ Drum, Baga (Guinea-Bissau).
Paris, Musée du Quai Branly.

Large, animal-skin drums called timba are used only by men and played mostly during the initiation rites of the Simo secret society. The horse, an animal rare in Africa, is a symbol of power.

The xylophone is one of the instruments played by the griots, the Mande bards. It is also found in central Africa, under the name of marimba.

▲ A xylophone (*balafon*) player, Bobo (Burkina Faso).

The keyboard consists of sticks of wood tied together and attached to a wood base, and empty pumpkins that act as sound boxes. The xylophone is usually tuned on a five-tone scale.

Sometimes the pumpkins are perforated and the opening covered with spider's webs (or other more modern materials), which act as vibrating membranes. The xylophone is played with two small hammers. It is also played in bands of three balafons *and drums.*

Twenty-one leather strings are arranged on the handle, in two parallel rows (a row of ten and one of eleven), and fastened to a bridge that is perpendicular to the soundbox; there are four possible tunings.

The kora *is held vertically: with the little or middle finger, the musician grasps the handle on each side of the soundbox and plays by plucking the strings with the index fingers and the thumbs.*

This string instrument has a soundbox built with half a pumpkin, over which an animal skin has been stretched. This is one of the symbolic instruments of West Africa's griots.

▲ Mamadou Diabate and his *kora* (Mali).

On the wooden posts of the great sacred hut of the Bandjoun chieftaincy, built in 2001 and destroyed in a 2005 fire, were carved several traditional instruments, such as the balafon, *drums, and castanets, in dancing scenes. Each dance pertained to a specific ritual, mask, or secret society.*

Besides the traditional instruments, contemporary, internationally known Cameroonian singers and musicians were also portrayed, such as the jazz saxophonist Manu Dibango and the singer-songwriter André Marie Talla, a native son of Bandjoun.

▲ House of Happiness, carved post with jazz musician figures, Bandjoun (Cameroon).

*One post was dedicated to the double bell (*kwi'fo, *"the king's assistant"), the most sacred of all instruments because it releases great quantities of vital energy (*ke*) that can be manipulated. It is the symbol of the Nyleng society, which comprises the sons and nephews of the king and the progeny of the farmer population that the hunters – from whom the reigning dynasty descends – found upon their arrival in the area.*

"The scene is ready for a real cultural trend to emerge that is no longer exotic" (Manu Dibango)

Contemporary Music

Geographic locations
Western, central, eastern, southern Africa

Related entries
Griots, traditional music

Much of contemporary pop music has African roots, though beginning in the 1950s African musicians and artists also exerted a direct influence with their world tours and entry into the international music market, starting with Miriam Makeba, Ibrahim Abdullah (Dollar Brand), and Manu Dibango. Of course, inter-cultural relations are mutual, and African music has also been influenced by its exposure to the West. For example, High Life music, born on the Gold Coast (today's Ghana) in the 1920s, fused percussion-rhythm Akan dance with jazz. Nigeria's Afrorock and Afrobeat, popularized in the 1960s by Fela Kuti, fused High Life, American free jazz, and funk. Similarly, contemporary Congolese music (known as Congolese rumba) has its roots in the colonial period, from the fusion of a local dance (*maringa*) with Latin American rhythms, such as rumba, merengue, bolero, cha cha, and *pachanga*, and the use

of the Spanish guitar. And *jaliya*, which is griot Mande music, from a mostly aristocratic, elite genre, has become pop, played on the radio and TV and sung by pop artists. The search for wider markets encourages the formation of multi-ethnic and multi-language bands, even if they offend the ethnic policies of their countries.

▶ The musician Mori Kanté.

Born in Johannesburg, South Africa, in 1932, Miriam Makeba left her country in 1960, when she was invited to attend the Venice Film Festival for the screening of an anti-apartheid documentary, Come Back, Africa. *She continued traveling, and in 1963 the Pretoria government stripped her of her citizenship after she testified against apartheid before the United Nations.*

She found success in the U.S., but left after her stormy marriage to the civil rights and Black Panther leader Stokely Carmichael. She moved to Guinea, where she was appointed representative to the U.N. from 1964 to 1975. In 1990 Miriam Makeba returned to South Africa at the invitation of President Nelson Mandela.

Miriam Makeba started her singing career in the 1950s with the Manhattan Brothers band and later with the Skylarks, mixing jazz and traditional South African music. In 1956 she composed her most famous song, "Pata Pata," which brought international renown, and in 1966 she won a Grammy Award with Harry Belafonte for their LP An Evening with Belafonte/Makeba.

▲ The singer Miriam Makeba.

Manu Dibango, the Cameroonian saxophonist, was born in 1934 and began his career in Brussels and Paris in the 1950s. He became known internationally in 1972 with Soul Makossa. *An eclectic artist, he has performed in many genres. In 1985 he launched the "Tam-tams for Ethiopia" drive to raise funds for that famine-ravaged country; many African artists such as Mory Kante and Salif Keita took part in the effort.*

In his autobiography, Trois kilos de café *(translated as* Three Kilos of Coffee *by Beth G. Raps), Manu Dibango writes: "In music there's no past and no future, just present. I have to compose the music of my own period, not of yesterday. People have always found me 'versatile' and accused me of 'pillaging.' 'Vampire Makossa' – I accept the judgment. How can you create if you don't immerse yourself in the material of your times? No creator can avoid being a vampire; painting, literature, and the informational arts function just as music does."*

▲ The musician Manu Dibango.

Born in Mali from a noble family, Salif Keita became a singer against his family's wishes, since for the Mande people the musical profession is reserved to the griots, a lower caste. An albino in a country that viewed albinos with suspicion, he moved to Montreuil, near Paris. In recent years he returned to Bamako, where he opened a night club and a recording studio.

Salif Keita debuted in the 1960s with the Rail Band du Buffet de la Gare, a Mali band that played a traditional Mandingo repertoire, and the Ambassadeurs du Motel, who were inspired by French songs, English pop, soul, tango, and especially Cuban music. He recorded his first album, Mandjou, in Abidjan in 1979; in 1987 his hi-tech record Soro was among the first to launch "world music." In 1988 he wrote the score for Souleymane Cissé's film Yeelen.

▲ The musician Salif Keita.

Born in Dakar, Senegal, in 1959, Youssou N'Dour is among the best-known performers of contemporary "world music." He likes to sing mbalax, *a fusion of Senegalese, Cuban, reggae, and pop music. His collaboration with Peter Gabriel in 1983 gave him international renown; he became famous with* Wommat (The Guide) *in 1994. He won a Grammy Award in 2005.*

His religious beliefs play an important part in his music. Youssou N'Dour is a follower of Cheikh Amadou Bamba and the West African griot tradition. He is also a savvy businessman who owns a recording company, a newspaper, a radio station, and a night club.

▲ The singer Youssou N'Dour.

Jamaican reggae was adapted to the African context with songs of social protest sung in Diula, Baoulé, French, and English. Alpha Blondy became an international name with Rasta Poue (1984) and Cococody Rock. His songs denounce apartheid, dictatorship, corruption, and tribalism, and promote messages of religious ecumenism. But they also celebrate politicians such as Felix Houphouet-Boigny, the president of the Ivory Coast.

Alpha Blondy (his real name is Sydou Koné) was born in Dimbrokro, Ivory Coast, in 1953. He moved to the United States, where he began to write reggae-inspired music. Unable to get a recording contract, he returned home and spent the next two years in a psychiatric hospital to treat his depression. After being discharged, he recorded his first record, Jah Glory, in 1983.

"Bloodshed in Africa / Bloodshed in Africa / What a shame, what a shame / It's a bloody shame, oh yeah! / It's a mighty shame, oh Lord! / See Babylonians are coming around / And messing around / With my people's mind / I can't stand it / No I won't bear it ..."

▲ The musician Alpha Blondy.

"If you cannot dance, go watch the monkeys in the forest"
(Kongo proverb, Democratic Republic of the Congo)

Dance

Geographic locations
Western, central,
eastern, southern
Africa

Related entries
Maasai, hunters and
warriors, voodoo,
body arts, traditional
music, theater

▼ Men dancing, Yacouba
(Ivory Coast).

African dance stresses group dancing, rather than individual or couples dancing. In contrast, masks may dance alone or as a couple, but this is reserved for exceptional events, and the dancer's identity usually remains hidden because the dance is the manifestation of a spirit. Poly-rhythmic music accompanies dancing – for example, different drums may each have their own rhythm. The dancer's movements correspond, as each part of the body, chest and pelvis in particular, acts independently, following up to four different rhythms at once. Often, the dancer is also the musician, with rattles in his hands and hanging from different parts of the body, generating sound as he moves. Dance is important not just as a social pastime, but religiously and politically as well. During dances for special events, such as funerals, ceremonies that evoke mythical primordial times, and propitiatory hunting rituals, figures are traced on the ground to separate the sacred space from the profane. Dance embodies the ethos of a culture. Dance groups also serve to strengthen one's ethnic identity and a feeling of belonging, for example, in urban areas that have suffered sweeping change.

Dance is one way of connecting with the gods to seek their favor, repair relationships, or ward off their wrath. Pleasing the gods and the ancestors ensures their support.

The link between dance and the opening to the sacred rests on the bodily experience of expanding or losing one's self in the dance, making it a symbol of what is beyond ordinary experience.

Dance can be a channel for the transmission of extraordinary powers; it can induce a state of trance that leads the deity to manifest itself in the dancer's body and possess it. Sometimes this experience is reached through the mask, which modifies the body's appearance and its movements.

▲ Voodoo worshippers dancing, Ouidah (Benin).

For the Dogon, "the masked dancers are the world; and when they dance in a public place, they are dancing the progress of the world and the world-order" (Griaule, 1970). The Kanaga mask in particular represents the world as created by God: the vertical stick is the axis linking heaven and earth, while the circular movement recalls the act of creation.

Masks sanction the end of mourning (dama) by dancing first on the terrace of the deceased's home, then in the village square. In the evening they lead the soul into the bush, from where it will reach the land of its ancestors, thus bringing closure to the deceased and the family.

▲ Dance of the Kanaga masks, Dogon (Mali).

The Kanaga mask dance uses abrupt left-to-right movements to reenact the ancestors' reaction to the insect that bit the ark on which they had been lowered to earth. Thus the first dispute broke out on earth, and the masks' song relives the memory by warning the insect: "Watch out!" At the same time, the cry drives women and children away. Each mask has its particular chant: that of the first Kanaga mask in the dancing line summarizes them all.

The Kanaga masks appear in acrobatic dances that are highly appreciated by tourists today; the Dogon put on shows for them that relive Dogon traditions. The dancer's skill lies in brushing the ground with the mask without breaking its arms.

Warrior dances express a man's strength and self-control, his power of taking, giving, and saving life (by killing, impregnating, or saving the enemy). They usually imitate and ritualize battle gestures.

With these dances the young Maasai warriors prove their strength and nimbleness with high jumps in place.

Warrior dances are performed to celebrate group and individual status (the entry into adult life of a generation of youths, or the battle slaying of an enemy by a valiant warrior). They are feats of virility, for vigor and resistance are seductive to women; a form of physical and emotional training for war, for they stir up the spirits and promote cohesion; and a religious act, a sort of energy-releasing prayer or sacrificial gesture. Finally, they are a political act, for they pay homage to a chief or channel the warriors' tension into a ritualized expression of violence.

▲ Warrior dance, Maasai (Kenya).

"Why then didn't you name me, like every other human being? ... You could have made a person out of me.... Alas, I am only a piece of wood" (Mitsogho tale, Gabon)

Theater

Theater has its roots in ritual, being performed in a space where everyday conventions are suspended. Mask dancing has a theatrical quality and when it loses its sacred character becomes theater. Both masks and puppets deal with movement and metamorphosis, and because they often originate from rituals about the dead and the bush spirits, even when just entertaining, they evoke something beyond mere spectacle. The disruption of the organic fluidity of normal bodily movements (heightened by changes in the voice) that is typical of mask and puppet shows and dance steps makes the theater a bridge between life and death. Because of the immediacy of its communication, theater also played an important role during decolonization, with the presentation of historical plays and figures of past leaders, such as Shaka Zulu or Ovonramwen, a Benin king. In Nigeria, the Yoruban popular theater that arose in the 1930s evoked myths, the poetry of *ifa* divination, and the pre-colonial past to help promote anti-colonial nationalism. One of theater's contemporary themes is everyday life in African cities, a topic that has also been the subject of recent Nigerian filmmaking.

Geographic locations
Western, central, eastern, southern Africa

Related entries
Mande, Nigerian region, body arts, literature, dance

◀ Puppet, Kuyu (Democratic Republic of the Congo).

331

This puppet represents the ideal of feminine beauty: the emphasis is on the breasts and the hairdo, which frames the slender face shaped by the perpendicular lines of the forehead and the nose.

▲ Puppet, Bamana (Mali).
New York, Friede Collection.

These puppets are mute; sometimes they perform on boats in the river. Their origin goes back to the mid-19th century. Around the end of the 19th century, the tradition was handed down by the fishing communities to the farming communities. Today puppets are used by the Bozo and Somono young fishermen's societies, and by the Bamana and Marka farmers' societies. The puppets perform at the opening of the fishing or farming season, and at harvest time.

Theatrical groups are formed by young men who compete against each other with both puppets and masks. A good performance will blend tradition and innovation, predictability and surprise. New characters are constantly added to the repertory, even "stealing" them from neighboring villages.

▲ Puppet, Bamana (Mali).
Private Collection.

Each mask or puppet performs accompanied by a song that introduces the character with praise and in the context of myths and legends as well as contemporary political or social issues. Some puppets represent historical characters, such as pre-colonial warriors, European soldiers, or even Charles de Gaulle. The horse is a symbol of power.

This type of carved box is placed on top of a bamboo frame covered with raffia and fabric on feast days.

This puppet's traits recall Al-Burak, the winged horse on which Muhammad flew from Mecca to Jerusalem before rising to heaven to face God during his night ascension. The image of Al-Burak is popular in Sierra Leone and Guinea with Muslims, Christians, and followers of traditional beliefs. Drawings and masks with its likeness are used to ward off witchcraft.

In Africa, puppets are moved not just with the hands, but often with the head, knees, feet, or the entire body. Many statuettes are also used as puppets. Even the actor's body parts can become puppets when he isolates them from the rest of his body, treating them as independent objects, as happens in many African dances with the movement of the dancer's hands, breasts, belly, or buttocks.

▲ Puppet, Baga (Guinea).
Paris, Musée du Quai Branly.

White, red, and black make up the basic color triad of African cultures: white is often associated with health and goodness, and black with disease and witchcraft. The color red is ambivalent, for it refers to an energy that can be used both ways.

This mask is moved by a stick inserted in the body: a patch of fabric on the neck hides the mechanism.

The puppet is held by a stick protruding from the base.

▲ Puppet, Ogoni (Nigeria). Private Collection.

This type of puppet was used by members of Amanikpo, a secret society, and moved by an elder; it was used only in shows for the initiated.

Human Habitats

Dogon
Nankani
Kumasi
Abomey
Tamberma and Somba
Fali
Musgum
Kraal
African Cities

◀ Granary door, Senufo (Ivory
Coast). Private Collection.

"Seen from above, the village is the image of the ancestor's house, with its eighty niches, and of the great blanket of the dead, with its white and black squares" (M. Griaule)

Dogon

Geographic locations
Mali, western Africa

Central elements
Anthropomorphism of
village layout, houses,
togu na

Related entries
Granary of the Pure
Earth, *nommo* genies,
farmers, dance

Different kinds of spaces are visible in a Dogon village: some are public, such as the square and the market place, others private, such as the men's meeting place, the house where the male members of the Awa society store their masks, or the house for menstruating women. Additionally, sites are set aside for altars, the cemetery, forges, pottery-making stoves, and waste disposal. Generally, these sites or buildings are laid out following an anthropomorphic principle that draws the parts into an organic unity that echoes the myth of the Dogons' origin as a people, and the layout of the space also recalls events of yore. Thus the village should stretch from north to south, in the shape of a man lying face up. The elders' council house (*togu na*) would be the head, the houses for menstruating women the hands, the large family compounds (*ginna*) the chest and belly, and the village altars the feet. In reality, since the Dogon landscape varies – moving from west to east it changes from highland to cliffs to sandy plain – the actual layout must follow the lay of the land, as well as historical events, so that the myth becomes a retrospective reading that imposes order and coherence on past events.

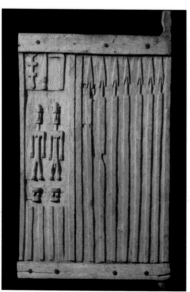

▶ Granary door shutter, Dogon (Mali).

*Banani is a four-part settlement linked together
by an ancestor. The Dogon villages were built
on the Bandiagara slopes for defensive purposes:
the people fled there to escape Mossi raids.
When the French came and peace was restored
to the area, new villages were built on the plain.*

*The homes are surrounded by walls. The rooms
and the granaries face a central inner court where
tools and implements are stored and meals are
prepared. The kitchen and bedrooms are on the
ground floor; a wooden ladder leads to the second
floor, where other bedrooms or storage rooms are
located, and to the terrace, where the harvest is
spread out to dry. The number of rooms and
granaries depends on the number of wives.*

▲ A Banani village, Dogon (Mali).

The roof of the men's house is several yards thick and consists of layers of millet stalks, an efficient form of insulation from the sun's rays. Because it is a perishable material, the roof must be rebuilt periodically by all the villagers and even by volunteers from nearby villages.

Common to all togu na *constructions is the very low roof that forces men into a sitting position. The Dogon have different explanations for this peculiarity: it is for defense from enemies on horseback, who cannot enter the house; for protection from the sun and the heat; or to reinforce the sayings that "one fights standing" and "one can never fight while sitting."*

The supporting walls and pillars made of wood, stone, or banco *(a mix of clay, water, and straw) are frequently decorated with symbolic motifs. While forbidden to enter the* togu na, *women are represented in the many fertility symbolisms.*

The togu na ("great shelter" or "mother's shelter") is where the "seated" word is spoken: an easy, meditative conversation among men. Visible from a distance, it represents the "head" of the village, the first building raised when founding a village. The elders make their decisions there, managing the life of the community and meting out traditional justice. In villages built on cliffs, the togu na is also a defense observation point.

▲ Men's house (*togu na*), Banani village, Dogon (Mali).

According to Ogotemmeli, a Dogon elder, "the façade and its eight rows of ten niches stand for the eight ancestors and their progeny, as numerous as the fingers of their hands." In the niches live the ancestors; they are arrayed in order of primogeniture, starting from the top row.

The façade and its checkered design symbolize the shroud in which the dead are wrapped, and evoke the orderly arrangement of the farmed fields. They also evoke Sirige, a large mask called "the many-storied house," whose lines recall the architecture of the Dogon house.

The pinnacles on top of the façade are altars to the ancestors. In principle, there should be eight, but sometimes the number differs, depending on the size of the house.

The spaces are symbolically viewed as male and female, according to an anthropomorphic model that sees the entrance door as the man's penis, the central room and the storage rooms on each side as the woman's body lying on her back in the sexual embrace.

▲ House (*ginna*), Sangha, Dogon (Mali).

The horse is one metamorphosis of the nommo genie; having reached the earth, in this guise he pulled the world's ark.

The different figures of this togu na should probably be understood as parts of a commemoration of the dama ceremony, when the souls of the deceased are driven out of the village and led to the land of the ancestors.

A carving portraying a Valu mask: this is the antelope killed by the Dogon hunters, which projects vital energy (nyama); the mask is a receptacle for it that also placates it.

A Fulani woman, her female parts displayed. The Fulani are historic enemies of the Dogon people.

A mask on stilts.

A carving portraying a Kanaga mask. The identifying feature of this mask is the upper part in a "Lorraine cross," a symbol of the Creator God, who with one hand points up to the sky and with the other, down to earth. The cross takes on additional meanings in different initiation levels of the Awa mask society.

▲ Drawing of posts of Seddourou's togu na, Dogon (Mali) (from Spini and Spini, 2003).

"If you help a child climb a tree, everyone will enjoy the fruit"
(Nankani proverb, Ghana)

Nankani

The Nankani people live on both sides of the border dividing Ghana from Burkina Faso. Their villages have scattered, walled family compounds surrounded by tilled fields. Because they are also built for defense, the compounds are laid out in a circle, and each house is connected to the next by continuous solid walls that have only one gate. The entrance to each house, protected by a wall, faces the main gate and is located so that someone inside the home can hit an attacker without being seen. The space is symbolically laid out in a male section (the outdoor area and the livestock yard, which is immediately inside the gate) and a female area (towards the center of the compound). The circular shape of the women's quarters recalls the jars used to store food, and is also a metaphor for the female womb. The doors to the women's quarters metaphorically recall the form of a vagina. The house is a reproductive and nourishing space centered around female fertility. Neighboring tribes such as the Kassena and the Nuna have similar but still distinct designs and layouts.

Geographic locations
Ghana, Burkina Faso, western Africa

Central elements
Male and female spaces, residential and defensive structures, mural painting

Related entry
Volta populations

▼ Painted house, Kassena (Ghana).

*In the dry savannah regions
the terrace is used for defense,
and also to dry food staples.*

*Houses are constructed by both
men and women: the men build
the walls and the women paint
the exterior of the house and
the inside rooms.*

▲ House terraces, Nankani
(Burkina Faso).

The triangle details are called "filed teeth" when the triangles point downward, or "dove's neck" when they point upward.

The vertical lozenge pattern recalls the harness that supports the sacred pumpkins carefully kept by the women at home. When a woman dies, her pumpkins are broken, releasing her soul.

▲ House façade, Nankani (Burkina Faso).

The geometric decorations are built on a dark-light chromatic contrast. They are painted in horizontal bands, in an arrangement that recalls the plants in a farmed field; the circular progress of the design, virtually endless, is associated with the snake that bites its tail and augurs family longevity.

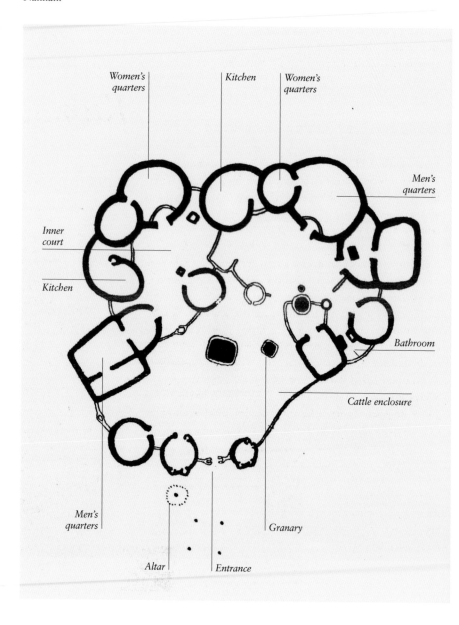

▲ Plan of a family residence,
Nankani (Burkina Faso)
(from Visona, 2001).

"Today … we were led to a large courtyard, where the king, surrounded by insignia, sat at the end of two long rows of councilors, chiefs and captains" (E. T. Bodwich)

Kumasi

In the 18th and 19th centuries, Kumasi, the capital of the Ashanti kingdom, was a lively commercial center with more than twenty thousand residents, which traded with trans-Saharan merchants and the Europeans depots scattered along the coast. In the 17th century, the Ashanti, who had conquered the southern kingdoms of Denkyira and Akwamu, copied their organization, also leaving the existing functionaries in place. Around the middle of the 18th century, the king (*ashantene*) Osei Kwadwo extended direct control of the capital over the subjected populations of his kingdom: the land was subdivided into administrative units managed by lower officials, and closer supervision was exercised over the extraction of gold and the ivory and kola-nut trades. The king also established a treasury, using literate Muslim officials. The streets of Kumasi were up to three hundred feet wide and had two-story houses. It was a violent city that was frequently set on fire during power struggles and fights for food supplies, which reached the city only irregularly. The market square, where parades and public ceremonies were held, was near the royal palace. Scattered around the city were stepped platforms on which the king sat, surrounded by his dignitaries when he made public appearances.

People
Ashanti

Geographic locations
Ghana, western Africa

Central elements
Capital of the Ashanti kingdom, shrines, houses, decorative and symbolic motifs

Related entries
Akan peoples, African religions, Black Islam

▼ Inside the Abirim shrine, Ashanti (Ghana).

The origin of the Ashanti wall decorations is unknown, but they definitely flourished in the 19th century. Many of these designs seem to have no meaning, or perhaps it was unknown outside royal and court circles and has since been lost. The lozenge design is usually interpreted as a mirror, while the zigzag lines are "climbing snakes." Possibly, they are adaptations of Islamic decorations engraved on artifacts brought to Kumasi by Muslim merchants.

The walls were built with trellises held together with clay, then plastered over and painted. In the 20th century, they have been replaced with cement. The shrines containing the altar to a deity differ from houses in their exterior decorations, which portray powerful animals such as the crocodile or the lion.

Inside a shrine are two courts: one to lodge the priests, the other for ceremonies. In the latter, three rooms laid out on three sides – where the priests, the musicians, and the faithful, respectively, stand – open onto the court, while the fourth side is the richly decorated wall of the chamber where the altar sits.

▲ Shrine (*abosomfie*),
Ashanti (Ghana).

Regular houses have only one inner court; larger ones have three or even four. The royal palace had ten or twelve courts, with walls variously decorated and connecting doors. The "stone palace" of the Ashanti king, built in 1822, copied the design of European forts. The use of pillars is probably inspired by European architecture; the fretwork surfaces are in the North African style.

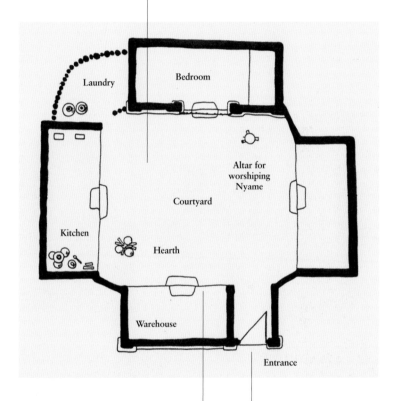

Laundry

Bedroom

Altar for worshiping Nyame

Courtyard

Kitchen

Hearth

Warehouse

Entrance

A typical Ashanti house consists of rooms arranged around the four sides of a central court; the rooms frequently have only three walls and open directly on the court. Some houses have two or three stories and can hold up to eighty people or thereabouts. The side facing the street sometimes has storefronts or trade shops or a balcony that is reached by climbing a few steps from the street.

The main entrance to the house is not located on the main façade but on a side, with access from an alley, to guarantee privacy. Everyday family activities, such as cooking, eating, gossiping, and discussing family business, take place in the inner courts.

▲ Plan of a house, Ashanti (Ghana) (from Oliver, 1975).

The walls are built of bamboo trellises and wood, plastered with clay.

Palm-leaf roof

The upper part of the walls is plastered with white clay.

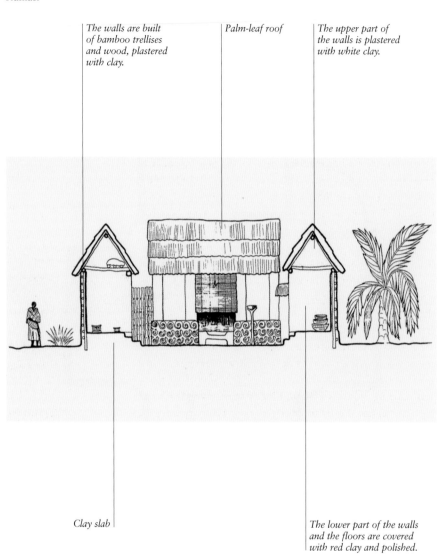

Clay slab

The lower part of the walls and the floors are covered with red clay and polished.

▲ Cross section of a traditional house, Ashanti (Ghana) (from Oliver, 1975).

"The fearless knife gave birth to Gu [the war god], and vengeance goes on" (proverb about Glele, the Fon king)

Abomey

In the center of Abomey, the capital of the Fon kingdom of Dahomey, stood the royal palace, encircled by tall walls. In the square facing it were the market and the panther temple, dedicated to the animal that was considered the king's double. Around the palace stood the quarters that made up the royal citadel, surrounded by fifteen-foot walls with several gates locked by large wooden doors. Here were the homes of the wives, the "Amazon" royal guard, the court craftsmen's guilds, and the slaves. On the other side of the walled compound were the palaces of the princes and their families. Streets radiated from the palace and crossed the city in the direction of Allada, the city where the ruling dynasty had its roots, and Kana, where the king had his country residence. The site occupied by the royal compound was meant to be expanded. For this purpose, according to popular tradition, King Agadja (1708–1740) had his men measure the distance that separated him from the coast with 23,502 bamboo canes, each fifteen feet long. The very construction of the palace followed this imperative, for it was customary for each new king to expand the boundaries of his predecessor and build his palace next to the dead king's, in an east-to-west progression that recorded the changes in dynastic space-time.

People
Fon

Geographic locations
Benin, western Africa

Chronology
17th–19th centuries:
Dahomey kingdom

Central elements
Dahomey kingdom,
royal palace,
bas-reliefs, dynastic
space-time

Related entries
Hunters and warriors,
voodoo, *asen*

▼ King Behanzin of
Abomey (Benin)
with his wives and
ministers, 2005.

The bas-reliefs are set in niches dug into the palace walls and pillars. They are made with soil from termites' nests, which is elastic and waterproof, mixed with palm oil. Oral sources date these reliefs to King Agadja, who ruled from 1708 to 1740. The horse and the lion are both symbols of King Glele (1858–1889).

▲ Bas-reliefs in the Abomey palace, Fon (Benin).

Usually the reliefs are arranged vertically in three frames and have distinct themes: the bottom relief refers to the current king through one of his "strong names" (names that express his destiny, as revealed in the fa divination rites); the middle one portrays war and conquest scenes; the uppermost relief pays homage to the ancestors and the deities that guard the palace.

Founded in the 17th century, the Fon kingdom spread its power in the following century to reach the coast and engaged in the slave trade. It reached its splendor in the 19th century under King Guezo (1818–1858). Pressured by the slave abolitionist movement, it partially reverted to an agriculture-based economy. At the end of the 19th century King Behanzin tried to resist the French conquest, but failed.

This enormous red fabric tent was forty-five feet high; it was decorated with fabric appliqués of bull's heads, human heads, and skulls. The king and his court sat under it.

A train of six thousand bearers leave the palace for the market square; they carry the royal treasure to be displayed to the people.

The parasols around the pavilion mark the presence of dignitaries and chieftains.

▲ Frederick Forbes, engraving of a procession before the royal pavilion (Abomey), 1851.

King Guezo's Palace

A. *Exterior court;* **B.** *King's quarters with two rooms for him and his wives on the first floor; the king received guests in another building nearby;* **C.** *Open vestibule of the inner court from which the king and his dignitaries viewed the dances held in the exterior court;* **D.** *Inner court reserved for solemn receptions and ancestor worship;* **E.** *Three-section building: on one side is the room of the king's woman servant; on the other side, the room where the king took his meals and slept; in the center, a hall where the king received family, functionaries, and important foreigners;* **F.** *Anvil altar; because the iron anvil is imperishable, it is a symbol of royal power and the exclusive place where the king worships;* **G.** *Throne room; during the ceremonies the thrones of the different kings were placed before the altar and the ruling king sat progressively on each one;* **H.** *"Pearl House"; I. "Panther House," the double animal of the Fon king.*

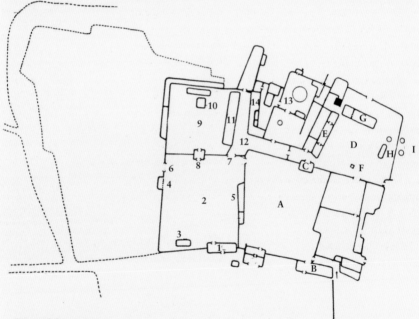

King Glele's Palace

1. *Open vestibule accessing the exterior court;* **2.** *Exterior court;* **3.** *Quarters for the servants of the palace minister* (adjabo); **4.** *Princesses' apartment, dedicated to ancestor worship;* **5.** *Hall for receiving foreigners;* **6.** *Access door to the Amazons' court;* **7.** *"Door to the Other World," through which the offers to be placed on Glele's tomb were passed;* **8.** *Building used as vestibule to the inner court, where the king met with the council of ministers;* **9.** *Inner court;* **10.** *"Pearl House," a shrine built by each new king for his deceased predecessor; built by Guezo's son Agoli-Ago;* **11.** *Treasure room;* **12.** *Hallway connecting Guezo's and Glele's inner courts, signifying continuity between the two kingdoms;* **13.** *Glele's tomb;* **14.** *The king's wives' quarters.*

▲ Plan of the palaces of King Guezo and King Glele, Abomey (Benin) (from Fassassi, 1978).

The Tamberma people call themselves Betammaribé, "those who know how to build"

Tamberma and Somba

The fortress-houses known as *tata* are common to several peoples, such as the Tamberma in northern Togo and the Somba of northern Benin. The Somba include several tribes, such as the Betiabé, Betammaribé, and Besorbé, who live in the foothills and slopes of the Atacora mountain range, where they once took shelter to escape the raids of the Bariba, warriors who came from the east and founded the Borgou kingdom in today's northern Benin. The *tata* is a multi-functional, fortified compound with a living area, a shelter for animals, a granary, and a shrine. The façade symbolically looks west, the direction from which the Somba migrations came, while the back looks east, the unlucky direction from which come all the evils that could strike the village. The northern and southern sides have a gendered significance: the northern-looking spaces are set aside for women and house chores, while the southern ones are for the men.

Geographic locations
Togo, Benin, western Africa

Central elements
Fortified house

Related entries
Chiefless societies, male and female, farmers

◀ Woman in front of her house, Tamberma (Togo).

The number of buildings and towers (from three to nine) varies depending on the owner's wealth and the size of his family.

▲ A *tata* village, Tamberma (Togo).

Built for defense,
these houses
have no
windows; the air
comes from an
opening in the
roof that is also
a vent for the
hearth smoke.

The building material (banco) is a clay mixture. For the
granary towers, which have thinner walls, termites' nest soil is
used, mixed with straw. The walls are built by arranging
twelve-inch layers of banco up to a height of twelve feet, then
plastering them with dirt mixed with water and dung. Finally,
the walls are waterproofed with a coat of karaté butter.

The conical roofs are covered with millet stalks or woven straw supported by a wood or stalk frame.

The terrace is reached by a wooden ladder leaned against the wall, to be removed in case of danger.

The terrace roof is made with wooden beams and woven lianas plastered with a coat of banco. *The terrace is a woman's space, where she cooks and stores food staples. The bedrooms and granaries also open onto the terrace. Sometimes the silos are divided into interior compartments.*

▲ The terrace of a *tata*, Tamberma (Togo).

"Thus we go from man to the cosmos and from the cosmos to man, both always present in the entire house and in each of its elements" (Jean-Paul Lebeuf)

Fali

For the Fali people of northern Cameroon, the living space is a web of references that link the human microcosm to the universal macrocosm, male to female, the turtle to the toad. In fact, the universe was born from the balance between the cosmic eggs of the toad (the female principle) and the turtle (the male principle): the former rotated east to west and the latter west to east, with the contents of each egg moving in an opposite direction from that of the shell. The world was born from this collision. Each further differentiation was born from the vibrations of these opposite yet complementary principles. For the Fali house, the generating movement is represented by the interaction between the cylindrical masonry walls (female) and the conical straw roof (male), rotating in opposite directions. The layout of the dwelling units, which reflects differences between social groups, follows an anthropomorphic pattern. Especially important is the granary, almost as tall as a man and shaped like a human body, with a head, neck, body, and feet (the stones that support it and raise it from the ground).

Geographic locations
Cameroon, western Africa

Central elements
Cosmological symbolism, anthropomorphism, zoomorphism

Related entries
Chiefless societies, male and female, farmers

◄ Pumpkin shell patched with twine decorated with a red bead, Fali (Cameroon).

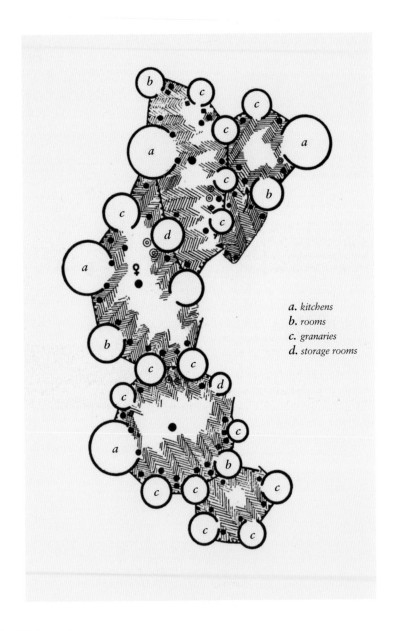

a. *kitchens*
b. *rooms*
c. *granaries*
d. *storage rooms*

▲ Plan of the house of a
polygamist, Fali (Cameroon)
(from Guidoni, 1975).

The size of the family compound and the number of huts within it vary with the age of the head of household and therefore with the number of his wives and children: first the compound expands; then, after the wives die and the children marry, it becomes smaller.

From the bed to the shelves, all the furniture is built-in and is part of the architecture, made from a mix of straw and clay.

▲ Front and cross section of a bedroom, Fali (Cameroon) (from Guidoni, 1975).

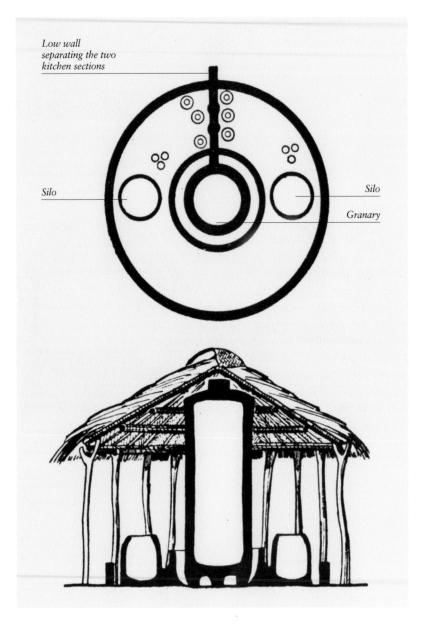

▲ Front and cross section of a
granary and kitchens, Fali
(Cameroon) (from Guidoni, 1975).

"Such formal perfection recalls the construction of an insect colony, or a fruit such as a pinecone or a pineapple"
(André Gide)

Musgum

For the past three hundred years or more, the Musgum, a fishing and herding tribe, have made their home in the alluvial plains along the border between Cameroon and Chad. Their homes (*tòlék*), built with a mixture of straw and mud, stand eighteen to forty-five feet tall, with a diameter of between fifteen and thirty feet. Several houses are grouped on the lot where several generations of the same family live. Although they began to decrease visibly, beginning in the 1930s with the French occupation, and almost disappeared, Musgum houses have seen a revival in recent years, as the natives try to rediscover their traditions and attract tourism, aided by international heritage-protecting organizations. The French author André Gide (*Travels in the Congo*) contributed to this revival by exalting the houses' beauty: he wrote of buildings so perfect that they seem works of nature, without superfluous decoration (the reliefs on the walls are used for climbing to the top), moved by an almost mathematical necessity. Built like upside-down vases, they have an opening on top to let the light shine in.

Geographic locations
Cameroon, Chad,
western Africa

Central elements
Architecture and
cultural identity

▼ Houses, Musgum
(Cameroon).

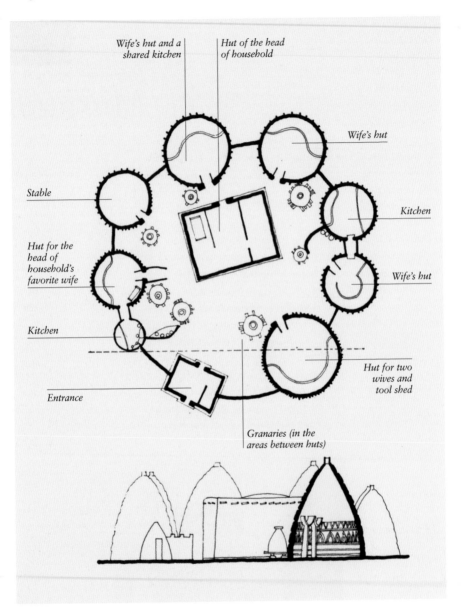

Wife's hut and a shared kitchen

Hut of the head of household

Wife's hut

Stable

Kitchen

Hut for the head of household's favorite wife

Wife's hut

Kitchen

Hut for two wives and tool shed

Entrance

Granaries (in the areas between huts)

▲ Plan and cross section of a family compound, Musgum (Cameroon) (from Guidoni, 1975).

"Two bulls cannot live in the same kraal" (Tswana proverb, Botswana)

Kraal

The model settlement of eastern Africa's herding populations, the kraal is a large, round enclosure with the cattle in the center and the homes lined up around the inside perimeter. Some kraals are permanent (like those of the Tsonga farmers of Mozambique), but more often they are semi-permanent (such as those of the Maasai herders of Tanzania), or mobile (like those of the nomadic Zulu clans). The ring with only one entrance is clearly designed for defense. There are separate spaces for people and cattle: "noble" sites (clean, where people live) and inferior ones (dirty, where the animals are kept). The Ba-ila villages in southern Zambia are shaped like a ring with inner concentric circles, each one occupied by an extended family and its livestock; the animals are next to the entrance, and the homes are farther inside. This transition from inside to outside, from lower-status places to high-status ones, is reflected in the size of the buildings: small warehouses are at the entrance, and farther back is the larger house where the male head of household lives.

Geographic locations
Eastern and
southern Africa

Central elements
Ring-like design,
space partitioning

Related entries
Maasai, Nguni, farmers

◀ Village in Kwa, Zulu, Natal (South Africa).

Zulu settlements consist of a central area at the top western part of the compound where the head of household, his mother, his children, the shrine to his ancestors, and the cattle yard (to which women have no access) are located, and a peripheral area at the lower eastern part where the wives live. The women's huts are arranged in a horseshoe pattern according to their status, with the upper-ranking ones on the right.

The domed huts are built with branches, clay, and manure.

The size and layout of the kraal changes over time, as the children grow and start their own families, so that each of the side huts can in turn become the center of a new kraal. In principle, the original center continues to be the center of the settlement, but in fact, as the head of household dies, the new kraals become independent.

▲ George French Angas, lithograph of a Zulu kraal near Umlazi, Natal (South Africa), 1849.

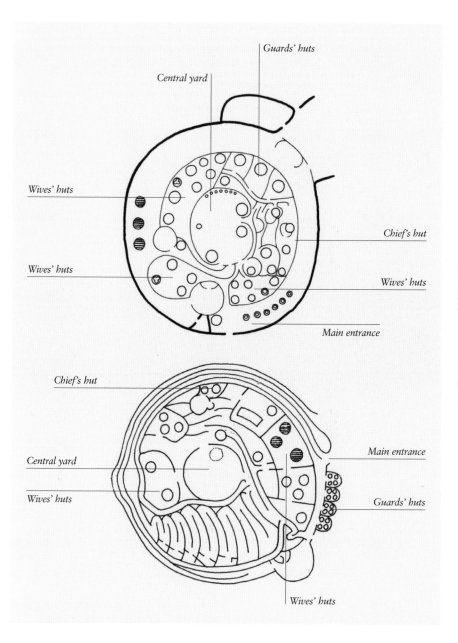

▲ Plans of kraals (Namibia)
(from Guidoni, 1975).

Some kraals were maze-like, with the chief's and the wives' huts in the innermost, more elevated area of the settlement. Here also stood the sacred grave of the ancestors and the sacrificial altar. The king owned several of these military camps for his Zulu army regiments and moved from one to the other. The regiments quartered in the capital were located at the right or the left of the large central house, depending on their status ("right-hand" or "left-hand" regiments).

In addition to their villages, the Maasai also had specific military camps for housing the young warriors, built along the kraal model but without a stockade.

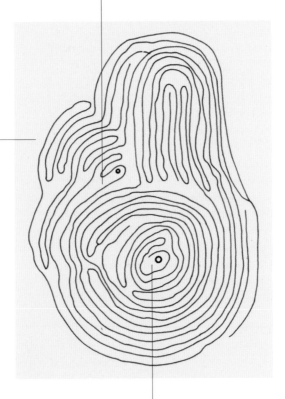

▲ Plan of a Zulu kraal (South Africa) (from Guidoni, 1975).

In the 19th century, the Zulu kraal developed into a true permanent military structure, from which the king could control his lands. In this case, the central yard was not set aside for the livestock, but for troop exercises and court ceremonies. Around it, in concentric circles, were the warriors' huts and those of their families. The number of residents could reach several thousand.

"The cities created by the whites become peopled with blacks, and this is actually the first African revolution" (George Balandier)

African Cities

The traditional image of Africa that lingers in the West is that of a rural continent without an urban component. In actuality, Africa has an ancient urban tradition that survives today in the commercial cities of Senegambia, Mali, Ghana, and Nigeria. It is true, however, that the colonial settlements were a stark break from the past, and at least in principle introduced the idea of an urban plan based on a geometric rationality: many of the present-day chaotic African metropolises developed from them. Naturally, the cities were built with the needs of the colonial powers in mind, intended to guarantee the separation of race and class, rather than the needs of the locals. For this reason, some post-colonial nations decided to found new capitals, moving the political center from the coast to the hinterland, in an attempt to reconfigure the country's space to meet the demands of African nationalism and find an indigenous path to modernity. Today, African cities keep growing, but their growth is not driven by economic expansion as much as by the increasing poverty of the countryside, which is caught in the vise of the global economy. Criminal violence, neo-tribalism, and solidarity networks intersect in the cities, along with inefficiency, corruption, social and political demands, and new artistic forms and ideas.

Geographic locations
Western, central, eastern, southern Africa

Central elements
Urbanization, colonial heritage, insecurity

Related entries
Colonialism, post-colonialism, witchcraft

▼ Weapons in Kinshasa (Democratic Republic of the Congo), 1997.

African shantytowns are born of a dire need, but are also examples of an inventive appropriation of spaces and materials: the building of makeshift housing that keeps changing according to the available materials and the personal histories and dreams of its residents.

Lagos is home to over ten million people; it grows by 13 percent every year without any kind of planning. As in many a megalopolis in the Southern Hemisphere, the skyscrapers of the administrative and financial center rise next to miserable bidonvilles. The post-war modernizing plans that were inspired by functionalist architecture have become tools of social transformation, and frequently of disintegration: for example, the small apartments built for Western-type nuclear families are inadequate for the extended African family.

Lagos became the capital of Nigeria in 1917. Nigeria itself is a creation of British colonialism that brought together under the same political framework more than two hundred and fifty different ethnicities. In 1992, the federal capital was moved to Abudia, a city born out of nowhere, from a plan drawn by the Japanese architect Kenzo Tange. With the shrinking of oil revenues, it now lies mostly unfinished. Its location inland was thought to better represent the unity of a nation devastated by the Biafran civil war: it was to act as a symbolic break with the colonial past, unlike Lagos, which is a product of it.

▲ View of Lagos (Nigeria).

Bester's paintings capture the hopes and disappointments of South Africa. Under the apartheid regime, his art reinforced identity pride; in the post-apartheid period, it denounces injustice and the desire to forget. In his collages, urban reality inserts itself as "found objects" picked up in the garbage.

The township of Soweto (an acronym for South Western Township) lies southwest of Johannesburg; it has a population of about two million people. Among its residents were Nelson Mandela and Bishop Desmond Tutu. In the 1950s, the Pretoria government turned it into a ghetto for the blacks who were pushing into the white districts of the city.

In the 1950s, the blacks were confined to townships and homelands. Not all the social and mental barriers have come down with the end of apartheid. In Johannesburg, the whites live increasingly entrenched in their districts, move about in cars, and walk only in the shopping malls. Crime is on the rise and many offices and buildings have shut down, though the streets now teem with black peddlers.

▲ Willie Bester, *Homage to Steve Biko*, 1992.

Children and minors under eighteen account for 45 percent of South Africa's population. In a country with a 40 percent unemployment rate, and where 20 percent of adults are HIV-positive, the populations of street children and child prostitutes are on the rise, fueled by abject poverty and the fear of infection. In Johannesburg, the victims are primarily children without kin, freshly arrived from the hinterland.

Children are not considered minors in need of protection (nor do they see themselves as such), but as individuals who play an increasingly active role: they are street peddlers, soldiers, little girls accused of seducing men to castrate them. Inter-generational and gender conflict use the language of witchcraft, fomented by fundamentalist and Pentecostal sects.

▲ Children living in water mains, Johannesburg (South Africa).

With poverty, violence increases and children, often accused of sorcery, become innocent scapegoats. Many of the children living on the streets of Kinshasa were deserted by their parents after neighbors accused them of causing disease, misfortunes, or deaths. Children are organizing in bands where one rises in rank by "killing" or "eating" human beings.

Kinshasa was founded as Leopoldville in 1881 by Henry Morton Stanley. In 1960 it had four hundred thousand residents. Now it is home to six million people, and its population is expected to increase to twenty-five million by 2025. The hopes of the 1960s have evaporated, and Kin-la-belle ("Kinshasa the beautiful") has become Kin-la-poubelle ("Kinshasa the trash can").

Kingelez works in Kinshasa. His architectural models are utopian visions of a free, fair city. There is nostalgia in them for the Kinshasa that could have been, and a phantasmagoric celebration of the consumerism from which most Africans are cut off.

▲ Bodys Isek Kingelez, *Projet pour le Kinshasa du troisième millénaire*, 1997.

In Kinshasa the business and office district is in the northern section, where the "white town" and its skyscrapers are. The residential district of Gombé along the Congo River houses embassies and the mansions of the Congolese and Western elites. Passing through the old, decaying neighborhoods, one finds new, makeshift towns, cities inside the city, that have a semi-rural character.

References

Map of Pre-colonial Sub-Saharan Africa
Chronology
Museums
Index
Bibliography
Photo Credits

◀ *Kifwebe* mask, Songye
(Democratic Republic of the
Congo). Private Collection.

Map of Pre-colonial Sub-Saharan Africa

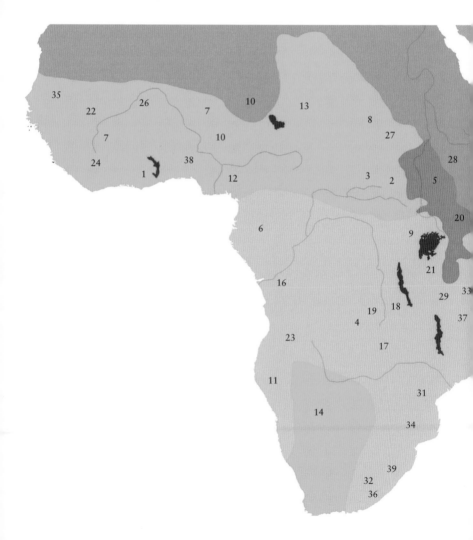

1. Akan
2. Azande
3. Banda
4. Chokwe
5. Dinka
6. Fang
7. Fulani
8. Fur
9. Ganda
10. Hausa
11. Herero
12. Igbo
13. Kanuri
14. Khoisan
15. Kikuyu
16. Kongo
17. Lozi
18. Luba
19. Lunda
20. Luo
21. Maasai
22. Malinke
23. Mbundu
24. Mende
25. Merina
26. Mossi
27. Nuba
28. Nuer
29. Nyamwezi
30. Sakalava
31. Shona
32. Sotho
33. Swahili
34. Tswana
35. Wolof
36. Xhosa
37. Yao
38. Yoruba
39. Zulu

Chronology

25,000 BC: Namibia, oldest rock painting.

6th century BC–5th century AD: Nok culture (Nigeria).

250 BC–1400 AD: Djenné-Jeno is founded and abandoned (the ancient Djenné, Mali).

300?–1075: Founding and fall of the Ghanaian empire.

9th–11th centuries: Igbo-Ukwu tombs and bronze artifacts.

9th–15th centuries: Djenné terracotta statues.

9th–16th centuries: Rise and fall of the Shongay kingdom (1591).

12th–16th centuries: Ife (Nigeria) bronze sculpture.

13th–early 16th centuries: Founding and fall of the Mali empire.

14th century: Mamprusi kingdom.

14th–15th centuries: Zenith of Great Zimbabwe's power.

14th–19th centuries: Rise and fall of the Benin kingdom (1897).

15th–16th centuries: The Dogon settle on the Bandiagara (Mali) cliffs.

15th–17th centuries: Rise of the Akan kingdoms (Ghana).

15th–17th centuries: Expansion of the Kongo kingdom.

1482–1665: The Portuguese trade with Kongo.

17th–18th centuries: Rise and zenith of the Illossi kingdoms.

17th–mid-19th centuries: Expansion and fall of the Lunda kingdom.

17th–end 19th centuries: Development and fall of the Kuba kingdom.

1680–1830: Oyo's Yoruba kingdom becomes politically important.

End 17th–end 19th centuries: Rise and crisis of the Luba kingdom.

18th century: Buganda becomes the leading Great Lakes kingdom.

18th century: The Baoulé migrate from Ghana to the Ivory Coast.

18th century: Development of the Merina kingdom in Madagascar.

Early 18th–early 19th centuries: Rise of Segou's and Kaarta's Bamana kingdoms (Mali).

18th–19th centuries: Expansion of the Ashanti kingdom.

18th–end 19th centuries: Rise and fall of the Fon kingdom of Dahomey.

19th century: Fulani jihad.

19th century: Sokoto caliphate.

1800–1870: The Fang people migrate to Gabon.

1816–1828: Shaka founds the Zulu kingdom.

1830–1900: The Chokwe kingdom rises in Angola.

1885: At the Berlin Conference, Africa is partitioned among the European powers.

1952–1956: Mau Mau rebellion.

1957: The Gold Coast becomes independent and changes its name to Ghana.

1990: Mandela is released and the African National Congress becomes legal in South Africa.

1994: End of the South African apartheid regime.

1995: Hutu militia massacre the Tutsi in Rwanda.

1999: A civilian government is restored in Nigeria after a long military regime.

Museums

Abomey (Benin), History Museum
www.epa-prema.net/abomey
Founded by the French in 1943, this museum is located in the palaces of Guezo and Glele, the Fon kings. It houses about one thousand objects that mostly belonged to the kings of Dahomey: thrones, weapons, altars, and insignia, still used by the royal family. It was restructured in 1997.

Bamako, Musée National du Mali
www.mnm-mali.org
The museum was founded in 1953 as a branch of the Institut Français d'Afrique Noire. Most of the early collection consisted of artifacts excavated by the archaeologist Szumoski, who created the museum. When Mali achieved independence, the museum was given its present name. After the 1970s crisis when the collection was dismantled, the museum was rebuilt in the 1980s. The current collection comprises an archaeological and an ethnographic wing, with mostly Dogon, Bamana, and Senufo artifacts. There is also a collection of audiovisual recordings of local cultural events.

Berlin, Ethnologisches Museum
www.smb.spk-berlin.de
Founded in 1873, the museum houses about half a million artifacts from all parts of the world. The African Wing was updated in 2005 and renamed "Art of Africa." Germany was in colonial Africa for only a short time, and the collection is mostly the work of its first director, Adolf Bastian. Other important museums of German colonialism are Stuttgart's Linden Museum and the Museum für Volkerkunde in Munich.

Grassland, Cameroonian Chiefdoms Museums
These four small museums were established through the effort of an Italian non-government organization, COE of Milan. They house the treasures of the Bandjoun, Baham, Babungo, and Mankon chiefdoms of the Grasslands. The local chiefs control the museum and take out the objects they need for their traditional ceremonies.

Lagos, National Museum of Nigeria
This museum houses important archaeological findings from the Nigerian Nok, Igbo-Ukwu, Ife, and Esie cultures, as well as bronzes from the kingdom of Benin that it reacquired on the international market. The selection of ethnological objects represents the many populations of Nigeria.

London, British Museum
www.thebritishmuseum.ac.uk
The African collection at the British Museum, formerly housed in the Museum of Mankind, was moved in 2001 to its current location in the Sainsbury Galleries: there, six hundred objects are on display from a collection of over two hundred thousand artifacts. They include works from Nigeria (Benin bronzes and the Talbot Collection), Ghana, and the Democratic Republic of the Congo (Torday Collection). In addition to traditional and archaeological items, contemporary artworks are displayed near the entrance to underscore the contemporary, open nature of African cultures. Other important English museums of African artifacts are Pitt Rivers in Oxford and Horniman in London.

New York, Metropolitan Museum of Art
www.metmuseum.org
The extensive number of African objects at the Metropolitan includes the generous 1969 gift of Nelson A. Rockefeller. There are eminent artifacts from all parts of Africa, including an ivory mask from the kingdom of Benin, some famous Dogon and Bamana statues, and a Luba seat by the "Buli Master" (19th century). Since 1982 they have been housed in the Rockefeller Wing together with pre-Colombian artifacts from Oceania. Another important acquisition was the Klaus Pers Collection, which includes 16th and 19th century objects from the kingdom of Benin, housed in the Benenson Gallery, which opened to the public in 1996.

New York, Museum for African Arts
www.africanart.org
The Center for African Arts was founded in 1984 to promote temporary exhibitions of African art. Over forty shows have been held so far on various subjects and with innovative approaches. In 1992 it was renamed the Museum for African Arts and moved to permanent premises. A new area for temporary exhibitions of traditional and contemporary African art is expected to open at the end of 2009.

New York, Studio Museum of Harlem
www.studiomuseuminharlem.org
The museum opened in 1967; it organizes exhibitions on contemporary African and Afro-American culture. In 1979 it acquired a permanent collection of about fifteen hundred works divided into three

sections: 19th and 20th century Afro-American art, 20th century African and Caribbean art, and traditional African art and objects.

Paris, Musée du Quai Branly
www.quaibranly.fr
Inaugurated in 2006, the museum collection consists of about three hundred thousand objects from Oceania, the Americas, Asia, and Africa. Thirty-five hundred are on permanent display, and about one thousand of these are from Africa. The latter are the collections of the Musée de l'Homme and the Musée National des Arts d'Afrique et d'Océanie. Some pieces were collected by the anthropologist Marcel Griaule and his students starting in the 1930s; others are from the Pierre Savorgnan de Brazza Collection from the late 19th century and the Pierre Harter (1928-1991) collection. The artifacts are displayed by region and theme and are primarily from Mali, Ivory Coast, Nigeria, Gabon, Democratic Republic of the Congo, and Cameroon. The museum has multimedia rooms, libraries, and a theater. Other French museums with African collections are the Musée Dapper in Paris and the Musée d'Arts Africains, Océaniens et Amérindiens of Marseilles.

Rome, Museo Nazionale Preistorico Etnografico Luigi Pigorini
www.pigorini.arti.beniculturali.it
Founded in 1876, the museum is located in Rome's EUR district. It houses collections of artifacts from pre-history, proto-history, and non-European cultures. The African wing was reinstalled in 1994 and organized in three parts: the discovery of the western African coast, the

exploration of the continent's interior, and the "discovery" of African art in the early 20th century. A special area is dedicated to ancient African weapons.

Tervuren (Belgium), Musée Royal de l'Afrique Centrale
www.africamuseum.be
This museum opened in 1910. In addition to the African fauna and tropical woods sections, it houses the richest collection in the world of ethnographic artifacts from central Africa, most of them from the Democratic Republic of the Congo, northern Angola, Rwanda, and Burundi. The museum will be totally reorganized in 2010, moving from a by now obsolete European approach to one planned in close cooperation with African cultural institutions. Other Belgian museums containing African artifacts are the Gand University Museum and the Antwerp Ethnographic Museum.

Vienna, Museum für Volkerkunde
www.ethno-museum.ac.at
The collection has thirty-seven thousand objects, half of which were acquired before 1927. Among the many valuable artifacts are bronzes from the kingdom of Benin, Afro-Portuguese carved ivory salt shakers and horns from the 15th and 16th centuries, works from Tanzania and the Great Lakes region collected at the end of the 19th century by Oscar Baumann, Cameroonian sculpture collected from 1907 to 1913 from the Rudolf and Helen Oldenburg collection, and items from the collection of Hans Meyer, a geographer.

Washington, National Museum of Africa Art
www.africa.si.edu

This museum was founded in 1964 under the sponsorship of the Smithsonian Institution and has about seven thousand objects from sub-Saharan Africa, divided into five sections: sub-Saharan African sculpture, art of Benin, pottery from central Africa, archaeological findings from the ancient Nubian city of Kerma, and artistic everyday crafts. It is also home to Eliot Elisofon's photographic archive and a library with over twenty-five thousand books on African art. Other American museums of interest are the American Museum of Natural History of New York, the Los Angeles Fowler Museum, and the University of Iowa Museum of Art.

Zurich, Rietberg Museum
www.rietberg.ch
The Rietberg Museum was founded in 1952 in the Wesendonck mansion in order to house the collection that Baron Eduard von der Heydt had donated to the city. It comprises works from Africa, Asia, and pre-Columbian America. The African collection reflects the baron's taste for elegantly formed objects and includes objects from Mali (Dogon), the Ivory Coast (Senufo, Guro, Dan, Baoulé), the kingdom of Benin, Cameroon (a famous *Batcham* mask), Gabon (Fang), and the Democratic Republic of the Congo (Luba, Songye, Vili). In 2007 the museum inaugurated a new wing. The Museum del Kulturen of Basel also houses a collection of African artifacts, as does the Musée Barbier-Mueller of Geneva.

Index

Abomey, 351
African Christianity, 226
African Cities, 369
African Religions, 180
Age-sets and Initiation, 134
Akan Peoples, 31
Asen, 237
Beads, 288
Black Islam, 221
Blacksmiths, 142
Body Arts, 278
Chiefless Societies, 131
Chokwe, 47
Colonialism, 167
Contemporary Music, 320
Contemporary Visual Arts, 308
Dance, 326
Divination, 183
Dogon, 338
Egungun Masks, 239
Eshu, the Rogue God, 209
Fali, 359
Fang and Kota Reliquaries, 247
Farmers, 252
Filmmaking, 311
Food, 264
Fulani (Peul), 28
Funerals in Ghana, 232
Granary of the Pure Earth, 189
Grassland Chiefdoms, 127
Griots, 151
Guinea's Western Coast, 12
Herders, 257
Hunters and Warriors, 153
Images of Power, 175
Kikuyu, 78
Kingdoms and Empires of the
    Sudan, 114
Kingdoms of Niger, 119
Kingdoms of the Great Lakes,
    124
Kongo, 42
Kraal, 365
Kuba, 56
Kumasi, 347
Lega, 68
Literature, 298
Luba-Lunda, 51
Maasai, 74

Madagascar, 89
Makonde, 82
Male and Female, 158
Mami Wata, 217
Mande, 17
Mangbetu, 64
Mbuti, 71
Musgum, 363
Nankani, 343
Ndebele, 102
Nguni, 106
Nigerian Region, 36
Nommo Genies, 193
Nyamwezi, 80
Ogboni Cult, 243
Oral Tradition and Writing, 293
Post-colonialism, 171
San, 93
Secret Societies, 138
Shango, the Thunder God, 205
Shona, 98
Sickness and Healing, 269
Skull Worship, 245
Slavery, 162
Swahili, 85
Tamberma and Somba, 355
Theater, 331
Trade, 260
Traditional Artists, 302
Traditional Music, 314
Twin Worship, 202
Volta Populations, 22
Voodoo, 213
Water Spirits, 196
Weaving and Clothing, 283
Witchcraft, 275
Women Potters, 146
Zande, 60

Bibliography

Africa

Histoire générale de l'Afrique, Presence Africaine, EDICEF, UNESCO 1997.
Amselle J.P. and M'Bokolo E. (eds.), Au coeur de l'ethnie, La Découverte, Paris 1995.
Balandier G., Società e dissenso, Dedalo, Bari 1977.
Balandier G., Sociologie actuelle de l'Afrique noire. Dynamique des changements sociaux en Afrique centrale, PUF, Paris 1955.
Bedaux R.A. et al., Vallées du Niger, Editions de la Réunion des Musées Nationaux, Paris 1993.
Bernardi B., Africa. Tradizione e modernità, Carocci, Rome 1998.
Bernardi B., Africanistica: le culture orali dell'Africa, Angeli, Milan 2006.
Bovill E.W., The Golden Trade of the Moors, Oxford University Press, Oxford 1968.
Calchi Novati G. and Valsecchi P., Africa: la storia ritrovata: dalle prime forme politiche alle indipendenze nazionali, Carocci, Rome 2005.
Cartry C. (eds.), La notion de personne en Afrique noire, CNRS, Paris 1981.
Chrétien J.P. and Prunier G. (eds.), Les ethnies ont une histoire, Karthala-ACCT, Paris 1989.
Coquery-Vidravitch, The Process of Urbanization in Africa (From the Origins to the Beginning of Independence), in "African Studies Review" 34, 1991.
Cornevin M., Secrets du continent africain revelés par l'archéologie, Maisonneuve et Larose, Paris 1998.
Daget S. and Renault E., Les traites negrières en Afrique, Karthala, Paris 1985.

Davidson B., Africa. Storia di un continente, Mondadori, Milan 1966.
Davidson B., La civiltà africana. Introduzione a una storia culturale dell'Africa, Einaudi, Turin 1972.
Davidson B., Madre nera. L'Africa e il commercio degli schiavi, Einaudi, Turin 1974.
Enwezor O., The Short Century. Independence and Liberation Movements in Africa, 1945-1994, Prestel, Munich, London and New York 2001.
Fage J.D. and Oliver R., The Cambridge History of Africa, Cambridge University Press, Cambridge 1975-1986.
Falk Moore S., Antropologia e Africa, Cortina, Milan 2004.
Garlacke P., Early Art and Architecture of Africa, Oxford University Press, Oxford 2002.
Gentili A.M., Il leone e il cacciatore. Storia dell'Africa subsahariana, La Nuova Italia Scientifica, Rome 1995.
Grunne (de) B., The Birth of Art in Africa, Nok Statuary in Nigeria, Biro, Paris 1998.
Grunne (de) B., Terres cuites anciennes de l'Ouest africain, Institut Supérieur d'Archéologie et d'Histoire de l'Art, Louvain 1980.
Insoll T., The Archaeology of Islam in Sub-Saharan Africa, Cambridge University Press, Cambridge 2003.
Jewsiewicky B. and Newbury D. (eds.), African Historiographies, Sage Publ., London 1985.
Ki-Zerbo J., Storia dell'Africa nera: un continente fra la preistoria e il futuro, Einaudi, Turin 1977.
Kopytoff I., The African Frontier: the Reproduction of Traditional Societies, Indiana

University Press, Bloomington 1987.
Mbembe A., Postcolonialism, Meltemi, Rome 2005.
Mudimbe V.Y., The Invention of Africa, Indiana University Press, Bloomington 1988.
Murdock G.P., Africa: its Peoples and their Cultural History, McGraw Hill, New York 1959.
Shaw S., The Archaeology of Africa, Routledge, London 1993.
Vansina J., Art History in Africa, Longman, London and New York 1984.

Religions, power, everyday life, and the arts

Anderson M.G. and Peek P.M., Ways of the Rivers. Arts and Environment of the Niger Delta, Fowler Museum of Cultural History, Los Angeles 2002.
Antongini G. and Spini T.G., Les palais royaux d'Abomey: espace, architecture, dynamique socio-anthropologique, Centre du patrimoine mondial, Paris 1995.
Arnoldi M.J., Playing with Time, Art and Performance in Central Mali, Indiana University Press, Bloomington 1995.
Arnoldi M.J., Geary C.M., and Hardin K.I, African Material Culture, Indiana University Press, Bloomington and Indianapolis 1996.
Auge M., Génie du paganisme, Gallimard, Paris 1992.
Auge M. and Herzlich C., Il senso del male. Antropologia, storia, sociologia della malattia, Il Saggiatore, Milan 1986.
Azevedo (d') W., The Traditional Artist in African Societies, Indiana University Press, Bloomington 1973.
Banham M., A History of Theatre

in Africa, Cambridge University Press, Cambridge 2004.

Barber K., Popular Arts in Africa, "African studies review" 30, 1987.

Barber K. (ed.), Readings in African Popular Culture, Indiana University Press, Bloomington and Indianapolis 1997.

Bargna I., Arte africana, Jaca Book, Milan 2003.

Bargna I., Arte in Africa, Jaca Book, Milan 2007.

Barlet O., Il cinema africano. Lo sguardo in questione, L'Harmattan Italia, Turin 1998.

Bascom W., Ifa Divination. Communication Between Gods and Men in West Africa, Indiana University Press, Bloomington 1969.

Bastin M.L., La sculpture Tchokwe, Chaffin, Meudon 1982.

Battestini S., Ecriture et texte. Contribution africaine, Les Presses de l'Université Laval, Présence africaine, Paris 1997.

Baxter P. and Alamagor U., Age, Generation and Time. Some Features of East African Age Organization, St. Martin's Press, New York 1979.

Bay E.G., Women and Work in Africa, Westview Press, Boulder 1982.

Bayart J.F., Globalizzazione e mutamento politico nell'Africa sub-sahariana (1989-2005), "Afriche e Orienti" 2, 2006.

Bayart J.F., L'Etat en Afrique. La politique du ventre, Fayard, Paris 1999.

Bayart J.F., Geschière P., and Nyamnjoh E., Autochtonie, démocratie et citoyenneté en Afrique, "Critique Internationale" 10, 2001.

Bedaux R.M.A. and Van der Waals J.D., Regards sur les Dogon du Mali, Rijksmuseum voor Volkenkunde Leyde, Editions Snoeck, Gand 2003.

Bender W., La musique africaine contemporaine, L'Harmattan, Paris 1992.

Beneduce R., Trance e possessione in Africa. Corpi, mimesi, storia, Bollati Boringhieri, Turin 2002.

Berns M., Art, History and Gender: Women and Clay in West Africa, "African Archeological Review" 11, 1993.

Beumers E. and Koloss H.J., Kings of Africa, Foundation Kings of Africa, Maastricht 1992.

Bilot et al., Masques du Pays dogon, Biro, Paris 2003.

Blandin A., Afrique de l'Ouest: Bronzes et autres alliages, Marignan, 1988.

Blier Preston S., African Vodun: Art, Psychology, and Power, The University of Chicago Press, Chicago 1996.

Bloch M., Un tentativo di incontro. Il concetto di "paesaggio" fra gli Zafimaniry del Madagascar, in U. Fabietti, Il sapere dell'antropologia. Pensare, comprendere, descrivere l'Altro, Mursia, Milan 1993.

Bocola S., Sièges africains, Réunion des musées nationaux, Paris 1994.

Boeck (de) F., Le "deuxième monde" et les "enfants sorciers" en République démocratique du Congo, "Politique africaine" 80, 2000.

Bohannan P. and Dalton G., Markets in Africa, Northwestern University Press, Evanston, 1962.

Boone S.A., Radiance from the Water: Ideals of Feminine Beauty in Mende Art, Yale University Press, New Haven, 1986.

Brambilla C. (ed.), Letterature dell'Africa, Jaca Book, Milan 1994.

Bravmann R.A., African Islam, Smithsonian Institution Press, Washington and London 1983.

Bravmann R.A., Islam and Tribal Art in West Africa, Cambridge University Press, Cambridge 1980.

Biebuyck D., The Lega: Art, Initiation and Moral Philosophy, University of California Press, Berkeley 1969.

Cafuri R., La concezione della storia nel regno del Danxome inscritta nella capitale Abomey, "Africa" XLIX (2): 260-274.

Chastanet M., Fauvelle-Aymar F.X., and Juhe-Beaulaton D., Cuisine et société en Afrique, histoire, saveurs, savoir-faire, Karthala, Paris 2002.

Child S. T. and Killick D., Indigenous African Metallurgy: Nature and Culture, "Annual Review of Anthropology" 22, 1993.

Colais E., Il cinema nero africano. Dalla parola all'immagine, Bulzoni, Rome 1999.

Cole H. and Aniakor C., Igbo Art. Community and Cosmos, University of California Press, Berkeley 1984.

Cole H. and Ross D.H., Arts of Ghana, University of California Press, Berkeley 1977.

Comaroff J., Of Revelation and Revolution: Christianity, Colonialism, and Consciousness in South Africa, University of Chicago Press, Chicago 1991.

Coquet M., Tissus africains, Biro, Paris 1993.

Cornet J., L'art royal kuba, Sipiel, Milan 1982.

Darkowska-Nidzgorski O. and Nidzgorski D., Marionnettes et Masques au coeur du théâtre africain, Sepia, Saint-Maur 1998.

De Surgy A., *La voie des fétiches*, L'Harmattan, Paris 1995.

Drewal H.I., Pemberton J. III, and Abiodun R., *Yoruba. Nine Centuries of African Art and Thought*, Center for African Art, New York 1989.

Evans-Pritchard E.E., *I Nuer: un'anarchia ordinata*, Angeli, Milan 1991.

Evans-Pritchard E.E., *Stregoneria, oracoli e magia tra gli Azande*, Cortina, Milan 2002.

Falgayrettes C., *Cuillers sculptures*, Editions Dapper, Paris 1991.

Fassassi M.A., *L'architecture en Afrique noire. Cosmoarchitecture*, Maspero, Paris 1978.

Fernandez J.W., *Africanization, Europeanization, Christianization*, "History of Religions" 18, 1979.

Fortes M. and Evans-Pritchard E.E. (eds.), *African Political Systems*, Oxford University Press, London 1940.

Frank B.E., *More than Wives and Mothers. The Artistry of Mande Potters*, "African Arts" 4, 1994.

Fraser D. and Cole H.M., *African Art and Leadership*, University of Wisconsin Press, Madison 1972.

Gariazzo G., *Breve storia del cinema africano*, Lindau, Turin 2001.

Geschière P., *Sorcellerie et politique en Afrique. La viande des autres*, Karthala, Paris 1995.

Girshick Ben Amos P., *The Art of Benin*, British Museum Press, London 1995.

Goody J., *Cooking, Cuisine and Class: A Study in Comparative Sociology*, Cambridge University Press, Cambridge 1982.

Griaule M., *Conversations with Ogotemmêli: An Introduction to Dogon Religious Ideas*, Oxford University Press, London 1970.

Griaule M. and Dieterlen G., *Le renard pâle*, Institut d'Ethnologie, Paris, 1965.

Guidoni E., *Architettura primitiva*, Electa, Milan 1975.

Héritier F., *Maschile/femminile. Il pensiero della differenza*, Laterza, Bari 2000.

Herreman F., *Material differences. Art and Identity in Africa*, Museum for African Art, New York 2003.

Heusch (de) L., *Le sacrifice dans les religions africaines*, Gallimard, Paris 1986.

Jewsiewicki B., *Mami Wata. La peinture urbaine au Congo*, Gallimard, Paris 2003.

Jewsiewicki B. et al., *Art et politique en Afrique noire*, Ass. canadienne des études africaines, Safi 1989.

Kasfir S., *Contemporary African Art*, Thames & Hudson, London 2000.

Kwabena Nkeita J.H., *The Music of Africa*, Norton, New York 1974.

Lamb V., *West African Weaving*, Duckworth, London 1975.

Larkin B., *Indian Films and Nigerian Lovers: media and the creation of parallel modernities*, "Africa" 67, 1997.

Latouche S., *L'altra Africa. Tra dono e mercato*, Bollati Boringhieri, Turin 1997.

Latouche S., *La planète des naufragés: essai sur l'après-développment*, La Découverte, Paris 1991.

Layton R., *Antropologia dell'arte*, Feltrinelli, Milan, 1983.

Lebeuf J.P., *L'habitation des Fali montagnards du Camerun septentrional*, Hachette, Paris 1961.

Lewis I.M. (ed.), *Islam in Tropical Africa*, Indiana University Press, Bloomington 1966.

MacGaffey W., *Astonishment and Power*, Washington, D.C. 1993.

Mayr L., *Regni africani*, Feltrinelli, Milan 1981.

Mbiti J.S., *African Religion and Philosophy*, Heinemann, Oxford 1989.

McLeod M.D., *The Asante*, The Trustees of the British Museum, London 1981.

McNaughton P.R., *The Mande Blacksmiths: Knowledge, Power and Art in West Africa*, Indiana University Press, Bloomington 1988.

Meillassoux C., *Antropologia della schiavitù*, Mursia, Milan 1986.

Meyer B., *Christianity in Africa: From African Independent to Pentecostal Charismatic Churches*, "Annual Review of Anthropology" 33, 2004.

Meyer L., *Les Arts des métaux en Afrique noire*, Sepia, Saint-Maur 1997.

Meyer P., *Kunst und Religion der Lobi*, Rietberg Museum, Zurich 1981.

Mitchell J.C., *La danza della Kakela. Aspetti dei rapporti sociali tra gli Africani in una comunità urbana della Rhodesia del nord*, in V. Maher, *Questioni di etnicità*, Rosenberg & Sellier, Turin 1994.

Monteil V., *L'Islam noir*, Seuil, Paris 1964.

Musée d'Arts Africains, Océaniens, Amérindiens de Marseille/Skira, Milan 1997.

Mveng E., *Identità africana e cristianesimo*, SEI, Turin 1990.

Nicolas A. and Sourrieu M. (eds.), *Les dessins bamoun*, Skira, Milan 1997.

Nooter M. and Roberts A.F., *Luba Art and the Making of History*, Museum for African Art,

New York, Prestel, Munich 1996.

Notué J.P. and Perrois L., *Rois et sculpteurs de l'ouest Cameroun. La panthère et la mygale*, Karthala Orstom, Paris 1997.

Oliver P., *Shelter, Sign & Symbol*, Barrie & Jenkins, London 1975.

Parodi da Passano G. (ed.), *Evhé-Ouatchi. Un'estetica del disordine*, Centro Studi Archeologia Africana, Milan 2004.

Phillips T., *Africa. The Art of a Continent*, Prestel, Munich and New York 1995.

Picton J. and Mack J., *African Textiles*, British Museum Publ., London 1989.

Piga A., *L'islam in Africa. Sufismo e jihad fra storia e antropologia*, Bollati Boringhieri, Turin 2003.

Pradelle de Latour C.H., *Le crâne qui parle. Ethnopsychanalise en pays bamiléké*, EPEL, Paris 1997.

Price S., *Afro-American Arts of Suriname Rain Forest*, University of California Press, Berkeley 1980.

Prussin L., *Hatumere. Islamic Design in West Africa*, University of California Press, Berkeley 1986.

Remotti F., *Luoghi e corpi: antropologia dello spazio, del tempo e del potere*, Bollati Boringhieri, Turin 1993.

Ravenhill P., *The Self and the Other: Personhood and Images among the Baoulé, Côte d'Ivoire*, Fowler Museum of Cultural History, University of California, Los Angeles 1994.

Rollard P., "La maison ba'mbenga: un champ sémantique? (pour un étude de l'espace pygmée)", in *Espaces des autres. Lectures anthropologiques d'architecture*, Editions de la Villette, Paris 1987.

Ross D.H., *Queen Victoria for*

Twenty-Five Pounds: The Iconography of a Breasted Drum from Southern Ghana, "Art Journal" 47, 2, 1988.

Roy C., *Art of Upper Volta*, Chaffin, Meudon 1987.

Rubin W. (ed.), *Il primitivismo nell'arte del XX secolo*, Mondadori, Milan 1985.

Schweinfurth G., *Au coeur de l'Afrique 1867–1871. Voyages et découvertes dans les régions inexplorées de l'Afrique centrale*, Hachette, Paris 1875.

Sieber R. and Herreman F., *Hair in African Art and Culture*, The Museum for African Art, New York, Prestel, Munich 2000.

Spini T. and Spini S., *Togu Na. La casa della parola*, Bollati Boringhieri, Turin 2003.

Tenaille F., *Le swing du caméléon. Musiques et chansons africaines, 1950-2000*, Actes Sud, Arles 2000.

Thompson R.F., *African Art in motion*, University of California Press, Berkeley 1974.

Thompson R.F., *Flash of the Spirit. African and Afro-American Art and Philosophy*, Vintage Books, New York 1984.

Turner V., *La foresta dei simboli*, Morcelliana, Brescia 1992.

Vansina J., *The Children of Woot. A History of the Kuba Peoples*, The University of Wisconsin Press, Madison 1978.

Visona M.B. et al., *A History of Art in Africa*, Thames & Hudson, London 2001.

Vivan I., *Letteratura africana. Interpreti rituali. Il romanzo dell'Africa nera*, Dedalo, Bari 1978.

Vivan I., *Il Nuovo Sudafrica dalle strettoie dell'apartheid alle complessità della democrazia*, La Nuova Italia, Florence 1996.

Vogel S., *Africa Explorers. 20th Century African Arts*, Museum of African Art, New York 1991.

Vogel S., *Baoulé: African Art / Western Eyes*, Yale University Press, New Haven 1997.

Warnier J.P., *L'esprit d'entreprise au Cameroun*, Karthala, Paris 1993.

Wersijver G. et al., *Masterpieces from Central Africa*, Prestel, Munich and New York 1996.

Willet F., *Arte africana*, Einaudi, Turin 1978.

Williams D., *Icon and Image*, Allen Lane, London 1974.

Wole S., *Teatro africano*, Einaudi, Turin 1987.

Zahan D., *Religion, spiritualité et pensée africaines*, Payot, Paris 1970.

Photo Credits